D1314358

Children Learning to Read:
International Concerns

Volume 2

Curriculum and Assessment Issues:
Messages for Teachers

Children Learning to Read: International Concerns Volume 1

Emergent and Developing Reading: Messages for Teachers

Edited by Pamela Owen and Peter Pumfrey

Children Learning to Read:
International Concerns

Volume 2

Curriculum and Assessment Issues:
Messages for Teachers

Edited by

Pamela Owen and Peter Pumfrey

 The Falmer Press

(A member of the Taylor & Francis Group)
London • Washington, D.C.

UK   The Falmer Press, 4 John Street, London WC1N 2ET
USA   The Falmer Press, Taylor & Francis Inc., 1900 Frost Road, Suite 101, Bristol, PA 19007

First published in 1995

A catalogue record for this book is available from the British Library

Library of Congress Cataloging-in-Publication Data are available on request

ISBN 0 7507 0365 2 cased
ISBN 0 7507 0366 0 paper

Jacket design by Caroline Archer

Typeset in 11/13pt Garamond by
Graphicraft Typesetters Ltd., Hong Kong.

Printed in Great Britain by Burgess Science Press, Basingstoke on paper which has a specified pH value on final paper manufacture of not less than 7.5 and is therefore 'acid free'.

Contents

Contents

Acknowledgments

The editors are indebted to the University Sector College of St Martin's, Lancaster, for hosting the 1993 International Reading Conference 'How Do Children Learn To Read?' in response to the International Association for the Evaluation of Educational Achievement (IEA) Reading Literacy Study.

The conference, following from the preceding Lancaster Conference on *What Counts As Being Able To Read?*, brought together professionals from many different countries and disciplines. The aims of these meetings included sharing information on common concerns and engaging in dialogues focused on advancing an understanding of the nature of literacy, its emergence, related pedagogic concerns and assessment issues.

The importance of integrating theory, research and practice was underlined. In order to help improve practice, each contributor was asked to provide a concluding section identifying 'Messages for Teachers'. The present two-volume series is an outcome of the above process. Each contributor's considerable investment of his or her time and expertise is acknowledged.

In conclusion, the editors gratefully acknowledge the professional skill, commitment and hard work of Libby Osborn, Secretary to the English Department at St Martin's College, and Jackie Day and Jocelyne Cox of Falmer Press, in preparing the manuscripts.

List of Tables and Figures

Tables

Figures

List of Tables and Figures

Abbreviations

ACER	Australian Council for Educational Reasearch
ANOVA	Analysis of Variance
a.o.	amongst others
APU	Assessment of Performance Unit
ASLPR	Australian Second Language Proficiency Rating Scale
BAS	British Ability Scales
BC	British Columbia
CDI	Composite Development Index
CERI	Centre for Educational Research and Innovation
CFAS	Centre for Formative Assessment Studies
CS	Cut Spelling
CVC	Consonant-Vowel-Consonant
DAS	Differential Ability Scales
DES	Department of Education and Science
DfE	Department for Education
DIFINT	Internal Differences
DIST	Distance measure
EP	Equal-Plus
ESRC	Economic and Social Science Research Council
ETS	Educational Testing Services
GNP	Gross National Product
HMI	Her Majesty's Inspectorate
ICC	International Coordinating Centre
ICC	Item Characteristic Curve
IEA	International Association for the Evaluation of Educational Achievement
IRT	Item Response Theory
i.t.a.	Initial Teaching Alphabet
ITDISCR	Item Discrimination
KS1	Key Stage 1
LEA	Local Educational Authority
L2	Second Language
MC	Multiple Response Category

MRC	Medical Research Council
NC	National Curriculum
NC EN2	National Curriculum for English Profile Component 2
NISEAC	Northern Ireland Schools Examination and Assessment Council
NFER	National Foundation for Educational Research
NRCs	National Research Coordinators
NUT	National Union of Teachers
OFSTED	Office for Standards in Education
RP	Received Pronunciation
SAT	Standard Assessment Task
SCAA	Schools Council for Assessment and Achievement
SEAC	Schools Curriculum and Assessment Authority
SoA	Statement of Attainment
STAIR	Standard Test and Assessment Implementation Research
TEEXT	Test of External variable
TESHAPE	Test of Shape
THETOT	Theta parameter for the Total data set
TO	Traditional Orthography
TORCH	Test Of Reading Comprehension
TV	Television
US(A)	United States (of America)
UNESCO	United Nations Educational, Scientific and Cultural Organisation

Introduction: International Concerns and Controversies

P. Pumfrey and P. Owen

Summary

The perceived importance of literacy in general and reading in particular is common in societies across the world. Despite contextual differences, there are numerous common concerns and controversies. From these, three areas are identified. The first is developing an improved understanding of the nature of children's early reading development. The second is the consideration of ways in which children's reading can be encouraged. (These two areas are addressed in Volume 1.) In this volume issues of curriculum and assessment in the context of professional accountability are addressed.

How much is the ability to read worth? To be illiterate in most contemporary societies is to be marginalized and disadvantaged. Anyone who arrives in a country where lack of knowledge of the language prevents their reading the most basic written signs, will appreciate the metaphorical imprisonments attributable to their ignorance of the language. Literacy is both a contributor to, and an amplifier of, human abilities. To argue that, in the era of information technology, learning to read is preparing children for the nineteenth, rather than the twenty-first century, is to misunderstand the nature of human thought and its development. Literacy liberates.

In countries across the world, standards of literacy and the processes underpinning them are of central interest to politicians, parents, professionals and pupils. The editors and contributors to this series are well aware of the controversial, complex interrelated and changing nature of views held concerning the receptive and expressive aspects of language involved in the emergence, development and assessment of literacy. Our focus on reading does not deny the importance of other modes of language. Reading is but one facet of literacy; literacy merely one component of communication and communication one part of child development.

Optimizing pupils' reading attainments depends crucially on professionals' understanding of child development and the conditions that facilitate reading as a thinking process. In this there are reciprocal relationships between advances in theory, research and practice. Mutual benefits are likely to accrue when professionals from different countries and disciplines are able to identify literacy-related issues of common concern and share experiences of promising developments. For all teachers, knowing *why* we use particular methods and materials and their effectiveness in specified circumstances, integrates theory, its applications and their evaluation.

Moves towards an interactive model integrating the unjustifiably polarized 'top–down' versus 'bottom–up' positions concerning the nature of emergent reading, its development, teaching and assessment are taking place. In respect of the first two of these, Chapter 1 in Volume 1 provides a constructive synthesis. This does not mean that important controversies do not continue. In the advancement of knowledge in all fields, the dialectic involving hypothesis, antithesis and synthesis is ever alive. The liveliness of the continuing debate on, for example, emergent and developing reading is immediately apparent when one compares the stances represented in Chapters 6 and 7 in Volume 1. The same is true in relation to assessment issues addressed in Chapters 7 to 12 in Volume 2.

In considering the merits of the cases presented in each of the chapters in both volumes, it is important to identify the author's implicit or explicit assumptions concerning the nature of reading, its development, teaching and assessment (for example, Volume 2, Chapter 2). The theoretical coherence of a contributor's case can also be considered in relation to the quality and extent of evidence adduced in support. Further, in the interests of reaching a balanced judgment, a consideration of the contributions made by different authors based on alternative theoretical stances and from different professional specialisms cannot be ignored.

Some of the chapters are based on researches carried out over many years and with considerable numbers of subjects; others report recent findings from smaller-scale studies. Some chapters are descriptive of what is deemed promising practice.

With confidence, we assert that no individual has a freehold on validity. The words of Bacon continue to give important messages. 'Read not to contradict and confute, nor to believe and take for granted, nor to find talk and discourse, but to weigh and consider' (Bacon 1561–1626: Essay 50 'Of Studies').

There are three major common concerns of those professionals involved in how children become literate and by what means such achievements can be appraised. These are:

- developing understanding of the nature of children's emergent reading;
- considering ways in which children's emergent and subsequent reading can be developed; and
- the assessment and improvement of reading processes and standards.

From these extensive fields, evidence drawn from the work of colleagues in many countries suggests that, within these concerns, shared understandings are gradually emerging from research and practice. Inevitably, there are also ongoing theoretical controversies that have important implications for practice in the classroom. The 'top–down' versus 'bottom–up' theories of reading development exemplify one controversy that appears to be nearing a resolution in an interactive model. These (inevitably partial) understandings cannot be ignored if we are to increase our ability to conceptualize, control and optimize the development of children's standards of literacy in general and reading in particular.

There is no claim that collectively the specific topics addressed by contributors represent a comprehensive coverage of critical issues. However, to remain unaware of the work being done in countries other than one's own would be irresponsibly insular. There is a growing consensus that, irrespective of the country, culture or language, the topics identified above merit inclusion in both the initial training of teachers and in continuing professional development.

This series is distinctive on the combined basis of four major counts. Firstly, it is internationally oriented. It provides a somewhat overlooked international perspectives on the three issues identified above. Evidence drawn from the following countries is presented: Australia; Canada; Denmark; England; France; Germany; Greece; Guam; Hungary; Israel; Italy; Jamaica; Japan; New Zealand; Northern Ireland; Scotland; Spain; and the USA. Reports on reading attainments across the thirty-two school systems and twenty-one language groups included in the International Association for the Evaluation of Educational Achievement (IEA) reading-literacy study are also reported and discussed.

Secondly, it is interdisciplinary. Professionals from complementary fields describe promising developments from their respective viewpoints:

teachers; teacher-trainers; psychologists; advisers; inspectors; administrators; statisticians; and research workers.

Thirdly, it contains messages for teachers and mentors concerning their regular work with pupils on encouraging literacy. In relation to improving and assessing reading, it combines *what* can profitably be done with *why* this is the case.

Fourthly, it addresses international issues of accountability. Research studies and promising classroom practice from around the world are reported highlighting implications for the design, implementation, improvement and evaluation of reading programs.

With the increasingly multicultural character of societies across the world, the two volumes are planned to appeal to an international readership, although predominantly in English-speaking countries. It is expected that the contents of both books will be of interest, albeit differentially, to the following groups.

- teachers in mainstream primary schools;
- teachers in special schools and units;
- LEA advisory and support staff;
- educational and child psychologists;
- students on initial teacher-training courses;
- teacher-trainers and school-based mentors; and
- research workers.

The strength of the two volumes is that they bring together, under the three international concerns identified, the work of professionals in different countries. Volumes 1 and 2 provide complementary information from colleagues with similar professional concerns working in different cultural contexts. The aim is to build bridges between theory, research and practice.

The genesis of this two-volume series derives from the editors' longstanding involvements in seeking to understand more fully, and thereby improve, the learning and teaching of literacy in general and reading attainments and progress in particular, of pupils in schools. Our work as teachers in mainstream secondary and primary schools, special schools and units, language and reading specialists in support services, research workers, academics and authors provides the basis for our involvements. Our contributions to initial training courses taken by teachers, coupled with the provision of courses of advanced training for qualified and experienced teachers, underline our personal commitments.

Over many years, our activities have led to the establishment of extensive professional contacts with colleagues in many countries engaged in similar work. Reflecting on our wide network of contacts and on common professional concerns and controversies, led to the present two volumes.

In the twenty-four chapters comprising this series, we have presented a selection of articles that provide information on research and practice. Each book is in two parts. Part 1 in Volume 1 concerns the importance of phonological awareness. Part 2 addresses wider concerns related to the development of children's reading. In Volume 2, Part 1 focuses on curriculum concerns and Part 2 deals with aspects of accountability and assessment. These contributions bear on some of the most important current concerns and controversies from the broad fields constituting emergent and developing reading and curriculum and assessment issues. Each of the chapters has a common structure. All authors have identified from their contributions a number of important 'messages for teachers'.

In Volume 2, the six chapters comprising Part 1 continue with a range of curriculum concerns. These include considerations of what is meant by literacy in different cultural contexts and demonstrate changes in current thinking about the nature of the concept and the materials and methods likely to enhance the acquisition of literacy. This affects how children's learning can be enhanced in culturally diverse communities. The two final chapters in this section return to a perennial controversy concerning ways in which the writing systems in different countries may affect standards of literacy. The six chapters in Part 2 are devoted to assessment issues. The pioneer work being carried out at the University of Manchester School of Education, that in progress at the Royal Melbourne Institute of Technology, and the work of the Ministry of Education and Culture in Israel, are arousing increasing international interest. The section concludes with two chapters based on the work of the International Association for the Evaluation of Educational Achievement reading-literacy study.

In conclusion, we know, but find unconvincing, the reasons for non-participation by the UK in this major international research. Did *your* country take part in the IEA reading-literacy study? If not, do you know why not? How true is it that ignorance can provide a (misguided and short-term) bliss? Perhaps fear of international comparisons of the educational efficacy of educational systems in promoting literacy will remain a central international concern for a long time.

Part 1

Curriculum Concerns

Chapter 1

Expanding the Dimensions of World Literacy

C. Foley

Summary

The ultimate goal of reading instruction should be to produce young people who can read fluently and who choose to do so for both pleasure and information. It is argued in this chapter that expanding the dimensions of world literacy to make it work better for more learners will best be facilitated by singling out and addressing facets of reading instruction which make for enjoyable literacy activities. The importance of making reading instruction enjoyable must remain at the centre of the world-literacy movement as its dimensions expand in an effort to understand better not only how children learn to read but why children choose to read.

Introduction

Examination of educational programmes and practices should provoke professionals to ask, 'Why would children enjoy reading instruction?' The ultimate goal of reading instruction should be to graduate young people who can read and write fluently and who choose to do so in order to improve their lives personally, as well as politically (e.g., improve their status and influence). Yet, the current worldwide pattern of teaching and assessing and then, based on some standardized criterion, determining whether literacy has been achieved, often ignores the importance of children's interest in, and enthusiasm for, literary activities.

Past and present efforts by nations to achieve minimal levels of literacy for the majority of their populations have focused on the pedagogy of numerous years of structured, redundant reading and writing instructional methodologies often delivered via boring and inappropriate reading texts. The results have been unsatisfactory. Students who do eventually 'measure up' on a skills test established for accountability purposes can still fail the true test of literacy by avoiding reading, writing and learning activities following their years of formal schooling. For students truly to enjoy language endeavours, enjoyable experiences and growth must occur early in life, during the very process of learning to read. Then, as adults, individuals will be more likely to participate in literary activities daily, despite busy home and work schedules.

Educators, through dialogue, continuously examine and expand the dimensions of world literacy. Past focuses have included finding ideal instructional approaches and developing effective teacher-training programmes. Establishing national standards, determining key skills to be measured and designing tests to assess proficiency levels are additional areas that have been given considerable attention. While the manner in which comparisons will be made amongst students in New York and Chicago, New South Wales and Queensland, England and Germany, forms an important foundation in the examination of, and quest for, world literacy, it is only one facet of the international movement. Great progress has been made in the study of how children learn to read; yet, new questions and focuses have also emerged, causing the dimensions of world-literacy dialogue and research to expand. Three examples of interesting issues related to reading materials and instruction that prompt further exploration are the use of: multicultural literature which mirrors the faces in the classroom; reading materials which equitably and realistically portray males and females; and reading instructional approaches which interest and motivate young learners.

In expanding the first dimension of world literacy, which pertains to the use of multicultural literature in the classroom, the ethnic representation in children's reading materials must consider the ethnic backgrounds of students in the classroom. All students need opportunities to read a vast array of texts to which they can relate culturally in order to develop positive self-perceptions and strong personal identities. Required reading materials should include selections with characters from various ethnic groups who are depicted in realistic settings and situations if children's understanding of the many cultures that surround them is to be strengthened. When reading materials used in the classroom favour one ethnic group over the numerous other student populations present, students from the minority, non or underrepresented cultures may be unable or unwilling to relate to the characters in the texts. Limited ability or desire to relate can ultimately result in lowered interest and comprehension. Negative, subliminal messages concerning societal values are sent to all readers, as well.

Have instructional reading materials changed over the years to better mirror the faces in today's classrooms? Basal-reading programs that have dominated reading instruction in American schools for over seventy years have influenced the cognitive and affective development of youngsters, causing them to reflect at times upon their very self-worth (Heymsfeld, 1989). Smith (1986) recognized that pupils who do not progress satisfactorily in these popularly used reading programs probably experience difficulty due to a mismatch between their experiential backgrounds and the prior knowledge required to comprehend the texts. In other words, students who were at one time categorized as poor achievers are now described as limited in their experiential background knowledge. Research demonstrates that students rely on their cultural backgrounds as well as on the cultural points of view presented in passages to comprehend a text (Pritchard, 1990). Shannon (1989b) suggests that basal-reading programs and standardized reading measures have fed a dual American myth, that minority and low socio-economic groups of students are responsible for the difficulties that they experience in learning to read while children from middle and upper-class homes are successful in learning to read because they are able to complete the basal program and pass the standardized achievement measures administered.

In American schools, shifts in demographics over time indicate that significant changes in the ethnic composition of the classroom have occurred. The prediction is that soon one of every three American children will come from an other-culture or non-English speaking home. Furthermore, the minority school-age population will increase from 25 per cent noted in the 1980s to 42 per cent during the 1990s (Commission on Minority Participation in Education and American Life, 1988). In large urban areas, 80 to 90 per cent of the American school-age population will be non-white (Astin, 1982; Gonzalez, 1990).

A second dimension related to the use of basal-reading materials that needs further attention is the large discrepancy in the portrayal ratio of females to males, a discrepancy which has existed for over four decades. In a 1977 study examining the sex of central or main characters in 1964–76 basal readers (Racism and Sexism Resource Center for Educators, 1977), 70 per cent of the basal characters were males. In another 1970s study examining the frequency of females and males appearing in 134 textbooks in stories with mastery themes (stories in which the central characters displayed qualities such as ingenuity, creativity, bravery, perseverance, achievement, adventurousness, curiosity, autonomy and self-respect) the ratio of text characters was similar: one female to three males (Women on Words and Images, 1975). However, stories with themes of passivity and dependence featured females six times as often as males, even when the females depicted could have been portrayed as appropriately handling the story situations presented. Females were featured primarily as mothers or job holders, but rarely as both in the instructional materials being used in the classroom.

Students at all grade levels need to be immersed in texts in which females and males are equivalently represented and realistically portrayed. Reading materials must depict the ever-changing, expanding and divergent roles of males and females, as well, in order to improve human relationships. The sexist role conditioning of earlier days must not be encouraged or reinforced in the 1990s through reading textbook representations of females and males or the ultimate result will be further divisiveness. Females deserve to be portrayed in instructional texts as leaders, decision makers and problem solvers. Girls should appear as often as boys in main-character roles and in a variety of story structures.

Students need to be motivated to read. Academic achievement is influenced by interest. Most school subjects are taught via textbooks. Thus, the appeal of text selections is crucial. Students are able to understand and retain subject matter when they identify with the characters and the events. Most importantly, students are more interested and involved in reading selections where characters appear to be real to them. In a study conducted by McArthur and Eisen (1976), students were found to stay on task longer and remember stories of achievement when the characters were of the same sex as the reader. In addition, the students were most likely to accept a female character in a story to be achievement-oriented if they had previously read a selection in which a female achieved. The more exposure the students had to non-sexist materials, the more they were influenced by, and able to retain, the values and attitudes of the materials. Despite such findings, society and textbook publishers continue to practise the wide use of male role models in books, television and other media.

A third dimension of literacy which needs to expand further is that of classroom reading instruction. A wide repertoire of instructional strategies needs to be utilized by teachers to stimulate students to learn and to involve them more actively in the reading process. If years of instruction are indeed necessary to reach maturity in reading, as has been suggested by the 'basal kindergarten through eighth grade' instructional approach, then efforts to maintain student interest over time and to adjust instruction for those who do not experience success, must be made. American basal programs have relied totally upon simplistic, instructional routines in the past, rather than capitalizing on novelty during daily lessons. Two facts which are not always considered are that learning occurs when information is presented via new or unusual techniques and some students are more difficult to motivate than others. Reading instruction cannot continue to require students to partake in redundant exercises over lengthy periods of time, as has been the case in the USA with the daily, nine-year regimented use of the directed-reading lesson (Betts, 1946).

Guam, a USA territory in the Pacific, struggles with the reality of an island-wide, mandated basal-reading instructional approach which is not meeting the needs of their unique American school population — a population which is not predominantly Caucasian middle-class, not predominantly male and not always challenged by the traditional basal-reading lesson. To better understand the research presented in this chapter, a brief history of Guam's educational system follows.

Guam's Educational System

Guam became a possession of the United States in 1898. Previously, the Spanish provided education to the children of Guam in their native language of Chamarro. Under USA control, the public educational system was Americanized and all classroom instruction was conducted in English. Instruction changed a third time with the Japanese occupation of Guam during World War II; during this time span, lessons were conducted in Japanese. The American system of education was reinstated upon Guam's liberation from Japan in 1944. The current political leaning, toward becoming a Commonwealth, could potentially result in yet another instructional swing for this small island population.

Presently, as a territory of the USA, Guam follows federal regulations regarding education. Classroom practices reveal a purely American instructional methodology. In reading, the basal approach, which has long dominated reading instruction in mainland schools (Flood and Lapp, 1986), is also the adopted, island-wide instructional program in Guam. Similarly, since the American public demands the administration of national, standardized reading assessments in the belief that the success of a school is reflected by the placement of its students on such measures, standardized achievement tests are also administered to Guamanian students (Shannon, 1989a). However, the large number of students 'at risk' in the middle and high schools and the consistently low scores of local students of all ages on mainland-normed measures have caused speculation that Guam's educational system is somehow 'substandard' compared with that of the continental USA.

Guam's deflated standardized test scores may be attributed, at least in part, to the use of the American system of basal-reading instruction and standardized assessment, both of which are insensitive to the experiential backgrounds of Pacific islanders and Asians, small minority groups within America's contiguous borders but majority populations in Guam. Instructional practices advocated by the basal publishers might ignore the learning styles of the local students or their needs to become mature readers. Educators, such as Spencer (1990), have criticized the rigorous marketing efforts of publishers in the Micronesian region to sell instructional programmes to Guam and surrounding island school districts which are obviously 'inappropriate' because they are not geared to these unique populations of students.

To grasp the multicultural mix in Guam and the male–female ratio, demographics are presented for the 1990–1 middle-school population. The demographic breakdown of this student population of 6,095 reveals that the indigenous Chamarro student population was the largest, with 3,145 Chamarros from Guam and 129 from nearby islands (twenty-nine from Rota, twenty-one from Tinian and seventy-nine from Saipan). The second predominant ethnic group in the sixth to eighth grades were Filipinos, with 1,648 students. The remaining ethnic groups identified included: 580 Caucasians, ninety-seven African-Americans, forty-five Koreans, thirty-five Chinese, twenty-one Japanese, seventeen Hispanics and fifteen Native American Indians. In addition, 194 students came from the Federated States of Micronesia, 100 from Belau and thirty-one from other surrounding islands. Of the remaining fifty-nine middle-school students, forty-six were from 'other' Asian countries and thirteen from 'other' regions of the world. Guam's middle-school population is almost evenly divided with 3,517 males and 3,478 females (Department of Education, 1991).

A reasonable expectation would be for the characters in the instructional reading texts used in Guam to be similarly distributed by ethnicity and sex to the population serviced for the best possible educational scenario to occur. In addition to noticeable problems with the character representation in the reading materials being used, classroom teachers in Guam also note reading instructional practices that are ineffective with their population. To address the three dimensions of world literacy targeted in this chapter, ethnic representation in reading materials, male and female representation in reading materials and reading instructional practices, a selection of recent studies are presented. All stem from the efforts of concerned and dedicated educators in the Guam school system who are attempting to improve reading comprehension and spark student interest during reading and content-area instruction.

Method

The first study discussed in this chapter focuses on Guam's unique multicultural middle-school population and the materials adopted for island-wide usage (Campbell, 1993). Campbell examined three seventh-grade basal-reading programs piloted in the middle schools to determine how sensitive the programs were to the classrooms' ethnic mix and distribution of males and females. The seventh-grade basal texts were: Houghton Mifflin's *Bright Glory from The Literature Experience Program* (Pikulski *et al.*, 1991), McDougal, Littell's *Red Level* from *Vistas in Reading Literature* (Chaparro and Trost, 1989) and Silver Burdett and Ginn's *Star Walk from World of Reading* (Pearson *et al.*, 1989). The basal characters from all the stories in the three readers, with the exception of animal stories, poems and skills articles, were examined to determine their ethnicity and sex, the type of selection in which they appeared and the role that they played.

Numerous studies have been conducted to examine instructional issues. Other studies shared in this chapter focused on the use of reading instructional variations which might stimulate student interest and increase comprehension. The first study conducted by a fifth-grade instructor in a northern Guam elementary school was prompted when the teacher noted three basal reading activities which were largely ineffective with the Chamarro and Filipino students in her classroom (Foley, Farra and Chang, 1991). These activities included the initial silent-reading seatwork task, the completion of a large number of seatwork pages and the written completion of the 'Focus on Comprehension' questions found at the end of each selection. The instructor decided to streamline the weekly basal lesson and replace these activities with taped repeated reading (Chomsky, 1976) and paired repeated reading (Koskinen and Blum, 1986) for one-half of the class who became the experimental group. The control group continued to receive the regular basal program, as they had throughout their elementary school careers.

In a similar study, middle-school science teachers also experimented with the taped-reading strategy in an effort to coax and to assist their reluctant and remedial readers to complete content-area homework reading assignments. To encourage their students to read the required text, these teachers made audio tapes of the assigned textbook passages and then made them available for checkout by the students. As a result, taped reading sessions were possible in each student's home. The question posed by these content-area teachers was a simple one: Would the students complete the reading homework assignments if provided with an instructional support system?

At the high-school level, McDonald (1993) experimented with a similar instructional variation, 'taped read-along', to teach literature. In addition to the taped read-along variation, McDonald also implemented 'story impressions' (McGinley and Denner, 1987), an instructional prereading strategy which utilizes prediction and links the reading and writing processes, to get her secondary students more actively involved in the reading process. Once again, the research of a local classroom teacher examined alternative instructional strategies that might appeal to her unique mix of students. Like other Guam educators who were choosing to vary the instructional classroom approach to reading tasks, McDonald recognized a need to increase student comprehension of required textbook readings. In her study, three groups of students, deemed to be equivalent, based on findings from the Kruskal-Wallis test used to analyse the comprehension pretest scores of the groups, were assigned to one of three reading instructional approaches for a five-week period during which five literature selections were read. The control group received the traditional high-school instructional approach as detailed in the teacher's manual; the students read the selection silently and then answered the textbook comprehension questions. Students in treatment group two (taped read-along) listened to a taped recording of the literature selection and read along in their books. They then answered the comprehension questions. Students in treatment group three (story impressions in a taped read-along format) discussed what the story might be about using the given story clues, wrote a story guess, listened to the taped recording of the literature selection while reading along in their books, compared/contrasted the story guess with the actual story and then answered the comprehension questions. Each of the three groups rated how much they liked or disliked the strategy used weekly at the completion of the instructional activities.

Not all the variations to traditional and often repetitive classroom-reading instruction implemented in Guam's classrooms by educators who felt that learning could be more enjoyable and more effective employed the taped reading element. A middle-school teacher (Bismonte, Foley and Petty, in press) substituted a single instructional component of the basal directed-reading lesson, the vocabulary activities, with 'possible sentences' (Moore and Moore, 1986). This is a strategy in which students make predictions about the relationships between unknown words and then use the text to evaluate and refine their vocabulary knowledge. One group of students, the control group, continued to receive the traditional basal instruction, while the others, who became the experimental group, received the modified basal approach. Only differences in vocabulary were examined in this research design.

To improve students' summary writing and comprehension of science text, a fifth-grade teacher in a southern Guam school (O'Mallan, Foley and Lewis, 1993) compared the use of the guided reading procedure (Manzo, 1975) with the traditional content-area instructional approach. Pupils in the experimental group were taught to recall orally a science text read silently and to then confirm, organize and note relationships amongst the recalled facts prior to writing a summary of the text. At the same elementary school, a second instructor focused on social-studies instruction (Benito, Foley, Lewis and Prescott, 1993) providing metacognitive instruction and practice in question–answer relationships (Raphael, 1982) to third, fourth and fifth graders to improve textbook comprehension. This instructional variation was a drastic deviation from the traditional basal-reading instruction received by the control group. In all the aforementioned research studies which examined traditional classroom instruction in search of more promising approaches to reading, the findings were promising.

Results

Results of the Campbell study related to the first dimension, ethnicity, revealed that characters in today's middle-school basal readers greatly resemble those found in basals a decade ago (Logan and Garcia, 1982). Column percentage scores (Table 1.1) permit the comparison of ethnic groups within a particular basal programme while row percentage scores permit ethnic comparisons across the three basal programmes included in this study.

Total row percentage scores in the Campbell study indicate that 70.59 per cent of the 415 basal characters examined were Caucasians (living either within or outside the continental United States). The second ethnic group most often depicted in the current seventh-grade basals was the Hispanic (12.77 per cent). African Americans ranked third with approximately one-half as many characters (6.27 per cent). Asians (3.61 per cent) and Native American Indians (3.61 per cent) comprised very small percentages of the total characters examined in the three sets of textbook selections. Japanese, Chinese and Vietnamese characters rarely appeared in the seventh-grade texts, and not a single Pacific islander was identified in the reading instructional materials being considered for island-wide adoption by Guam educators.

Row percentage scores reveal that of all the Hispanic characters found in the three programmes, more than one-half, 56.60 per cent, appeared in the McDougal, Littell series. The Houghton Mifflin programme had the least number of Hispanic characters (15.10 per cent). McDougal,

Table 1.1: Ethnicity of characters presented in three middle-school basal-reading series

Ethnicity	Houghton Mifflin			Basal-reading Series McDougal, Littell			Silver Burdett and Ginn			Total	
	N	Col. %	Row %	N	Col. %	Row %	N	Col. %	Row %	N	Row %
Total Caucasian*	75	72.12	25.60	133	71.12	45.39	85	68.55	29.01	293	70.59
Caucasian in USA	36	34.62	21.30	90	48.13	53.25	43	34.68	25.44	169	40.72
Caucasian out USA	39	37.50	31.45	43	22.99	34.68	42	33.87	33.87	124	29.88
African American	12	11.54	46.15	8	4.28	30.77	6	4.84	23.08	26	6.27
Hispanic	8	7.69	15.10	30	16.04	56.60	15	12.10	28.30	53	12.77
Native American Indian	3	2.88	20.00	11	5.88	73.33	1	.81	6.67	15	3.61
Chinese	3	2.88	60.00	0	0.00	0.00	2	1.61	40.00	5	1.20
Japanese	0	0.00	0.00	1	.53	16.67	5	4.03	83.33	6	1.45
Vietnamese	0	0.00	0.00	2	1.08	100.00	0	0.00	0.00	2	.48
Asian Other**	3	2.88	20.00	2	1.07	13.33	10	8.06	66.67	15	3.61
Pacific Islander	0	0.00	0.00	0	0.00	0.00	0	0.00	0.00	0	0.00
Totals: N and Col. %	104	25.06		187	45.06		124	29.88		415	

Notes: * Total Caucasian = Caucasian in USA + Caucasian out of USA.
       ** Thai (8); Mongolian (3); Indonesian (2); Iraqi (2).

Source: Campbell, E.D. (1993)

Littell had a relatively high representation of Native American Indians (73.33 per cent), as well, in comparison to the other two basal programs, Houghton Mifflin (20.00 per cent) and Silver Burdett and Ginn (6.67 per cent). Of the African Americans identified in the basal selections, 46.15 per cent appeared in the Houghton Mifflin reader; Silver Burdett and Ginn had the least number of African American characters (23.08 per cent). The Chinese were not represented at all in the McDougal, Littell program. Likewise, Japanese characters never appeared in the Houghton Mifflin reader. McDougal, Littell was the only publisher to include Vietnamese characters in the seventh-grade basal. None of the three series examined in the Campbell study portrayed a Pacific islander in a single reading selection. 'Other' Asian characters identified tended to be concentrated in a single basal selection and were predominantly Thai.

Table 1.2 presents results of the Campbell study related to the second dimension of literacy, the inclusion of female and male characters in the basals. Table 1.2 shows that McDougal, Littell had more story characters (187) than the other two programmes, Silver Burdett and Ginn (124) and Houghton Mifflin (104). Thus, the number of characters for both sexes in McDougal, Littell was greater than that of the other two reading series. Yet, the McDougal, Littell reader also displayed the largest discrepancy of males (135 characters or 72.19 per cent) to females (fifty-two characters or 27.81 per cent). Overall, percentage scores showed that males appeared as story characters much more frequently (69.64 per cent) than females (30.36 per cent) in the basal selections examined.

Table 1.2: Sex of characters by basal-reading series

Sex	Houghton Mifflin		McDougal, Littell		Silver Burdett and Ginn		Total	
	N	%	N	%	N	%	N	%
Males	71	68.27	135	72.19	83	66.94	289	69.64
Females	33	31.73	52	27.81	41	33.06	126	30.36
Totals	104		187		124		415	

Source: Campbell, E.D. (1993)

The Campbell study further assessed the treatment of the sexes by categorizing female and male characters by role: main character, supporting character or minor character (Table 1.3). Column percentages reveal that of the 129 characters depicted in main roles, 105 (81.39 per

Table 1.3: Character roles by sex for the three basal-reading programs

Sex	Total N	Main			Character Roles Supporting			Minor		
		N	Col. %	Row %	N	Col. %	Row %	N	Col. %	Row %
Males	289	105	81.39	36.33	100	63.29	34.60	84	65.67	29.07
Females	126	24	18.61	19.05	58	36.71	46.03	44	34.38	34.92
Totals	415	129			158			128		

Source: Campbell, E.D. (1993)

cent) were males while only twenty-four (18.61 per cent) were females. Even in supporting and minor character roles, males appeared twice as often as females. In supporting roles there were 100 male characters (63.29 per cent) in comparison to fifty-eight female characters (36.71 per cent). In minor roles, eighty-four males (65.67 per cent) appeared in comparison to forty-four females (34.38 per cent). Row percentages indicate that across the three series, males appeared predominantly in main and supporting roles (36.33 per cent and 34.60 per cent, respectively) while females were cast most often in supporting and minor roles (46.03 per cent and 34.92 per cent, respectively). Females played the least important character roles in the McDougal, Littell basal program where they were identified predominantly in minor character roles.

The final variable analysed in Campbell's study relating to the sex of the basal characters was the representation of females and males in the various story types found in the seventh-grade readers: real-life, myths and legends, biographies and autobiographies and science fiction and fantasies. Findings as set out as Table 1.4 column percentages indicate that the greatest number of both male and female characters appeared in the real-life selections (44.64 per cent and 48.41 per cent, respectively). However, row percentages indicate that, overall, the real-life selections contained more than twice as many male characters (129 or 67.89 per cent) as female characters (sixty-one or 32.11 per cent). The largest discrepancy between the sexes occurred in the myths and legends category where males (sixty-five or 80.25 per cent) were depicted four times more often than females (sixteen or 19.75 per cent). The best female representation was in the science fiction and fantasy category where 39.02 per cent of the characters were females. However, even this strongest female representation was not equivalent to that of the males, who appeared as characters in this story type 60.98 per cent of the time.

Table 1.4: Male and female representation in the four types of basal-reading selections

Type of Selection				Sex			
		Male			Female		
	N	Col. %	Row %	N	Col. %	Row %	Total
Real-life	129	44.64	67.89	61	48.41	32.11	190
Myths and legends	65	22.49	80.25	16	12.70	19.75	81
Biographies and autobiographies	45	15.57	72.58	17	13.49	27.42	62
Science fiction and fantasies	50	17.30	60.98	32	25.40	39.02	82
Totals	289			126			415

Source: Campbell, E.D. (1993)

Findings related to gains relevant to the third dimension of literacy, varying classroom-reading instruction to improve learning, were positive. In the Foley, Farra and Chang (1991) study, significant gains in oral reading comprehension occurred following an eight-week implementation of taped and paired repeated reading in place of three directed-reading lesson components considered to be ineffective with the Guamanian students. Teacher observations revealed that the supplemental reading strategies used with the experimental group in this study increased student interest, resulting in more effort being made during both the silent and oral readings of the basal selections. Students in the experimental group were described as more motivated and more on task during the taped and paired repeated readings than were the students in the control group who continued to receive and to avoid the three basal seatwork tasks included in the traditional instructional approach.

The science teachers who encouraged their middle-school students to complete home textbook-reading assignments by providing them with taped readings of the text assignments found this instructional variation to be successful initially when students began to ask if the next tape was available even before the textbook reading was assigned. In addition, the number of audio tapes available for checkout had to be increased to meet the growing student demand for the taped reading-homework component of the class.

Results of the McDonald (1993) study that employed two instructional variations to the traditional literature lesson, taped read-along and story impressions in a taped read-along format, suggested that, while the high-school students responded favorably to all three strategies the first time they were used, fluctuations occurred in the students' interest in the approaches over time. Table 1.5 presents the

Table 1.5: Percentage of students who liked the reading strategy used (N = 89)

Week	Traditional Silent Reading %	Reading Strategies Taped Read-along %	Story Impressions %
1	61.54	70.00	73.33
2	25.00	8.33	15.38
3	38.46	15.38	40.00
4	14.29	72.73	42.86
5	23.08	81.82	25.00
Average Rating	32.47	49.65	39.31

Source: McDonald, F.D. (1993)

percentage of students in each of the three groups who liked the reading strategy used to teach the literature selections over a five-week period.

A majority of the students in all three instructional groups initially rated the strategy used to teach the first literature selection positively. However, ratings of all three strategies plummeted by the second week of instruction. The traditional strategy received low-interest ratings for the remainder of the five-week study. 'Story impressions' ratings fluctuated but never regained the initial, positive response given after the first week of usage. The taped read-along strategy began to regain appeal following two weeks of lowered ratings, receiving the highest percentage of positive marks from students during the last two weeks of instruction. The average rating of all three strategies indicated that a majority of the students were not favorable to any of the instructional approaches implemented in this particular study.

To compare the comprehension of the three groups receiving the same literature selections via different instructional approaches, a one-factor analysis of variance (ANOVA) was used. Mean scores of both the taped read-along group, treatment group two, and the story impressions in a taped read-along format group, treatment group three, were statistically significant at a probability level of .0248 when compared to control group one who received the traditional instructional approach to literature. (See Tables 1.6 and 1.7).

A *post hoc* analysis indicated that both instructional variations were significantly better than the traditional approach used in the classroom. However as can be seen from Table 1.8, a significant difference in the student-comprehension scores was not found to exist between the two treatment groups.

The strongest finding in the O'Mallan, Foley and Lewis (1993) study was that the students, as a result of the guided reading-procedure instructional variation, paraphrased more while simultaneously decreasing

Table 1.6: Mean comprehension scores and standard deviations for the three instructional strategies

Group	Mean	S.D.
Control group 1		
Traditional strategy	6.67	1.67
Treatment group 2		
Taped read along strategy	7.76	1.09
Treatment group 3		
Story impressions strategy	7.71	1.90

Source: McDonald, F.D. (1993)

Table 1.7: Analysis of variance of effectiveness of alternative reading strategies

One Factor ANOVA	X$_i$: Group		Y$_1$: Comprehension Mean Score	
Source	DF	Sum Squares	Mean Squares	F-Test
Between groups	4	25.90	6.47	2.95 (p = .0248*)
Within groups	85	186.85	2.20	
Total	89	212.74		

* significant

Note: There were four treatment groups and one control group in the original study.
Source: McDonald, F.D. (1993)

Table 1.8: Fisher PLSD post hoc comparison between groups

One Factor ANOVA	X$_1$: Group	Y$_1$: Comprehension Mean Score
Comparison	Mean Difference	Fisher PLSD
Control 1 vs. Treatment 2	−1.09	1.07*
Control 1 vs. Treatment 3	−1.04	.98*
Treatment 2 vs. Treatment 3	−.05	1.07

* p < .05

Source: McDonald, F.D. (1993)

their tendency to plagiarize material read in their written summaries. And lastly, following the question–answer relationships/metacognitive instruction (Benito, Foley, Lewis and Prescott, 1993), the experimental group in this study correctly answered a significantly larger percentage of the comprehension items on the end-of-chapter social-studies test.

Discussion

The key finding of the Campbell (1993) study was that approximately two-thirds to three-fourths of the characters depicted in the seventh-grade basals were Caucasians, a minority group in Guam's middle-school population. The ethnic groups found predominantly in Guam, especially the indigenous Chamarros and the neighbouring Pacific islanders, never even appeared in the basal texts being considered for island-wide adoption. The Campbell findings revealed a modest increase in the representation of Hispanic characters and a slight decrease in the number of African American characters appearing in the current middle-school basal texts. In the Campbell study of three seventh-grade basals, only 6.27 per cent of the characters were African Americans. Klebacher (1984) found that 13.00 per cent of the characters in four fourth to sixth-grade basal readers were African American. In Logan and Garcia's (1982) study, Native American Indians comprised 3.40 per cent of the total basal characters. Similarly, in the Campbell study conducted eleven years later, 3.61 per cent of the basal characters were native American Indians. Though new ethnic groups (Asians, Chinese, Japanese and Vietnamese) emerged in the seventh-grade basal readers of the 1990s, they appeared in a small number of selections. The fact that Pacific islanders and Asians were seldom found is noteworthy considering Pacific islanders and Asians have more than doubled in population, from 3.5 million to 7.3 million, according to the USA 1990 census.

Relevant to the second dimension of literacy, Campbell found that males were depicted in basal-reading selections at the seventh-grade level two to three times more often than were females. Females are still seldom seen to be the problem solvers or story focus in the instructional reading materials used in American classrooms, according to current findings in the Campbell study. Again, basal-publishing companies have ignored the findings and demands for change made by earlier researchers (Racism and Sexism Resource Center for Educators, 1977; Women on Words and Images, 1975). The large discrepancy in the ratio of females to males and the similar discrepancy in the frequency of females and males in main roles has continued into the 1990s.

Relevant to the last dimension, instructional variation, the novelty of the method of taped reading was effective for a lengthy period of time at the elementary level during reading instruction and at the middle-school level during science instruction. In the fifth-grade classroom (Foley, Farra and Chang, 1991), gains were noted in comprehension for the group that used taped and paired repeated reading in place of instructional components of the basal felt to be ineffective with the Guamanian youngsters. In addition, student interest and willingness to stay on task during reading activites were also noted to increase as a result of the instructional change. At the middle-school level, students who previously had not completed science homework-reading tasks were found to become enthusiastic and positive when read-along tapes of the assigned texts were made available for overnight checkout.

In literature classes at the high-school level, the taped read-along strategy was the most interesting to the students of the three approaches used to provide instruction of required literature selections. Comprehension of the literature selections increased for both alternative approaches to the traditional classroom instruction, taped read-along and story impressions in a taped read-along format. However, results of the study confirmed the suspicions of some Guam secondary teachers that they have difficulty motivating high-school students to read assigned texts. While the students in the study initially responded favorably to all the strategies used, fluctuations occurred in their interest in the instructional approaches throughout the five-week span of the study.

The 'possible sentences' strategy used in place of the vocabulary component of the directed reading lesson resulted in students' improved comprehension of the key vocabulary terms targeted for instruction (Bismonte, Foley and Petty, in press). In addition to the students' increased abilities to pronounce and define the vocabulary terms, observations of the researchers and classroom teachers were that students in the experimental group were more interested during classroom instruction and more likely to complete homework-reading assignments than were those in the control group. In this particular study, the traditional approach, if conducted as directed by the teacher's manual, was also effective.

As a result of the guided-reading procedure instructional variation, fifth-graders paraphrased more while simultaneously decreased their tendency to plagiarize material in written summaries (O'Mallan, Foley and Lewis, 1993). This instructional result should greatly benefit participants in the study during their secondary-school years, when they will be required to write numerous reports without plagiarizing texts.

In the final study in which question–answer relationships and meta-cognition were employed to strengthen student comprehension of social-studies text (Benito, Foley, Lewis and Prescott, 1993), intermediate-aged pupils who averaged only one correct answer to the four items at the end-of-the-section comprehension check, doubled their performance on this measure following a five-week instructional period.

In the past five years, in all classrooms in which teachers implemented variations in reading or content-area instruction, students have experienced comprehension gains. Children in Guam's elementary and secondary classrooms responded positively to a number of diverse instructional strategies which deviated from the traditional approach to reading.

Messages for Teachers

Children spend an important part of their lives in school. They learn a range of basic skills including those of literacy. They also formulate social attitudes and behaviours. Self-esteem, academic success and attitudes toward ethnic groups are influenced by what students do not read as well as by what they *do* read. Subtle and overt values are transmitted through the contents of reading texts (Jackson, 1944; Fisher, 1965; Tauran, 1967; Litcher and Johnson, 1969).

For educators in Guam, the results of Campbell's study on ethnic and sex representation of characters in current middle-school basal readers suggest that mandated reading materials may make no effort to portray characters who are similar to the population of students actually using them. As a result, problems in areas such as comprehension and assessment could be expected — due to the mismatch between student and character experiential backgrounds. In the affective domain, an alarming message is being sent to the children concerning the value of their cultures. Will Guam's young people be able to acquire a love of reading when exposed, for the most part, to story characters unlike themselves?

Internationally, educators need to continue to examine closely the instructional reading materials being used in their classrooms to determine if they promote or inhibit learning and literacy. Cultural diversity in Guam, or in any democratic society in which equality of opportunity is acknowledged as a crucial objective, has important implications for educational policies and practice. As the findings from the small-scale researches in Guam reported above suggest, important lessons can be learned by teachers from the practices and research of colleagues in other culturally diverse societies. For example, cultural diversity and its pedagogic implications across an entire curriculum, and in relation to literacy in particular, are being systematically addressed at national, school and classroom levels in England and Wales (Pumfrey and Verma, 1993a; 1993b; Verma and Pumfrey, 1993a; 1994). Are the materials used in your school's literacy program culturally sensitive?

Research must extend further with the next cycle of ethnicity studies to include a new and quickly growing 'ethnic' population of interracial children. Interracial children form a growing group in today's classrooms; yet, this student population has seldom been included in ethnic-research endeavours.

Society is changing and the portrayal of the sexes must also change in the school curriculum. Literacy, as defined by academic achievement, is curtailed for females by the unfair depiction of them in the texts that they read. Stories that children are required to read must increase the number of females depicted in strong leadership roles. Today's females need achievement-oriented role models with whom they can identify. Males also must be presented in varied roles, free of the sexist labelling that occurs when they are cast in stereotyped roles. If the definition of literacy does expand to include 'fostering a love for reading and producing avid readers', then the need for immediate and drastic changes in the classroom materials used to teach reading will have to be addressed.

Students' self-esteems, values, aspirations and fears are influenced by the extent to which they identify with the characters and life situations experienced through print — especially if they become emotionally involved with the characters. Character identification leads students to mold their own behaviours after their model characters (Busch, 1972). If minority and female students cannot find characters and settings in stories with whom they can identify, their personality growth may become inhibited. They can also become disenchanted with school and ultimately become academic non-achievers (Poussaint, 1970). Reading materials used in schools worldwide should reflect the population of the local community and of a world in which judgment is not based on sex or ethnicity, but on an individual's character.

Educators, parents and children alike agree that learning to read is not an easy task for many pupils. Despite this, it is the primary facet of schooling where failure is unacceptable. In striving for world literacy, the definition of the concept must expand as the knowledge base and commitment to the cause grow. Establishing standards and then determining how to deliver instruction and measure success is only the beginning of the international quest for equality and an educated citizenry. All pupils who enjoy instruction will enhance their learning potential and, once truly motivated, will choose to use the skills learned. Avid reading and writing will stimulate further growth in literacy skills.

In establishing sound literacy goals for the 1990s, the foremost goal must be to instill in children a love for reading so that, ultimately, they will read. Enthusiastic, lifelong learners need to be graduating from secondary institutions worldwide. Educators who recognize the value of literary activities and make them enjoyable will have a much greater success rate than those who continue to view reading solely as a set of skills to be taught and mastered or a curriculum to be completed. The reality and commonality which bring international educators together is the fact that there can be found, in all nations, a group of unfortunate individuals who are either unable or unwilling to read and write. Strengthening the literacy levels of these students is perhaps the most demanding challenge faced in today's classrooms. This might be best accomplished by experimenting with instructional variations which could improve both student interest and comprehension during reading and content-area instruction.

Conclusion

Expanding the dimensions of world literacy to make it work better for more learners will best be facilitated by singling out and addressing facets which may be factors contributing to students' reading success or reading failure. The importance of making reading instruction relevant and enjoyable must at all times remain at the centre of the world-literacy movement as its dimensions expand and more pieces of the literacy puzzle are examined in an effort to better understand not only how children learn to read, but why children choose to read and what makes children love to read.

References

ASTIN, A.W. (1982) *Minorities in Higher Education: Recent Trends, Current Prospects, and Recommendations*, San Francisco, Jossey-Bass.

BENITO, Y.M., FOLEY, C.L., LEWIS, C.D. and PRESCOTT, P. (1993) 'The effect of instruction in question–answer relationships and metacognition on social studies comprehension', *Journal of Research in Reading*, **16**, 1, pp. 20–9.

BETTS, E.A. (1946) *Foundations of Reading Instruction*, New York, American Book.

BISMONTE, A.R., FOLEY, C.L. and PETTY, J.A. (in press) 'Effectiveness of possible sentences with middle school students in Guam', *Reading Improvement*.

BUSCH, F. (1972) 'Interest, relevance, and learning to read', in ZIMET, S.J. (Ed) *What Children Read in School: Critical Analysis of Primary Reading Textbooks*, Grune and Stratton, pp. 116–17.

CAMPBELL, E.D. (1993) *An Examination of Ethnic and Sex Representation in Three Seventh-Grade Basal Readers*, Mangilao, Guam, University of Guam.

CHAPARRO, J.L. and TROST, M.A. (1989) *Vistas in Reading Literature (Red Level)*, Evanston, IL, McDougal, Little and Co.

CHOMSKY, C. (1976) 'After decoding what?', *Language Arts*, **53**, pp. 288–96.

COMMISSION ON MINORITY PARTICIPATION IN EDUCATION AND AMERICAN LIFE (1988) *One Third of a Nation*, Washington, DC, American Council on Education.

DEPARTMENT OF EDUCATION (1991) *Active Ethnic Report: Middle Schools*. Agana, Guam, Government of Guam.

FISHER, F.L. (1965) *The Influence of Reading and Discussion on the Attitudes of Fifth Graders toward American Indians*, Berkeley, CA University of California.

FLOOD, J. and LAPP, D. (1986) 'Types of text: The match between what students read in basals and what they encounter in tests', *Reading Research Quarterly*, **21**, pp. 284–97.

FOLEY, C.L., FARRA, H.E. and CHANG, E.A. (1991) 'Supplementing a fifth-grade basal reading program with taped and paired repeated reading', *Journal of Reading Education*, **17**, 1, pp. 6–14.

GONZALEZ, R.D. (1990) 'When minority becomes majority: The changing face of English classrooms', *English Journal*, **79**, 1, pp. 15–23.

HEYMSFELD, C.R. (1989) 'Point/counterpoint: The value of basal readers', *Reading Today*, August/September, pp. 18–19.

JACKSON, E. (1944) 'Effects of reading upon attitudes toward the Negro race', *Library Quarterly*, **14**, pp. 52–3.

KLEBACHER, K. (1984) *Contemporary Children and Basal Reading Series*, Union City, NJ, Kean College of New Jersey.

KOSKINEN, P.S. and BLUM, I.H. (1986) 'Paired repeated reading: A classroom strategy for developing fluent reading', *The Reading Teacher*, **40**, pp. 70–5.

LITCHER, J. and JOHNSON, D.W. (1969) 'Changes in attitudes toward Negroes of White elementary school students after use of multiethnic readers', *Journal of Educational Psychology*, **60**, pp. 148–52.

LOGAN, J.W. and GARCIA, J. (1982) 'An Examination of Ethnic Content in Nine Current Basal Reading Series', Chicago, Paper presented at the Annual Meeting of the International Reading Association.

MANZO, A.V. (1975) 'Guided reading procedure', *Journal of Reading*, **18**, pp. 287–91.

MCARTHUR, L.Z. and EISEN, S.V. (1976) 'Achievements of male and female storybook characters as determinants of achievement by boys and girls', *Journal of Personality and Social Psychology*, **33**, pp. 470–3.

MCDONALD, F.D. (1993) *Use of Story Impressions in Guam High School Literature Classes*, Mangilao, Guam, University of Guam.

MCGINLEY, W.J. and DENNER, P.R. (1987) 'Story impressions: A prereading/writing activity', *Journal of Reading*, **31**, 3, pp. 248–53.

MOORE, D.W. and MOORE, S.A. (1986) 'Possible sentences', in DISHNER, E.K. *et al.* (Eds) *Reading in the Content Areas: Improving Classroom Instruction*, 2nd ed., Dubuque, IA, Kendall/Hunt.

O'MALLAN, R.P., FOLEY, C.L. and LEWIS, C.D. (1993) 'Effects of the guided reading procedure on fifth graders' summary writing and comprehension of science text', *Reading Improvement*, **30**, 4, pp. 194–201.

PEARSON, P.D., JOHNSON, D.D., CLYMER, T., INDRISANO, E., VENEZKY, R.L., BAUMANN, J.F., HIEBERT, E., TOTH, M., GRANT, C. and PARATORE, J. (1989) *World of Reading (Star Walk)*, Needham, MA, Silver Burdett and Ginn, Inc.

PIKULSKI, J.J., COOPER, J.D., DURR, W.K., AU, K.H., GREENLAW, J., LIPSON, M.Y., PAGE, S., VALENCIA, S.W., WIXSON, K.K., BARRERA, R.B., BUNYAN, R.P., CHAPARRO, J.L., COMAS, J.C., CRAWFORD, A.N., HILLERICH, R.L., JOHNSON, T.G, MASON, J.M. MASON,

P.A., NAGY, W.E., RENZULLI, J.S. and SCHIFINI, A. (1991) *The Literature Experience (Bright Glory)*, Boston, MA, Houghton Mifflin Co.

POUSSAINT, A. (1970) *What Students Perceive*, Washington, DC, United States Commission on Civil Rights.

PRITCHARD, R. (1990) 'The effects of cultural schemata on reading processing strategies', *Reading Research Quarterly*, **15**, 40, pp. 273–95.

RACISM AND SEXISM RESOURCE CENTER FOR EDUCATORS (1977) *Sexism and Racism in Popular Basal Readers 1964–1976*, New York, Author.

PUMFREY, P.D. and VERMA, G.K. (1993a) *Cultural Diversity and the Curriculum. The Foundation Subjects and Religous Education in Secondary Schools*, Volume 1, London, Falmer Press.

PUMFREY, P.D. and VERMA, G.K. (1993b) *Cultural Diversity and the Curriculum, The Foundation Subjects and Religous Education in Primary Schools*, Volume 3, London, Falmer Press.

RAPHAEL, T. (1982) *Improving Question–Answering Strategies for Performance through Instruction*, Urbana-Champaign, IL, University of Illinois, Center for the Study of Reading.

SHANNON, P. (1989a) *Broken Promises: Reading Instruction in Twentieth Century America*, New York, Bergin and Garvey.

SHANNON, P. (1989b) 'The struggle for control of literacy lessons', *Language Arts*, **60**, 6, pp. 628–34.

SMITH, F. (1986) *Insult to Intelligence: The Bureaucratic Invasion of Our Classrooms*, Portsmouth, NH, Heinemann Educational Books, Inc.

SPENCER, M.L. (1990) *Responsible Bookselling in the Developing Micronesian Pacific*, Mangilao, Guam, University of Guam, Micronesian Language Institute.

TAURAN, R.H. (1967) *The Influence of Reading on the Attitudes of Third Graders Toward Eskimos*, College Park, MD, University of Maryland.

VERMA, G.K. AND PUMFREY, P.D. (1993) *Cultural Diversity and the Curriculum Cross-curricular Contexts, Themes and Dimensions in Secondary Schools*, Volume 2, London, Falmer Press.

VERMA, G.K. and PUMFREY, P.D. (1994) *Cultural Diversity and the Curriculum Cross-curricular Contexts, Themes and Dimensions in Primary Schools*, Volume 4, London, Falmer Press.

WOMEN ON WORDS AND IMAGES (1975) *Dick and Jane as Victims: Sex Stereotyping in Children's Readers*, Authors, Princeton, New Jersey.

Chapter 2

Children's Learning and the New English Curriculum

B. Raban-Bisby

Summary

This chapter reviews the main features of the reading component of the new English Curriculum and judges how far these will influence teaching and children learning to read. The nature of evidence on how children learn to read is explored. It is argued that research paradigms too often determine the research questions about reading rather than the reverse which should be the case. This situation causes problems in the English Curriculum when coupled with vested interests pulling in different directions. Much work remains to be done to hold the ground between the different tensions and avoid a wilful disregard for theories of learning and their reality in the classroom.

Introduction

This chapter explores issues concerning children's learning within the context of their learning to read and then maps these on to the concept of learning which is becoming enshrined in the National Curriculum in England through teacher training and becoming embodied in the revised draft Order for English in particular.

The contributions of Piaget, Chomsky and Bruner to our thinking concerning how children learn to read have been ably demonstrated by Donaldson and Reid (1982). For instance, Piaget's notions (1955) of 'accommodation' and 'assimilation' provide a powerful model for counteracting notions of learning being the stringing of beads. Through using these two concepts we are able to get a more sophisticated sense of new knowledge transforming old knowledge structures, and a more organic grasp of the notion of development.

Chomsky's work (1957) has given us insight into the way children acquire language and use their knowledge about language to become increasingly efficient in their ability to identify linguistic probabilities from limited information. In addition to these powerful strategies, Bruner's research (1957) has highlighted the concept of 'perceptual recklessness' and reminds us to temper ideas of predictability in language with due regard to the perceptual features of the spoken or written stimulus.

Focus on Learning

Concepts of learning and causes of failure to learn are central to the concerns of reading teachers, and what they know from their own work with children above all else is that we all fail to learn what doesn't make sense to us. The problem, as Smith (1986) has pointed out, is not one of not being able to learn, but rather not being able to make sense of what we are trying to learn.

This belief comes from the experience that teachers are more effective when they make themselves understandable to the learner, no matter how little the learner knows. Because of this insight, interest has been focused on what has become known as 'prior knowledge'. This view of necessary prior knowledge, is based on the fact that it is easier to understand what people say or write when there is an existing understanding of what they are talking or writing about.

Work in the 1970s, for instance, illustrated that children categorized as 'low achievers' in school have limitations in their prior knowledge rather than any defective learning abilities (Anderson, Spiro and Montague, 1977). Where does this prior knowledge come from? It is not from systematic and specific instruction because that in turn requires prior knowledge. It comes from more general experience of the topic in which the learning is to take place. We learn by engaging in activities, where we are helped to understand what is going on, and helped to engage in the activities themselves.

Smith (op. cit.), refers to experimental evidence (Mandler, 1967) which illustrates this process, demonstrating how understanding, or the activity of making sense, leads to learning rather than the deliberate effort to, for instance, memorize. The activity which was investigated included three groups of subjects who were given cards with single words printed on them. One group was asked to memorize the words for a later test, one group was asked to categorize the words in whatever way they chose and to memorize the words for a later test, the third group were asked only to categorize the words.

Both groups who engaged in the categorization task did equally well in memorizing the words and did considerably better than the group asked to memorize the words alone. The activity of categorizing the words was a powerful means of imposing order and making sense of the activity. Indeed, in this investigation categorization was found to be far more salient in promoting learning than the nonsensical task of learning individual words.

Learning has always been a difficult topic for psychologists to research. How can experiments compare between subjects who will inevitably have different prior knowledge? Towards the end of the last century, experimental psychologists discovered that they could avoid all this difficulty if they restricted their studies to how individuals learned nonsense or meaningless syllables and words. No one can have prior knowledge of something from outside their experience, something that makes no sense. With nonsense, as Smith (op. cit.), has pointed out, everyone starts learning from scratch. There were no uncontrolled variables or individual differences to 'contaminate' the results. Experiments could now be replicated and experimental results verified. The nonsense syllable offered the researcher control.

The results of such research studies made possible the formulation of laws of learning, which could be represented by smooth curves on a graph and summarized by algebraic formulae. Indeed, the history of the experimental study of learning has been a struggle between researchers trying to devise better nonsense and subjects trying to make better sense of it. However, the fact that some laws of learning could be said to be based on nonsense has been generally ignored in the field of education during the first half of this century, although its influence can be found even now.

There are two common assumptions underlying this view of learning: on the one hand, to understand something you first must learn it, and on the other hand, that there is no point in studying something you already understand. Both these assumptions are wrong. Indeed the reverse is true. To understand something does not mean that we know it already, but that we can *relate* it to what we know already, that we can *make sense* of it. In order to learn you have first to understand. These erroneous assumptions confuse understanding with knowledge. We are capable of understanding things we do not already know and we probably do so every moment we are awake and not bored or bewildered. When we read something we understand, we make sense of it even though we did not know it already; and as a consequence we learn. The only thing we are likely to learn if we are confused or bored is that the text is confusing or boring. Smith (op.cit) continues, if children read material that is confusing and boring, they quickly learn that reading itself is confusing and boring and subsequently make little progress with literacy.

Developmentally, a growing understanding of the nature and uses of print does not occur in a vacuum. It depends on living in an environment where print is important. It depends on interactions with print which are a source of social and intellectual pleasure for both children and those around them. Indeed, researchers have pointed out that awareness of forms and functions and uses of print provides not just the motivation for learning to read, but the backdrop against which reading and writing are best learned. The likelihood that children will succeed in learning to read at school, therefore, depends most of all on how much they have already experienced about reading before they get there (Raban, 1984) and this is where children's prior knowledge comes from. This finding is also reflected in research findings from other countries (Clay, 1979; Ferreiro and Teborosky, 1983).

Styles of Research

What we know about children learning to read is based on evidence. The nature of this evidence emerges from a variety of different sources and gives practitioners a number of mixed messages as they look to research to inform their classroom actions, in particular, as they look for ways of helping children who are making slow progress with their reading.

An important source of this information comes from academic research, although this has not always been helpful. For instance, while attending a conference in America a few years ago, I was reminded that people, even those who share the same concerns, do not share the same views of the world or the way in which it is organized. What counts as evidence for one group is unconvincing for others; what is important for another group is seen as insignificant when viewed from a different perspective.

At this conference findings were reported from a large-scale study, a micro-analysis of classroom reading. In this research based on children aged 7–9 years, video recordings were being analysed in order to define, describe and seek the role of attentive behaviour in reading. It was hypothesized that increased attention on the part of the child would decrease oral-reading errors, and this decrease in errors would in turn lead to a better understanding of what was read.

These videos provided data which were being analysed in minute detail. The outcomes were being subjected to statistical analysis derived from models developed in the sphere of biomedical quantitative research. The time, effort, money and sheer ingenuity involved in this major research initiative was breath-taking and was beginning to yield tentative results:

- boys are more inattentive than girls;
- younger children are more likely to be inattentive;
- difficult texts increase inattention; and
- low-ability children tend to lose concentration.

Practitioners can be forgiven for asking if research of this complexity and sophistication really is necessary to find out things which are all quite clear to any teacher or parent. Here we see the beginnings of a dilemma, identified in this instance by what this researcher would count as evidence and the nature of that evidence.

What is at stake here are the questions: What is knowledge? — and, more importantly — Whose knowledge counts? If research, through its activity of systematic investigation has any role in contributing to our knowledge base, what we are finding in reading research is an uncompromising emphasis on a single set of assumptions about the world, the way we experience it and how we learn from this experience, and this in turn informs our research literature.

As someone with the responsibility for publishing an annual review of reading research in Britain, I have the opportunity for tracking prestigious journal articles and the outcome of research funding policies. In this country and elsewhere, studies which get published predominantly emanate from a single research paradigm. This paradigm rests in the empirical/analytic tradition and is based on assumptions taken directly from the physical and biological sciences, assumptions which, for instance, have given us theories of learning nonsense.

Examples of funded research embedded in this paradigm include the Economic and Social Science Research Council (ESRC) study which reports that when text is manipulated through misspellings and stimulus degradation, partially sighted subjects slow down their overall reading speed. Also the Medical Research Council (MRC) study which reports that partially hearing subjects are poor at judging rhyme.

The kind of pervasiveness enjoyed by this style of research can be illustrated by the percentage of papers published in the top international journals. For instance, in a survey of twenty-one volumes of *Reading Research Quarterly* 97 per cent of the articles are from this perspective, 99 per cent in the *Journal of Reading Behavior*, and 98 per cent in *Journal of Reading Research*. Even in those journals which do not attract such prestige, for instance, *Research in the Teaching of English* and *Language Arts* the percentages are 72 and 77 respectively (Shannon, 1989).

Taken together, the assumptions of the empirical/analytic tradition enable reading researchers to treat all questions as if they had a single answer to 'what is . . . ?':

- What is reading?
- What is the most effective way of teaching reading?
- What is learning?

Of course these questions are too complex to address directly in single studies, so questions like these get subdivided into components. For instance reading becomes attention, decoding, comprehension and then each of these subsystems is divided even further in the belief that the bits can be put back together again to address the major issues.

In an important sense, these researchers are unconcerned about the effects of their work on the total cultural and social framework of reading instruction. Their purpose is to investigate cognitive processes and develop rational systems for testing and validating their own hypotheses. Research paradigms, whilst providing opportunities to bring a particular order to the world, also set constraints on what researchers can see in that world, on the questions they consider legitimate and important, and on the techniques they choose to answer those questions (See Chapter 1).

Wilding (1988) has conducted extensive work on experiments relating to lexical decision tasks. In these tasks, subjects are required to reject or accept letter strings as words or non-words, He finds that this type of task, which appears to be currently central to psychological investigations of the reading process, needs modification if sense is to be made of the results. However, he acknowledges;

> it may be more justifiably argued that such complications move the investigation away from the original concerns of the research . . . and that the task will become even more unlike 'normal' reading. (Wilding, 1988)

Wilding also hints that lexical-decision task experiments may only have marginal relevance in the investigation of reading anyway. In a recent volume of *Reading Research Quarterly*, Anderson, Wilkinson and Mason (1990) have identified the problem in all of this. They state that reading research and teaching reading have been moving 'out of earshot' of each other. They continue by saying that research on reading reflects little of what has been discovered about reading.

What is being argued here is not that the dominant paradigm is necessarily wrong, but that this paradigm, because of elitist forces, is determining the research questions which it is legitimate to ask. The reverse, of course, should be the case. Research questions themselves should be determining the choice of paradigm and paradigmatic diversity should be the more common characteristic of academic reading research. Questions of 'What is . . . ?' clearly need to give way to questions of 'How do . . . ?':

How do children learn?
How do children learn to read?

An example of what is referred to here as paradigmatic diversity is to be found in the recently reported research from two teams at Harvard University headed by Jeanne Chall (Chall *et al.*, 1990) and Catherine Snow (Snow *et al.*, 1991) respectively. Both teams of researchers focused on the same sample of children, although they conducted their research in quite different ways according to their own paradigmatic preferences. While their findings are reported in separate books, the coincidence of their results is remarkable and when the books are studied together they provide a richness of confirmatory insight rare among academics.

What is clear to those of us working in the field of literacy, is that practice in certain respects has outstripped theory and experimental evidence, and there is a loss of faith in how the two communities of research and practice can relate and articulate their concerns. This has resulted in the unfortunate circumstances of the moment which sees reading researchers unable to combat the force of ill-informed concern about the teaching of reading in our school. Indeed we are being pushed to one side by a tyranny of ignorance and its unabashed confidence.

In an important sense we are unable to join the fray — our training has prepared us well for the university seminar and the conference symposium, but leaves us quite unprepared for the discourse of media which has neither the time nor the patience for considered debate and reviewing all factors. Such discourse as ours does not translate easily into banner headlines nor does it fit well into two minute radio and TV slots. Those who have these skills do make their voices heard, although they are not always the voices we would wish to hear.

Learning to Read

Brock (1990) has identified several of these voices, which he refers to as myths. One powerful and enduring voice continues to call out that:

reading is accurate decoding. This is what purports to be the 'common sense' view of reading. If text is made up of words and words are made up of letters, then start with the letters. Such a view has a long heritage. An instance of it can be found more recently in 1970 when the National Right to Read programme was launched in America. It was launched with all the euphoria of getting a person to the moon and back, and the same principles were to be adopted to teach reading.

As Smith (op. cit.), has pointed out, getting to the moon and back was rightly seen as a complex logistical problem. It was seen as a problem which was solved one step at a time, by breaking down the task, through systems analysis and linear programming, into manageable units, with each objective rigorously assessed for achievement, and with quality control monitored, the final objective could be reached. It was assumed that identical procedures would deliver literacy to all children, by teaching one small step at a time and constantly testing that each objective was successfully achieved. The intellectual and publishing muscle of America was called on to help reach this ambitious target.

Theories were developed to support and justify this new fragmented approach to education. In time the idea of subskills became raised to even greater heights and referred to as 'the basics' along with emotional assertions that education should return to them. It is a familiar story in this country too. The underlying argument remains the same: the pathway to successful achievement is a trail of meaningless fragments, and this view has been with us for a long time.

In the seventeenth century:

> the ordinary way to teach children to read is, after they have got some knowledge of their letters and a smattering of syllables and words, to make them name the letters, and spell the words till by often use they pronounce at least the shortest words at first sight. (Hoole, 1660)

In contrast, by 1893 Rice, a noted American radical who made an extensive survey of school practice including interviews with teachers, argues for the use of a variety of teaching methods in teaching reading. And in the fifteenth edition of the *Teachers' Manual of the Science and Art of Teaching* dated 1898 teachers are urged to consider good reading as good speaking;

> children cannot read what they do not understand, they cannot in such a case interpret the thought of the writer. (National Society's Depository, 1898)

Under the section in this book which addresses methods of teaching reading, it continues;

> The old fashioned way of teaching words (was) by beginning with letters and combining these letters into syllables and words. This method does not meet the difficulty that every 20th word in the English language presents. You will find that in practice you will have to combine methods. (op. cit.)

This was suggested 100 years ago and probably not for the first time even then.

Messages for Teachers

Children learn language, literacy and other things holistically; they do not learn in fragments of isolated skills. Language, whether spoken or written is a complex set of subsystems which interrelate. And they interrelate with increasing sophistication as development proceeds. Successful language learners begin with a reason for using language, and move gradually towards acquiring the forms which reveal those functions. As has been pointed out, children learn language; they learn to use language and go on to learn about language (Halliday, 1973).

Clay has been reminding us for more than twenty years of one of the major outcomes of her extensive observational studies of children learning to read and write.

> Children do not learn about language on any one level of organisation *before* they manipulate units at higher levels, although many teaching schemes believe that this is so. (Clay, 1975, p. 19)

Clearly, both skills of accurate decoding and comprehending messages in text are necessary. But while they are necessary conditions of literacy, they are not sufficient conditions fully to describe literacy. Literacy also involves the ability to respond critically, sensitively and with discrimination to what is read, heard and seen. Promoting approaches to uncritical literacy, which are encapsulated in the rigid teaching of a sight vocabulary or of phonics or the exclusive use of a single reading scheme can only again lead to a lowering of standards. One wonders whether it is one of the current political goals of education to produce critically literate people?

A now well-known DES memo, circulating the ministry at some time during the early 1980s said in part:

we are beginning to create aspirations which society cannot match . . . When young people drop off the education production line and cannot find work at all, or work which meets their abilities and expectations, then we are only creating frustration and perhaps disturbing social consequences. (DES cited by Simon, 1985)

The memo continues:

if we have a highly educated and idle population we may possibly anticipate more serious social conflict. People must be educated once more to know their place. (op. cit.)

Contrast this position with that currently predominating in America. Six goals have been set for education in the 1990s by the President. The target date is the year 2000. Three of them are worth mentioning in this context;

1. All children in America will start school ready to learn. (Implying, of course, that learning only takes place in school?)
4. US students will be first in the world in science and mathematics.
5. Every American adult will be literate . . .

These directives have been given against a backdrop of the report from the National Assessment of Educational Progress which indicates that US students achieved at roughly the same level in reading as they did twenty years ago — indeed much the same story as in this country. However, the US story is told against a background of phonics teaching and ours against a position which is held to be the reverse.

Brock (op. cit.) identifies further voices which claim that: *there is something called functional literacy which can be measured by standardized tests.*

In 1992 when the International Reading Association honoured the Director General of UNESCO, because worldwide illiteracy rates had dropped, it is worth reminding ourselves what functional literacy might mean. What is overlooked in the eagerness for worldwide literacy, is that there is not just a single commodity called 'functional literacy'. What is functional literacy for a car mechanic who consults complex technical manuals of engine specifications, may not be the functional literacy of a parent with a medicine bottle or an adult with a job specification and an application form. For instance, in Brice-Heath's study

(1983) of two communities in the Carolinas, she illustrates how telling stories in one community is a form of cultural sharing and in the other, stories are considered improper. In this sense, what does it mean to talk about rates of illiteracy, or rates of functional literacy in a national population? I, for instance, as a university professor, might be considered by most to be a literate person, but if my reading contexts are changed from educational research, current affairs, literary texts and so on, to income-tax returns, instructions on how to assemble a wardrobe, or computer manuals, even more recently, to lengthy documents from Senate House, then I am in deep trouble!

What we see happening here is that literacy needs to be defined by context, opportunity, and by experience and prior knowledge. To narrow down the complexity of literacy to arbitrarily chosen criteria of word recognition and the like is inappropriate. It pays little attention to historical changes and significantly different contextual circumstances that coexist within diverse communities. It also ignores the differing degrees of literacy competency operating within any one individual. To follow the road of arbitrarily chosen criteria will result in dropping standards not raising them, as we have seen in the current testing regime currently being put in place in England and Wales. It is worth remembering that the more observable an aspect of language behaviour, the easier it is to assess and the more likely it is to be trivial.

Conclusion

The issues raised in this chapter are enduring threads which have woven their way through our National Curriculum Council English-evaluation project (Raban *et al.*, 1993) and repeatedly I have been brought up against these tensions. Firstly, in a review of theories of learning, theories of teaching and theories of curriculum content; how far should these come together in practice or should be located apart from each other in some form of 'fitness of purpose'? In the English curriculum there are vested interests pulling in both directions.

Secondly, views of language which deal developmentally with the smallest units of observable behaviour first, and then build the curriculum through increasing levels of complexity, act in opposition to the ways in which children use language and the way they learn language, whether spoken or written. However, starting a curriculum pathway by acknowledging that children operate on all levels of language at once from the beginning, leaves us with a developmental and assessment framework which merely states that they get better as they make progress through school.

These issues are causing problems as the English Order is revised and redrafted because, since the beginnings of mass public education in Britain, the teaching of English as a whole has been a focus of keen political interest and political control. The definition of what is to count as English (speaking and listening, reading and writing) has always been a matter of conflict between contending interests. The views people have of what literacy involves, of what counts as being literate, of how we learn and teach literacy, what they see as 'real' or appropriate uses of literacy skills determine, both directly and indirectly, the realities of practice.

As dissatisfaction intensifies with regard to the products of our maintained schools by commerce and industry, in the public mind a return to the teaching of standard English and formal grammar along nineteenth-century lines has come to be equated with a rise in stand-ards, not only of literacy, but of morals and behaviour in society as a whole. This is the teaching which is perceived to characterize English teaching in our private schools and our best grammar schools of the past. As one commentator has commented in *The Sunday Times*:

> Grammar is the fastest rising topic in the Tory party firmament, now almost on a par with hanging and dole fraud . . . The na-tion's grammar stirs the juices. (*The Sunday Times*, November 1988)

There remains much work to be done to hold the ground between these tensions. This is especially so as we see teacher training reduced to a requirement for subject knowledge coupled with classroom-management skills alongside a wilful disregard for theories of learning and their reality in the classroom. With respect to the English curric-ulum, the recursive model of language development found in the current curriculum, rooted in research and matched by the experience of teach-ers, is eliminated by the recent proposals for a revised curriculum. In short, the new assessment statements, for instance, are even more ar-bitrary and remote from empirical evidence. The model of language and learning implicit in the proposed curriculum is that of developing language skills through conscious mastery of rules and much guided practice.

The long-term consequences if these proposals are implemented will be a narrowing of the curriculum with a heavy emphasis on cor-rectness above all else. The benefits which teachers have gained from a developmental approach will be lost as pressure is experienced to teach the conventions of speaking, listening, reading and writing to children who may not have enough experience to make these meaningful. The proposed National Curriculum for English, especially that part of it to be assessed, would if it were to be implemented, be one that ignored most of what has been discovered about the development and teaching of oral and written language over the last thirty years. It is based on an unreal vision of what children are like and how best they can be taught. The view of learning which it puts forward is one which assumes that learners are passive, compliant and of similar background experiences, interests and abilities. This is simply not true. To suggest that children come into classrooms as empty vessels is an insult to their different types of expertise and to their validly different experiences of the world.

If we want our children to understand the complexities of our societies and to engage in constructive dialogue about the world in which they live, we cannot ask them to leave their language, their experience and their culture on the doorsteps of our schools. More importantly, if we continue to allow ignorant pronouncements about the English curriculum to go unchallenged, we are in danger of producing a generation of young people whose own language has been devalued, whose self-esteem has been damaged and whose learning has been impeded.

If we as teachers attempt to funnel the richness and diversity of our classrooms into an inflexible, monocultural curriculum framed in a rigid adherence to, for instance, standard English for all purposes or phonics as the only method of teaching reading, then we deny what we know about the way people learn and we shall, at best, marginalize and, at worst, destroy the voices of our pupils. Their voices deserve our attention.

Cartmell (1993), during an investigation of English in institutions of higher education, asked how these departments saw the future of English studies. Their collective response was characterized by diversity. They saw new options coming on stream concerning cultural and media studies. They saw the widening of the canon of literary authors and texts to include more women and ethnic-minority writers. They perceived the study of English literature becoming the study of literatures in English. They saw English as an increasingly interdisciplinary study, with a fuller integration of language and literature studies within a view of 'literary' studies which would be sufficiently inclusive to embrace both canonical and non-canonical texts.

Staff in these university departments of English agreed that recent government proposals to proscribe what happens in schools' English curricula is a thunderstorm on their horizon. They were vociferous in wanting to combat this whenever it appeared. To this end, forty professors and lecturers of English signed a letter which appeared in the British press during 1993 strongly objecting to the proposed revisions to the school English curriculum. The proposals, they maintained;

> reject the consensus of professional opinion about the best practice in schools; they involve an unacceptable degree of political and statutory control over classroom teaching . . . a new curriculum which so misrepresents the subject of English is an inadequate preparation for its study at higher levels.

Finally, at university level there are exciting new developments and trends in the study of English leading to cultural and media studies, women's studies, creative writing and the study of other literatures in English. What we see happening here is that if the revised proposals are implemented then the study of English in schools will slowly but definitely be pushed out of line from the teaching of English at higher levels. There is a danger that such a disjunction will fracture our intellectual heritage, destroy homogeneity within the profession and strangle the freshness of discourse which characterizes the vitality and richness of English teaching.

References

ANDERSON, R.C., SPIRO, R.J. and MONTAGUE, W.E. (1977) (Eds) *School and the Acquisition of Knowledge*, Hilisdale, NJ, Erlbaum.

ANDERSON, R.C., WILKINSON, I.A.G. and MASON, J.M. (1990) 'A microanalysis of the small-group, guided reading lesson: Effects of an emphasis on global story meaning', *Reading Research Quarterly*, **26**, 4, pp. 417–41.

BRICE-HEATH, S. (1983) *Ways With Words*, Cambridge, Cambridge University Press.

BROCK, P. (1990) 'A review of some of the literary, political and mythological contexts of reform and regression in literacy education', paper presented at 15th Australian Reading Association National Conference, Social Context of Literacy, Canberra.

BRUNER, J.S. (1957) 'On perceptual recklessness', *Psychological Review*, **64**, pp. 123–52.

CARTMELL, D. (1993) 'Bright with occasional showers', *Times Higher Educational Supplement*, 7 December.

CHALL, J.S., JACOBS, V.A. and BALDWIN, L.E. (1990) *The Reading Crisis: Why Poor Children Fail*, Cambridge, MA, Harvard University Press.

CHOMSKY, N. (1957) *Aspects of a Theory of Syntax*, Cambridge, MA, MIT Press.

CLAY, M.M. (1975) *What Did I Write?*, London, Heinemann.

CLAY, M.M. (1979) *Reading: The Patterning of Complex Behaviour*, London, Heinemann.

DONALDSON, M. and REID, J. (1982) 'Language skills and reading', in HENDRY, A. (Ed) *Teaching Reading: The Key Issues*, London, Heinemann.

FERREIRO, E. and TEBOROSKY, A. (1983) *Literacy Before Schooling*, London, Heinemann.

HALLIDAY, M.A.K. (1973) *Exploration in the Function of Language*, London, Arnold.

HOOLE, C. (1660) *Discovery of the Old Art of Teaching School*, London, Andrew Crook.

MANDLER, G. (1967) 'Organisation and memory', in SPENCE, K.W. and SPENCE, J.T. (Eds) *The Psychology of Learning and Motivation*, New York, Academic Press.

NATIONAL SOCIETY'S DEPOSITORY (1898) *Teachers' Manual of the Science and Art of Teaching*, 15th ed., London, Spottiswoode and Co.

PIAGET, J. (1955) *The Child's Construction of Reality*, London, Routledge and Kegan Paul.

RABAN, B. (1984) Observing Children Learning to Read, Unpublished Ph.D, University of Reading.

RABAN, B., CLARK, U. and McINTYRE, J. (1993) *Evaluation of the Implementation of English in the National Curriculum at Key Stages 1, 2 and 3, 1991–93*, York, National Curriculum Council.

RICE, J.M. (1893) *The Public School System in the United States*, New York, Century.

RICE, J.M. (1912) *The Scientific Management of Education*, New York, Hinds, Noble and Eldridge.

SHANNON, P. (1989) 'Paradigmatic diversity within the reading research Community', *Journal of Reading Behaviour*, **21**, pp. 97–107.

SIMON, B. (1985) *Does Education Matter?*, Lawrence and Wishart.

SMITH, F. (1986) *Insult to Intelligence: The Bureaucratic Invasion of Our Classrooms*, Portsmouth, NH, Heinemann.

SNOW, C.E., BAMES, W.S., CHANDLER, J., GOODMAN, I.F. and HEMPHILL, L. (1991) *Unfulfilled Expectations: Home and School Influences on Literacy*, Cambridge, MA, Harvard University Press.

WILDING, J.M. (1988) 'The interaction of word frequency and stimulus quality in the lexical decision task, now you see it, now you don't,' *The Quarterly Journal of Experimental Psychology*, **8**, 1–2, pp. 51–66.

Chapter 3

The Ecology of Sense-making: The Literacy-learner's Dilemma

M. Bogle

Summary

Approaches generally applied in the development of literacy locally may be broadly described as skill-based. The underlying assumptions are taken as 'givens'. Methods of instruction, consistent with these approaches, achieve standards (determined through a primarily punitive approach to assessment) which cause much public concern. Data from observation and teacher information over two terms of instruction, provide the description of the status of the learner's experiences and knowledge especially with respect to language. The discussion brings into focus the function of support for, and validation of, the learner's dilemma in the effort after sense, and examines the concept of universals in literacy instruction and the relevance of the notion of context as dynamic.

Introduction

Some societies are experiencing a growing anxiety over standards of literacy. This anxiety has often been fed by the perception that standards are falling, and decision-makers in many instances have responded by embarking on national schemes targeting a rise in literacy levels. Those of us in countries categorized as 'Third World' have had our anxiety transformed into qualification for financial assistance from international agencies. Professionals in education have been expending much research energy, time and resources on literacy. Professionals in many other disciplines have, separately or in collaboration with their colleagues in education, brought the phenomenon of literacy into sharper focus. Currently, there is a heightened interest in *how* literacy is acquired —

an interest which has uncovered many issues. These issues enter the debate on the extent to which methods of instruction are responsible for standards in literacy. Some argue that in formal schooling at least, methods need to be informed by a somewhat more complete and coherent understanding of how children acquire literacy.

This chapter takes the view that learning to be literate is one instance of learning and operates on the basic principles of all learning. These principles define the learning environment; and individuals acquire patterns of operating these principles. Violations and disruptions of the principles and acquired patterns introduce dilemmas for a learner. Mismanagement of violations and disruptions introduce discontinuities into the process of learning and affect the nature of learning. Natural (versus 'contrived') learning situations allow potential violations and disruptions to be managed as sources of information in operating the principles and building patterns. Contrived learning situations can draw 'with benefit' on the operations in natural learning situations of which learning language use is an instance.

Conceptual Background

Brice-Heath (1983) identifies the relevance of the learner's knowledge of language-in-use to the process of learning to read. In her research, children who were able to *read to learn* did so in totally integrated contexts: the message and the situation of contact with print were dependent on each other. In this way patterns of language use were learnt through demonstration; and the elements of these situations lacked independence. Elements comprising language systems, message(s), situational context, purpose or intent, pairs of participants, processes of participation — negotiation and construction, medium of delivery, as well as non-language replications of the message(s) exist in dynamic interaction. She found the interaction to be such that when an element was isolated it was viewed as 'unknown' and therefore lacking significance. However, focusing attention in a way that retained the relatedness of language-in-use, became another demonstration of language-in-use. This simultaneously restored the isolated element to the status of 'known' and added new knowledge of that element. This offered the learner a perspective on the nature of literacy as well as on how one manages the process of learning to be literate.

Frank Smith (1983) argued for demonstrations, engagement and sensitivity as components of the approach to language learning in school.

This approach makes use of the learner's familiarity with the components in natural language learning.

This argument supports the demand for continuity between formal instruction on the one hand and the learner's language knowledge and experience with systems of communication and ways of using language on the other. Clay, writing in *Reading Today* comments on the value which meeting this demand has for achieving independence in learning and economy in teaching:

> They [learners] have abilities to initiate, construct, and actively consolidate their own learning. If we enlist these learning initiatives, then we do not have to teach so much . . . (Clay, 1993, p. 3)

Enlisting their learning initiatives requires some understanding of what the learner brings in respect of those elements comprising the natural learning situation. Enlisting their initiatives means providing for the needed continuities with, and support for, what the learner already knows about appealing to the totality of his or her prior knowledge and about allowing the context of situation to signal the relevance of what he or she knows for the task at hand. Enlisting their initiatives means allowing for the learner's ownership of the goal or goals to be achieved by the application of what he or she knows.

But enlisting their initiatives must simultaneously mean providing opportunities for the learner to have access to the facilitator's systems, thus providing the benefits of the experiences of others. This further demand is for a richness in the context of situation. This richness will allow the demonstration and exploration of the known signs and of the nature of connectedness at the same time that it provides for the seeking out of new connectedness, signals and perspectives.

From this vantage point, the issue in formal instruction toward literacy becomes that of identifying what it is that the learner brings and what the demands are of *making sense* — of perceiving a relevant and coherent whole in the contrived learning situation which characterizes school.

Questions and Issues: An Exploration

It seems useful to focus on these issues and demands as they are manifested in the practices and assumptions of literacy development in classrooms. A relevant question then becomes, What is demonstrated through the practices of classroom instruction? The ensuing question then is: What assumption underlies the choice of demonstration? A final question relates to the engagement of the learner in these demonstrations and assumptions.

The questions, concerns, and issues in this chapter are raised and explored with reference to a context broadly described linguistically as Creole. This, in general terms, labels a situation in which the language commonly in use is derived from languages in contact. The specific Creole context of this presentation is one with an English-related Creole in a situation where a standard form of English is the official language. Literacy is taught with respect to this official language.

The English-related Creole in focus was born in a socio-political power structure associated with slavery. While African slaves outnumbered masters, linguistically, slaves were not a single unified group. The perfection of the model of English offered by the motley crowd of masters and masters' representatives may have been equally discontinuous. Communicative needs and intents had therefore to fabricate bridges and blaze trails thus giving rise to new and different language forms with the resulting language essentially an oral form.

While currently, the linguistic situation may be described as a continuum with the Creole at one end and standard English at the other, and with sections of the population having access to the full scale, many have not mastered standard English. This has been the source of dissatisfaction with secondary school-leaving achievement assessed through examinations expected to be written in standard English. The quality of performance in English language on these examinations is largely interpreted in terms of literacy levels. Some claim that learners enter the secondary phase of the system with low levels of literacy and suggest a link between this and the quality of performance and achievement in the official language. Some examples of differences between the two language forms are presented in Table 3.1 while some issues related to the medium of presentation are suggested by the material in Table 3.2.

The exploration of literacy learning in this context was structured to provide a description of classroom practices and their assumptions with respect to literacy development. This is seen as representing one perspective on conditions and processes of literacy acquisition and providing a launching pad for negotiated staff development as a background against which to elaborate on the initial description of practices and assumptions. The choice of a language focus reflects the view of learning to be literate as learning the operations of the written form of language-in-use.

Table 3.1:   *Examples of Jamaican Creole — standard English differences*

	Jamaican Creole	Standard English
Phonology	bud	bird
	jinks	drinks
	jugs	drugs
	chiljen	children
	chuck	truck
	chavel	travel
Semantics	ignorant	irrascible
Syntax	a beat dem beat im	he was beaten/they *beat* him
	a im dem beat	they beat *him*
	a dem beat im	*they* beat him

Table 3.2:   *Attention to word boundaries*

Jamaican English		Standard English
one suppond a time	=	once upon a time
mixty motions	=	mixed emotions
a tired	=	attired
shed rule	=	schedule
to wide in	=	to widen
earth wake	=	earthquake

Source: Scripts from a regional examination taken at end of secondary school.
Note: Candidates are all from a linguistic context in which English is the official language while the majority of the population speak a Creole form and interact in a culture which is dominantly oral.

Method

A central and necessary concern of any investigation of literacy in the context outlined above is to find instructional paths to the success by which the achievement of schools is judged, which some need for social mobility and betterment, and about which many seem to care very little if at all they care. In general terms, research identifying standards of performance in relation to socio-economic status or to expenditure in education have not offered much direction for improvement and for instruction. There is a sense of the inadequacies of the usual form of research questions and the paradigms used to investigate them. The concern with norms or with predefined categories continues to beg questions and to sideline those learners who do not satisfy the norms or fit the categories. It seems that these learners deserve to be led to achieve whether or not they fit the categories. Research findings based on a control experimental-group paradigm point to a common curriculum as the road to achievement for all and raise the issue of the validity of assuming universals.

Against this background, the decision was taken to collect data with the capacity to describe the extent of the continuity (with respect to literacy) between learner knowledge and school practices and with an openness to seeing actual patterns rather than instances of a preconceived pattern or set of patterns. The part of the project reported here used school interviews and observation schedules and a series of performance tasks.

The schedules for school focused on the teachers' classroom practices as they relate to literacy:

- the nature of engagement with language;
- the roles of participants and patterns of goal selection;
- the structure of situations/events in which learners are engaged; and
- the concept of literacy and literacy learning projected.

The data were collected in the context of a model of staff development in which teacher participants individually select an aspect for development. A series of video tapes formed the basis of discussion of classroom practices with particular reference to teaching literacy development. These became the stimulus for selecting an aspect. Prior to this, teachers had provided a written description of their own practices for which they were encouraged to provide the rationale.

The teacher-participants were from two schools and were teachers of initial grades in the primary system (age group: 6–11+ years). The schools are in two distinctly different geographical locations: one deep rural and agricultural and the other approximately 120km away on the outskirts of a flourishing tourist resort and dependent on the resort for employment but self-sufficient with respect to social interaction and entertainment without being a closed community. The deep-rural school contributed three teachers while the other contributed two teachers.

From the performance tasks which learners were asked to do, information was sought on their access to language production:

- verbal response to picture stimulus;
- non-verbal response to picture stimulus;
- concept of use of language in writing; and
- application of knowledge of sound values attached to letter symbols used in writing and reading.

The picture stimuli allowed for labelling of objects, labelling of actions and explaining as verbal responses. In the other picture-stimulus task, learners were asked to draw something similar in function to the picture the identity of which they had satisfactorily established and the function of which they had accurately described (somewhat equivalent to the task of identifying a word with a targeted initial sound). Another of these tasks required the selection and reproduction of a solid shape needed to fix a cup which was not holding juice because it had no bottom.

To explore their concept of writing the children were encouraged to write their own stories which they could read to me. This task afforded the opportunity to check on their knowledge and use of the sound values of letter symbols in writing and in reading.

Results

From these data one arrives at descriptions and interpretations rather than results. From the gathered data, a recurring element of the practices aimed at literacy development is the use of picture reading in which the focus is on details of the picture or illustration. Care is usually given to seeing that the learners recognize these details as familiar. Learners generally provide verbal labels for objects in the picture or illustration. Pictures or illustrations normally carry a single-sentence caption learnt by repetition which is viewed as essential to learning. Attention to word forms is given in a different context and without reference to the words comprising the caption. Instruction targeting word recognition brings into focus words connected by their structure and with the unwritten requirement that they be monosyllabic. The stated objective is to teach the initial sounds and their representation. The task is set in the context of the teacher listing the target letters (e.g., *m, b, r, s*) and providing words with missing letters. The learners are to supply from the list of letters that which is missing from the words provided.

Underlying this structure of instruction is the view that letter-sound knowledge is a requirement for reading to begin. While much attention is given to the phonological system of language, the elements are detached from the meaning functions they routinely serve. Thus the practices seek to engage learners with language forms in the written medium. Attention to the communicative intent of language is delayed until mastery of sound-value representation is assured. Performance on the various tasks suggests that learners, if they have stored this representational information, either do not have access to it or do not know its purpose (see Sample J, Figure 3.1). Of course, these options need not be mutually exclusive.

Figure 3.1: Sample J: Silbert

Both the response to print and the response to the demand for print occurred as reproductions from memory without any apparent concern for accuracy (see Sample X, Figure 3.2). For some, the demand for print evoked a search for available copies of writing even when the learners were unable to read what was copied (see Sample Y, Figure 3.3). The writing was apparently not recognized as real language and the forms not seen as functional or to have any connection with a message (see Sample K, Figure 3.4).

The language of reference in the instructional practices was standard English which is not the first language of any of the learners. This means that learners have no language point of reference for the language system with which instruction is working. A dilemma exists here for learners facing form in isolation from function and without a point of reference. Perhaps the nature of the learner's problem is accessible if

M. Bogle

Figure 3.2:   Sample X: Larry

it is noted that the phonological system of the learner's language has
the capacity for producing the following as *homo*phones:

thought (/taught/) — taught
drugs (/jugs/)   — jugs
truck (/chuck/)   — chuck
trunk (/chunk/)   — chunk
hot (/hat/)   — hat

It is also true that the first language does not use a system of marking
number in action concept words. Hence the form distinction between
has and *have* is not salient so the relevance of the difference often
escapes even older learners.

Smith (op. cit.) observes that demonstrations, engagement and
sensitivity are crucial to learning. This, in a sense, describes the ecology
of sense-making which is what is central to learning. The distance
between the learner's language knowledge and the language knowledge
required by the emphasis of literacy instruction makes demonstrations
and engagement impossible and introduces the expectation of difficulty

Figure 3.3: Sample Y: Gary

Gary ach ive

come Roy you came and look for me

come little boy
I am going to look for Pam.
You come and look for Pam too
I am going to look here

Figure 3.4: Sample K: Latoya

Pat and Samplay Thex I am girl

and experience of failure. The absence of such expectation and experience is what Smith labels 'sensitivity'. Harste, Woodward and Burke (1984) observed demonstrations, engagement and sensitivity as a recurring underlay in successful oral-language learning and in literacy learning in learners in a range of ages.

The code emphasis which characterizes the practices in these situations has been argued by some theorists to be valuable in the beginning stages of reading (Chall, 1983; Perfetti, 1985). As a universal principle, it seems questionable in circumstances such as those of the learners described here. The environment defined by the learning context will need to be a modifying input in applying this as a principle. If, like the school, the home-belief system includes an acceptance of the principle then the learner's dilemma can be intensified.

It was observed that where the teacher's practices reflected a modification of this belief, the learner did not face the dilemma to the same extent. However, many of these learners appeared to be having difficulty overcoming the exposure to the more prevalent practices. The learners in that context were making reasoned demand for letter-sound help.

In addition to the above, classroom practices supported the role of the learner as passive and teachers as the sole judges of the quality of what is achieved. Learners' responses were accepted in relation to their freedom from 'mistakes'. Mistakes were observed to be reasons for condemnation rather than growth points. An emphasis on the code or the material can only result in teacher-selected goals in the circumstances of these learners; and access to standards of achievement is exclusive to the teacher. Garner (1990) argues that these conditions can be expected to be deterrents to strategy use. Hence, even if learners had ways of learning, the conditions defined by the classroom practices and assumptions do not invite or support their application.

On the performance tasks the learners were observed to be copying from a model even when they were to be writing their own 'stories'. They apparently did not expect their efforts to be acceptable if they did not conform to that which they had come to identify as the teacher's standards. In practice, all their writing was copying from the chalkboard written language generated by the teacher. The dilemma was that the children could accept no responsibility for writing as composing (see Sample F, Figure 3.5).

As can be deduced from the foregoing, the structure of the situations in which the learners were engaged could not be described as communicative. The component of *purpose* with reference to both the immediate context and the uses of language was missing (Halliday, 1973,

Figure 3.5: Sample F: O'Brien

See my name here.
My name;Pam.
My name is Roy.

Smith, op. cit.). There was, in a way the equivalent of gathering blocks but with nothing to build and no reason to build.

What is the concept of literacy and literacy learning being developed by these learners from these circumstances? These learners were not observed to have any interest in books and were without the texts provided by the system because they had destroyed the books. Very few displayed any interest in available writing; and even these few did not show sustained interest. Literacy activities were, by and large, school activities. Where practices were modified away from being materials-centred and towards being learner-centred, the learners showed an interest in 'reading each others' stories' and expected each to be saying something different. They even expected to be able to laugh when they read. While they were not attempting the use of writing for personal functions, they were more willing to do writing as composing *on demand* (see Sample D, Figure 3.6).

Figure 3.6: Sample D: Jermaine

It is not clear whether these learners are yet aware of how they can use much of what they have in order to learn to be literate. Learning to be literate is more something someone — the teacher — does to you than being something the reader (learner) is doing. The notion that treating small elements makes learning easier may need to be examined against the realities of natural learning situations. Bartlett (1932) cited by Ivan-Nejad, McKeachie and Berliner (1990) provided the background to the development of thought about the multisource nature of learning. This thinking identifies the problems imposed by the principle of simplification by isolation exemplified in the letter-sound code emphasis characterizing the practices observed. Embedding the concerns of this emphasis, according to the multisource theory, is to have the learning benefit from the multiple input of integration, (see Figure 3.7). The

Figure 3.7:   Models of routes to literacy

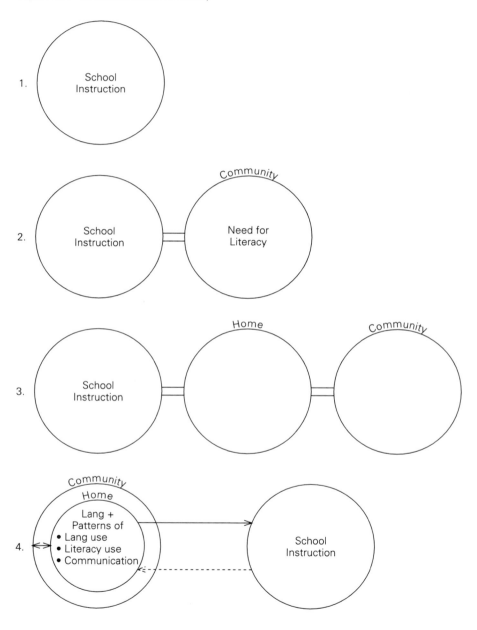

input from many sources simplifies the issues. Against this background, Resnick's (1987) distinctions between learning in school and out could explicate the learner's dilemma in aligning his ways of learning with the learning demands of school.

Messages for Teachers

As currently conceived, literacy is language-based and focuses on the written form. Therefore, in assisting literacy acquisition it seems important to recognize the status of the learner's knowledge of language. Perhaps the question to be answered is 'What does the learner know about language?' This may be limited to a description in terms of form and function. Knowing about language is not intended to refer to whether the learner can talk about language. Rather it refers to his or her ability to operate all the controls needed in the circumstances in which language is being used. In other words, how language is being used, for what purposes, and in what form, are important concerns.

In describing the status of that knowledge, it is necessary to establish the relationship between the language of literacy and the learner's language or languages. The learner's first or spoken language may not always be the language in which literacy is being acquired. Also, the learner may not have acquired literacy in his first language. Remember, too that the language known will be the only point of reference in the approach to written language; at the same time the learner may not know this or see the connection. It is from the points of connection that a learner's acquisition of literacy can be directed.

Some systems of language are not automatically and independently accessible even when the individual is a competent user of the language. The phonological system can be expected to be particularly troublesome; differences are known to exist even across groups in the same speech community. Where the writing system engages arbitrary symbols, the phonological system can be a source of confusion. (Consider the representations, *hope, rope, lope, sope (soap); reach, react.*) Attending to the representation of this system in isolation introduces a burden. The burden can be eased by attending to the system in the context of the purpose it serves, thus giving insight into letter functions.

Learners know something about learning: that the unknown must make a sense that solves the problem at hand . . . that provides the answer(s) needed for the next step or to complete the task. That is, the unknown takes its meaning from what is known. The learner needs to be able to retain this principle intact. He or she may need help to identify what he or she knows and how to use that knowledge. This will provide support for existing knowledge and anchor the new learning. What is known about language and its written form will need to be activated and utilized. Environmental print (which includes labels and packaging) can be a useful starting point.

Conclusion

As teachers we would do well to operate as learners in the teaching–learning situation as much as the learner in our charge. The idea is not new (Holmes, 1952). It is professionally challenging. Above all, it is eminently worthwhile. In that frame we can be part of the dynamic and expanding context which defines learning situations.

References

BRICE-HEATH, S. (1983) *Ways With Words*, Cambridge, Cambridge University Press.

CHALL, J.S. (1983) *Stages of Reading Development*, New York, McGraw-Hill.

CLAY, M. (1993) 'Reading Today', *International Reading Association*, February/March, p. 3.

GARNER, R. (1990) 'When children and adults do not use learning strategies: Towards a theory of settings', *Review of Educational Research*, **60**, 4, pp. 517–29.

HALLIDAY, M.A.K. (1973) *Exploration in the Function of Language*, London, Arnold.

HARSTE, J.C., WOODWARD, V.A. and BURKE, C.L. (1984) *Language Stories and Literacy Lessons*, Portsmouth, NH, Heinemann.

HOLMES, G. (1952) *The Idiot Teacher*, London, Faber & Faber.

IVAN-NEJAD, A., W.J., McKEACHIE and BERLINER, D.C. (1990) 'The multisource nature of learning: An introduction', *Review of Educational Research*, **60**, 4, pp. 509–15.

PERFETTI, C.A. (1985) *Reading Ability*, New York, Oxford University Press.

RESNICK, L.B. (1987) 'Learning in school and out', *Educational Researcher*, **16**, 9, pp. 13–20.

SMITH, F. (1983) *Essays Into Literacy*, Exeter, Heinemann.

Chapter 4

The Avon Collaborative Reading Study

T. Gorman

Summary

This chapter documents the evident success of a project mounted in a cluster of inner-city schools in Brighton, England in getting less able readers to enjoy reading more and to get better at it through effective group work. A large proportion of the children involved belonged to ethnic minorities. Results from the study suggest that pupils do not learn to produce or interpret language effectively simply by listening to a teacher talking. In the teaching of reading, collaborative work among pupils is essential.

Introduction

This study documents the evident success of a project mounted in a cluster of inner-city schools in Bristol in getting less able readers to enjoy reading more and to get better at it (Gorman *et al.*, 1993). A large proportion of the children involved belonged to ethnic minorities.

In 1992, Avon LEA obtained funding from the DfE to mount a programme in Whitefield Fishponds School and its main feeder primary schools to provide support for language-related activities, particularly reading, using an approach that helped pupils to work effectively in groups. The local authority invited the National Foundation for Educational Research (NFER) to advise on methods of evaluating the programme. Gorman, the former head of the Centre for Research in Language and Communication at NFER, was asked to carry out the evaluation. In this he had the assistance of John Trimble, an experienced teacher seconded to the project by Avon LEA.

The Evaluation

At the end of the Summer term in 1992, the general reading attainment of the pupils in Years 6 and 8 in the schools was assessed through an appropriate form of the *Reading Ability Series*, a nationally standardized test (Kispal, Gorman and Whetton, 1989). The mean score on the test of the primary pupils was 100.6. The information from the initial test was used by the teachers at both age levels to assemble pupils into mixed-ability groups. The groups of four to five children each included at least one less able reader and one good reader. Sixty groups of children were assessed at primary level and forty-nine at secondary.

In the following two terms, each pupil completed two additional purpose-designed tests. The activities involved focused on the interpretation of a poem, in one case, and a set of thematically related informative materials, including newspaper reports, in the other. The collaboration of the teachers involved and particularly of Jane Davies, the head of the Communications Faculty in the secondary school, was crucial in devising tests that related to schemes of work in use in the schools.

The 'Collaborative Reading' tests devised had three main components. The first involved *independent* reading. The pupils read the poem or reference materials individually and answered the questions linked to these. The second component involved *collaborative* reading. At this point pupils shared their responses and agreed on a joint response. The third component involved *review*. The children reviewed their individual responses in the light of the group discussion and made changes if they wished to. On the basis of the changes made it was possible to calculate what we termed a 'net improvement score' for each pupil.

The Results

As would be expected, pupils' scores on the tasks after discussion were, on average, significantly higher than those gained through independent reading. More interesting and less predictable, was the finding that on each task the net improvement score of the less able readers was higher than that of pupils in the other groups. That is to say, these pupils made a significantly greater number of accurate amendments after discussion than did pupils whose initial scores were relatively high.

Our initial assumption was that this pattern of response was a statistical artifact in that the 'good' readers — the pupils who made

Figure 4.1: *Primary non-fiction — Before and after: 3 groups on prescore*

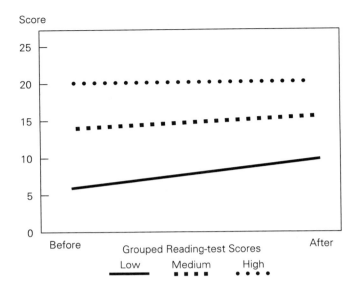

Note: Total possible score 24

Figure 4.2: *Primary non-fiction: Gain from experiment*

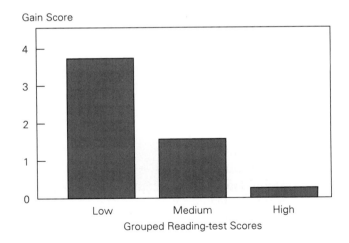

Figure 4.3: *Secondary poetry — Before and after: 3 groups on prescore*

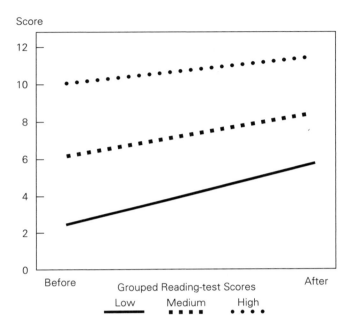

Note: Total possible score 14

Figure 4.4: *Secondary poetry: Gain from experiment*

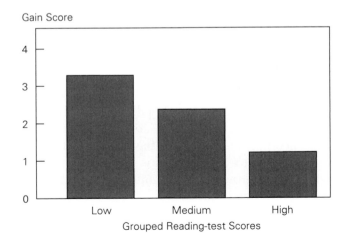

fewer errors initially — had less scope to improve. We therefore 'standardized' the scores (by dividing the number of accurate amendments by the number of errors made on first reading). The results still showed the group of low performers making significantly more improvement than the high performers on three of the four tasks. There is no question therefore that in reviewing and revising their responses, the less able readers applied what they had learnt through collaborative discussion more effectively than the more able readers did.

Figures 4.1–4.2 above show the pattern of response of primary pupils in completing the non-fiction task. Secondary pupils results in completing the poetry task are shown in Figures 4.3 and 4.4 below.

Interpreting the results

How can the results be explained? Earlier research has shown that, typically, less able readers are less willing than good readers to alter their initial interpretations of what they read. Having once arrived at an understanding of the meaning of a statement, they tend to adhere to it. To give an example of this lack of flexibility, consider the results of an Assessment of Performance Unit (APU) test (*That Sinking Feeling*) in which pupils were asked to interpret an extract from a story by Betsy Byars about a little girl (the narrator) who caused a raft made by her older brother and his friends to sink, after they had refused to let her play with them (Gorman and Kispal, 1987). When asked, the majority of the fifty-two pupils in the lowest performance band, and all but one boy in that group, said that the person telling the story was a boy, despite the linguistic and circumstantial evidence to the contrary, that was revealed as the story unfolded. (For example, her brother says 'I'll kill her', and her mother advises 'I shouldn't push your luck, madam'.)

Why then does collaborative reading encourage such pupils to be more open-minded and willing to alter initial impressions? There are three main reasons. Firstly, focused discussion helps pupils to understand both the meaning of what they have read and of the questions asked about it. It helps to clarify what is expected of them. Secondly, discussion with a small group of other children gives these pupils scope to develop and synthesize their own initial ideas about what they have read. In doing this, they gain confidence. Finally, the opportunity to formulate a written response collaboratively, removes their concern that they may make further errors in giving their response in writing. These are certainly some of the reasons why the less able readers in this study were galvanized by the process of collaborative reading to amend their initial interpretations of what they had read. The pupils' own comments show that, in the main, they enjoyed the experience; the teachers' observations suggest that the pupils became more adept at the process of collaborative reading as the terms proceeded. These are obvious benefits.

When an alternative form of the *Reading Ability Series* was completed by the primary pupils in March 1993 — after a period of seven months, including a Summer break — the results showed a significant improvement in the general reading performance of the group with a gain in mean score of approximately 2.0 standardized points. This may not be wholly attributable to the collaborative reading programme, but the programme would certainly have contributed to the change.

Group Work in the Teaching of Reading

Effective group work in classrooms is far less common than is generally supposed. The NFER survey of *The Teaching of Initial Literacy* (Cato *et al.*, 1992) showed that while the children in the classes observed were generally seated in groups, they seldom worked collaboratively within these groups; nor was it common for them to engage cooperatively in a task that required each pupil to provide a spoken or written response.

HMI reports and other studies have pointed out that although children sit in groups in the majority of infant and primary classrooms there is usually no specific demand for them to work together on a group task or undertaking (Tizard *et al.*, 1988). 'Typically', Neville Bennett has observed, 'pupils work *in* groups but not *as* groups' (Bennett, 1992). He added, 'The unfortunate outcome of that is a high level of low quality talk and a dearth of cooperative endeavour.'

In reviewing research on second-language acquisition, Peter Dickson noted that the increase in collaborative work in which learners work in groups or pairs has been a central feature of developments in classroom practice (Dickson, 1992). He added, 'Although there are strong educational reasons for group work it is also a necessary condition for creating more open interaction of the kind judged important for L2 development.' It has been established that group work leads to more talk. Moreover, compared with teacher-fronted work, peer-groups, particularly pairs, appear to offer the greatest opportunity for both receiving comprehensible input and producing comprehensible output. Peer-group work also provides the best opportunities for feedback. It is obvious that precisely the same considerations apply in teaching English to English speakers.

The Main Finding

The most important finding from this study relates to the significant extent to which less able readers were galvanized by the collaborative reading process to amend or correct their initial interpretations of what they read. They clearly benefit from the activity. Given the results, however, it would be sensible for teachers to devise group situations in which more able readers also have opportunities to read together collaboratively on specific occasions.

Messages for Teachers

The main messages for teachers that the collaborative reading project points to are these:

- Pupils need to be given frequent opportunities to work collaboratively on tasks in which the overall purpose or outcome, their individual responsibilities, and the form of response (spoken or written) required, are clear to them.
- The teachers' main jobs will be to select appropriate, interesting texts for reading; devise questions about the texts that focus on the main issues; and provide guidance about how pupils should respond to the text. In many cases this response will be spoken and directed to the class as a whole.
- Needless to say, the teacher will observe the activities of the groups and intervene when necessary, to facilitate the working of the groups.
- Normally, this observation of the process and outcomes of collaborative reading provides the basis for a teacher-led review of those issues that gave rise to differences of interpretation within the groups.

Conclusion

Sustained, individualized work is required in all areas of the curriculum but using language is essentially a cooperative activity. Speaking, reading and writing are best practised in cooperation and collaboration with other pupils and adults. This study demonstrates clearly that collaborative reading is a form of group work that is of particular benefit to less able readers, and one that pupils in general enjoy and from which they benefit.

References

BENNETT, N. (1992) *Managing Learning in the Primary Classroom*, Stoke-on-Trent of Trentham Books Ltd.

CATO, V., FERNANDES, C., GORMAN, T. and KISPAL, A. (1992) *The Teaching of Initial Literacy — How Do Teachers Do It?*, Slough, NFER.

DICKSON, P. (1992) *Using the Target Language in Modern Foreign Language Classrooms: A Review*, Slough, NFER.

GORMAN, T., HUTCHINSON, D. and TRIMBLE, J. (1993) *Reading in Reform: The Avon Collaborative Reading Project*, Slough, NFER.

GORMAN, T. and KISPAL, A. (1987) *The Assessment of Reading: Pupils Aged 11 and 15*, NFER-NELSON, Windsor.

KISPAL, A., GORMAN, T. and WHETTON, C. (1989) *Reading Ability Series, Levels A-F, Teacher's Handbook*, NFER-NELSON, Windsor.

TIZARD, B., BLATCHFORD, P., BURKE, J., FARQUHAR, C. and PLEWIS, I. (1988) *Young Children at School in the Inner City*, Erlbaum, London.

Chapter 5

Writing Systems in Different Languages: A Factor Affecting Literacy Standards?

C. Upward

Summary

Factors affecting literacy standards range from institutional through methodological to systemic. This chapter will consider the effect the English writing system has on literacy acquisition. Starting from the alphabetic principle, it will compare such systems as Italian, Latin, Japanese, American and British. The diverse facets of irregularity in English will be related to the learning process, the initial teaching alphabet, and the revised English Order of the National Curriculum. Finally, the issue will be placed in its historical and global context, and questions asked about educational priorities and the potential for reducing systemic obstacles to improved literacy standards in the future.

Note

To demonstrate certain aspects of its theme, this chapter is written in Cut Spelling (CS) (Upward, 1992a); some of its implications are considered in the final section. CS is a simplified, partially regularized orthography for English which removes three categories of misleading letters:

1. Letters irrelevant to pronunciation (e.g., *debt* becomes CS *det*).
2. Letters representing post-accentual schwa with L, M, N, R (e.g., *bottle, bottom, button, butter* become *bottl, bottm, buttn, buttr*); similarly in inflections and some suffixes (e.g., *waitd, waitng, fishs, eatbl, edbl*).
3. Most doubled consonants are written single (e.g., *bottl, bottm, buttn, buttr, accommodation* become *botl, botm, butn, butr, acomodation*).

Other simplifications reduce the use of capital letters and apostrophes. Additionally, three rules of letter-substitution apply:

1. The sound /f/ is spelt F (e.g., *fotograf, enuf*).
2. The sound of J is spelt J (e.g., *jymnast, jinjr, juj*).
3. IG pronounced as long Y is spelt Y (e.g., *high, height, sign* become *hy, hyt, syn*).

Readers unfamiliar with CS are recommended to ignore unusual spellings at first and read as fluently as possible. With a little practice, reading CS becomes perfectly easy.

This note is now repeated in CS to illustrate the system.

Note (Cut Spelng version)

To demnstrate certn aspects of its theme, this chaptr is ritn in Cut Spelng (CS); som of its implications ar considrd in th final section. CS is a simplifyd, partialy regulrized orthografy for english wich removes thre categris of misleadng letrs:

1. Letrs irelevnt to pronunciation (e.g., *debt* becoms CS *det*).
2. Letrs representng post-accentul shwa with L, M, N, R (e.g., *bottle, bottom, button, butter* becom *bottl, bottm, buttn, buttr*); simlrly in inflections and som sufixs (e.g., *waitd, waitng, fishs, eatbl, edbl*).
3. Most dubld consnnts ar ritn singl (e.g., *bottl, bottm, buttn, buttr, accommodation* becom *botl, botm, butn, butr, acomodation*).

Othr simplifications reduce th use of capitl letrs and apostrofes. Aditionly, three rules of letr-substitution aply:

1. Th sound /f/ is spelt F (e.g., *fotograf, enuf*).
2. Th sound of J is spelt J (e.g., *jymnast, jinjr, juj*).
3. IG pronounced as long Y is spelt Y (e.g., *high, height, sign* becom *hy, hyt, syn*).

Readrs unfamilir with CS ar recmendd to ignor unusul spelngs at first and read as fluently as posbl. With a litl practis, readng CS becoms perfectly esy.

Introduction: Systms and Standrds

Th aim of this chaptr is to encuraj al litracy workrs, wethr reserchrs, teachrs or lernrs, to take a criticl vew of th riting systms in wich litracy skils ar aquired, especialy in english. Th centrl question askd is: how far ar th dificltis faced by lernrs merely a product of particulr featurs of th riting systm concernd, rathr than inherent in th lernng process? This criticl vew reflects both th intrnationl perspectiv and th emfasis on fonics as th sycolojicl basis of alfabetic litracy, wich caractrize th presnt work as a hole. Such a vew must be expectd to gro in importnce, as th hyest standrds of litracy ar recognized to be vital for th prosperity and welbeing of al cuntris, as sycolojicly welfoundd litracy policis ar developd for educationl curicula, and as th needs of foren lernrs and users of english com to demand incresing atention.

Disatisfaction with th conditions of litracy aquisition in english is nothing new, indeed it has been a continuing theme in english education for over 400 years (Michael, 1987). Relativly recent is th awareness of th litracy needs of al children rathr than just of a privilejd class, as is awareness of th role of educationl standrds in determnng a cuntris ability to 'succeed' in a competitiv intrnationl environmnt. This latr considration especialy has led to sevrl comparativ studis of educationl standrds in difrnt cuntris, focusng in varying degrees on th specific aspect of litracy (CERI, 1992). Formost amongst these is th study by th International Association for the Evaluation of Educational Achievement (IEA, 1992a, 1992b, 1993) across thirty-two cuntris. It is th subject of Chaptr 12 of this volume. Comparisns between litracy standrds in difrnt cuntris ar dificlt to make because conditions vary so much, but th IEA statistics may alow som tentativ conclusions about th efect of difrnt riting systms, in particulr about th extent to wich mor dificlt riting systms corelate with loer standrds of litracy. Initial obsrvations from th survey wer that Finland, with an exeptionly regulr riting systm, acheved th hyest litracy standrds, wile Denmark, with a less regulr riting systm, fared less wel (Allerup, 1993). Certnly th hypothesis that iregulr riting systms ar hardr to lern, and that systms that ar hardr to lern wil inevitbly produce loer standrds of litracy, is hyly plausbl in lojic, and if a causl relationship can be demnstrated, ther wil be importnt implications for litracy policy in english.

Method: Clarifyng Concepts

This chaptr begins and ends with english, and it is therfor first necesry to take issu with and hopefuly help clarify a numbr of notions widely

Table 5.1: Thre senses of th word 'spelng'

1 Uses of word	2 Meanng in context	3 Wat is spelng?
'english spelng'	Conventions for riting words	= SYSTM
'practisng spelng'	Lernng how to rite words	= ACTIVITY
'atrocius spelng'	Floutng conventions	= ACURACY

held in th english speakng world about litracy in th english riting systm, wich efectivly means its spelng.

Th word 'spelng' itself is subject to confusion, ofn being equated with 'riting'. But insofar as it is th medium for litracy jenrly, spelng concerns readng as much as riting. *Table 5.1* anlyzs som importnt senses of 'spelng', colum 1 shoing varius uses of th word, colum 2 parafrasing ther meanngs, and colum 3 defining them in terms of elementry concepts. We shal in this chaptr be concernd chiefly with spelng as a systm wich has two functions: to enable riters to comit words to visbl form (brail and morse ar exeptions); and to enable readrs to recognize words in text. But a premis for both these functions is that th spelng systm must be lernt. Sycolojicly, th two functions constitute a unity, utilizing th same systm and oprating in th same minds, and wen one function is practisd, it reinforces comand of th othr. This unity is too ofn overlookd in english and th functions themselvs even confused. Thus th 1993 revised proposals for english in th english/welsh National Curriculum (Department for Education, 1993) seprate readng and riting as Atainmnt Target 2 and Atainmnt Target 3, but classify th task of chekng spelngs in a dictionry undr readng, not riting. That riting may be an efectiv way of inculcating syt vocablry for readng is typicly neglectd. We shal later note th success of italian children in lernng to read initialy by riting — an aproach wich has ocasionly also been found useful in english (Martin and Friedberg, 1986).

Givn this uncertnty about th concept itself, it is not surprising that recent perceptions of english spelng hav difrd markdly too. Befor th mid-twentieth century, linguists, including som ho had studid th forms and historicl evlution of english spelng in depth, mostly recognized that english spelng was hyly iregulr, even caotic.[1] Lately, howevr, many linguists hav been reluctnt to accept that english spelng cud be seriusly defectiv, and th fact of its evlution was somtimes taken to imply it must be ideertly adaptd to modrn needs (survival of th fitst?) (Chomsky and Halle, 1968). In prefrnce to 'caotic', a range of epithets such as 'polysystemic' (Albrow, 1972), 'logografic' (Sampson, 1985), 'morfofonemic' (Stubbs, 1980), or 'deep' (Aaron, 1989) hav been aplyd in an atemt to sujest som ordr in th systm. Posbly th pendulum is now beginng to swing bak — a very recent work at least professes neutrality on th question (Carney, 1994). Wethr ordr or disordr is in fact domnnt, may be jujd by evidnce presentd later in this chaptr.

Sycolojists hav been mor concernd with how lernrs internlize english spelng patrns. Evidnce has been garnrd particulrly from studis of th abnorml — th dificltis of dyslexics, th spelng of nonwords — and varius theoreticl modls hav been proposed. For instnce, th 'dual process modl' sujests that readrs treat regulr and iregulr spelngs difrntly, regulr spelngs being decoded 'orthograficly' (i.e., by interpretng th sound valus of th letrs), wile iregulr spelngs ar recognized 'lexicly' (i.e., hole words ar machd against ther imajs as stord in th readrs word-memry, or 'lexicn') (Henderson, 1984). Anothr modl proposes stajes in lernng to read, th beginr recognizing words as holes (a 'logografic' staje), th oldr readr decoding letrs into sounds (an 'alfabetic' staje), and th skild readr dealng with al aspects, regulr and iregulr, of th riting systm (an 'orthografic' staje rathr difrnt from that proposed by th dual process modl) (Sterling, 1992).

Ther ar som fairly obvius objections to such modls. English spelngs ar not esily divisbl into regulr and iregulr (e.g., *paid* is regulr by analojy with *raid* but iregulr by analojy with *played*). Yung and adult readrs alike read al familir spelngs autmaticly ('lexicograficly') on syt, but hav to decode ('alfabeticly') al unfamilir spelngs, regardless of regularity. Furthrmor, teachng methods may influence, perhaps even determn, how lernng proceeds: a fonic method or a structurd readng sceme may produce difrnt stajes or processes from a hole-word method or 'real books'. And behind al these objections is th question wethr a coherent description of lernng processes is posbl in english at al, wen th most varid iregularitis lurk as potential traps for th lernr at evry turn. To parafrase a sixteenth century observr of th problm: u canot discovr how children normly lern to walk if u only alow them to go on a tytrope or on ther hands (Hart, 1570).

A mor helpful modl for *norml* processes of litracy aquisition (i.e., in a reasnbly regulr riting systm) is implyd by Steven Rose's findngs about th natur of memry (Rose, 1992). His neurobiolojy tels us that sense impressions (e.g., of th spelng and sound of words) leve fysiologicl, chemicl and electricl traces in th brain. If these impressions ar repeatd, th traces ar reinforced, and synapses (links between nerv cels) ar developd as rutes wich facilitate subsequent reprocesng of those impressions. A regulr spelng systm wud thus constntly reinforce fewr synaptic links formd during lernng, but a hyly iregulr riting systm like english myt send mor complex mesajs to th brain, less stable synaptic links wud develop, and th resultng readng skils wud be that much less relybl (compare Magdalene Vernon's 'cognitiv confusion', Vernon, 1957). This 'synaptic' modl of th sycolojy of litracy aquisition is also perfectly compatbl with th 'evlutionry' acount of brain developmnt proposed by th Nobel prize winr Gerald Edelman. Evidnce of hyr standrds of litracy in regulr riting systms wud furthr confirm its apropriatness.

Educationists vews of english spelng ar equaly varid. Historicly, teachng methods hav ranjed from lernng th ABC, readng thru spelng, sylabic analysis, spelng lists, and dictations (Michael, 1987). Fonics is advocated today on th grounds that 'children lern much fastr wen they no th letr sounds and can work words out for themselvs' (Lloyd, 1992); but this is oposed by a 'hole word' aproach on th grounds that 'th mor words u no, th esir it is to recognize and lern othr words, based not on fonic corespondnces, but on sylabic and semantic resemblnces' (Smith, 1991). Th title of Margaret Peters book *Spelling: taught or caught?* implys a simlr dictomy (Peters, 1985). Nor is th british govrnmnt consistnt: its Kingman Report (DES, 1988) specifyd that 16-year-olds shud 'spel corectly', since 'spelng obeys rules', but its Cox Report (DES, 1989) stated that 'th aim canot be th corect unaidd spelng of any english word — ther ar too many . . . that can cach out even th best spelr' — in othr words, english spelng ofn dos not obey rules. Penalizing mispelngs in examnations wud thus stigmatize pupils for failng to acheve th imposbl.

How is it that english spelng, th worlds prime medium of ritn comunication, has jenrated such disagreemnt about its natur, about litracy aquisition, and about teachng methods? One mesaj of this chaptr is that th sheer iregularity of english spelng obstructs not merely lernrs, but also linguists, sycolojists and educationists atemtng to undrstand it. Because ther is so litl sense in th systm, it is hard to make much sense out of it. Th only way to explain english spelng is thru its chekrd histry. Ther we se letrs insertd in loan words to reflect ther languaj of orijn (e.g., в in *det*), or insertd merely by analojy (e.g., ʟ in *coud* by analojy with *would*), or 'by mistake' (e.g., ᴘ in *ptarmigan*), or one letr taken from french (e.g., ᴀ in *resistant*) conflictng with a difrnt letr taken from latn (ᴇ in *consistent*). We se formr alternativ spelngs surviving as anomlis (e.g., *speak/speech, deign/disdain*) cryng out to be harmnized. Th work of th sixteenth century scoolmastrs Coote and Mulcaster apart (Mulcaster, 1582; Coote, 1596), lernrs and users needs hav scarcely impinjd on th desyn of th systm at al, indeed since 1066 ther has been no coherent overal 'desyn'. Hence th title givn by th duch linguist Nolst Trenité to his 250-line rymng catlog of orthografic inconsistncis in english: *The Chaos* (Nolst Trenité, 1929).

Results: Consequences of Unpredictbl Spelng

That th authr of *The Chaos* was not a nativ speakr of english was no accidnt. Wher nativ speakrs, acustmd to th systm from ther erliest years, tend passivly to accept its iritations and frustrations, non-nativs litrat in othr languajs mor ofn react with impatience. Thus th linguist Mario Pei first recals th ese of litracy aquisition in italian, befor he moved to America at aje 7:

> U ar taut th alfabet, then u ar givn sequences of spoken and ritn sylabls . . . Ther ar a few confusing moments wen u ar taut to insert an н aftr c, g, sc, and an i aftr th same consnnts, to sho certn sounds befor front or bak vowls. Beyond that, yr ear is a gide to yr spelng if u speak standrd italian . . . Th word *spel* dos not exist in th italian vocablry, wich is a clu to th entire situation.

He then recounts (Yule, 1991) his dismay on meetng english, wich he has described as 'one of th worlds most awsm messes'.

Tho th polyglot hungarian Julius Nyikos was adult wen he migrated to th USA, his reclections ar simlr (Nyikos, 1987):

> I, as wel as evry othr hungarian child without serius lernng dificltis, lernd to read any and al hungarian texts fluently by th end of th first year of elementry scool . . . I lernd to read latn corectly at th aje of ten within one week, and jermn at elevn in less than a week. So did al th othr hungarian students studying in th Gymnasium that I atendd. At forteen I startd lernng to read and rite english, and made som progress. At university . . . I lernd to read and rite finish in a few ours, as did al my felo students. In 1949 . . . as soon as I arived in th United States, I resumed lernng to read and rite english, and I hav been making modrat but stedy progress since then. At this rate I hope to becom comfrtbl with english orthografy in anothr decade or so . . . (Nyikos, 1987)

(Se Volume 1, Chaptr 5 for a contempry acount from Hungry).

Wy shud non-nativ speakrs be mor struk by th dificlty of english spelng than nativ speakrs? An importnt reasn is that non-nativ speakrs hav an aditionl hurdl to overcom wen they lern english. For nativ speakrs, readng jenrly means relating spelngs on th paje to pronunciations alredy stord in memry. Non-nativ lernrs, howevr, mor comnly encountr spelngs th pronunciation of wich they canot so esily retreve from memry, and they ar therfor mor dependnt on spelng to sho pronunciation. That is

Table 5.2: *Spelng-induced mispronunciations by non-nativ speakrs of english*

Pronunciation Modl	Mispronounced Word
nation, sensational	national
baked, faked	naked
fear, hear, near	bear
undermined	determined
brother, mother	bother
cove, stove, drove	dove (= bird)
brown, gown, town	own
cowards, Howards	towards
woo	who

wy Nolst Trenités *The Chaos* laments th unpredictbl relationship between spelng and sound: corect pronunciation of th ritn english word is a minefield. Anothr aspect of th problm is seen in a widely used bilingul spanish and english dictionry (Smith, 1971): evry english word has its pronunciation sepratly spelt in th Intrnationl Fonetic Alfabet (itself inconvenient for most users to decyfr), but th pronunciation of the spanish words is transparent from ther norml spelng. Mispronunciation of english words by non-nativ speakrs is undrstandbly rife — *Table 5.2* givs som exampls of such spelng-induced errs. Not only non-nativ, but nativ speakrs too need spelng to sho pronunciation, and th failur of english spelng to do so relybly is seen to restrict litracy potential in varius ways. Even hyly litrat nativ speakrs hav th comn experience of discovrng as adults that they hav mispronounced certn words since childhood. Travlrs ar frequently nonplusd by th spelng of place names on maps or syns. Th less wel educated ar inhibitd from public speakng by fear of ridicule for mispronouncing. Dificlt spelngs hav been shown to deter yung peple from expandng ther activ vocablry (Moseley, 1989). Such limitations on litracy ar al consequences of iregulr spelng.

Yet th problm is not suficiently aknolejd. Al too typicl and influential was Chomsky and Halles remark that 'orthografy is a systm desynd for readrs ho no th languaj' (Chomsky and Halle, 1968), a statemnt to wich we must object in almost evry particulr. First, we alredy rejectd th notion of 'desyn' in modrn english spelng. Secnd, th esential systemic and sycolojicl unity of readng and riting means that orthografy must serv both readrs and riters: they hav an equal need for predictbl sound-symbl corespondnce, for decoding and encoding words respectivly. Third, no orthografy can be desynd only for peple ho no th languaj: evryone first aproachs languaj as a lernr, and we continu lernng thruout our lives. Most importnt of al, th role of english as a world languaj demands it shud also be desynd for those ho aproach th languaj as non-nativ speakrs. That is in evryones comunicativ intrest.

Interpretation: How Dificlty Afects Litracy

We hav repeatdly referd to th dificlty of th english riting systm arising from its lak of predictbl sound–symbl corespondnces, but we hav not yet made any very exact comparisns between languajs. A numbr of studis hav compared litracy aquisition across languajs, covrng th roman alfabet and othr alfabets such as cyrilic (both russian and serbian), hebrew and arabic, as wel as non-alfabetic systms such as th japnese sylabris, and chinese caractrs. J Downings colection *Comparative Reading* (se also his contempraneus paper 'Is Literacy Acquisition Easier in Some Languages than in Others?') (Downing, 1973a, 1973b) dos not make statisticl comparisns, but th gretr dificlty of english (or rathr th gretr ese of othr languajs) is repeatdly aluded to in remarks such as 'it seems to be jenrly beleved that children just do not find it dificlt to lern to read' in, for instnce, Finland, Jermny and Norway (p. 107). Othr studis, from America, (Tarnopol, L. and M., 1976, 1981; Stevenson *et al.*, 1985), particulrly compare litracy standrds in chinese, japnese and english; noteworthy from Britain is Henderson (1984).

A recent paper by th presnt authr (Upward, 1992c) and especialy one by Thorstad (1991) giv mor precise statisticl evidnce. Comparing spelng acuracy in english and jermn, th formr found that, in terms of mispelngs, english apeard almost sevn times mor dificlt than jerman, with redundnt letrs causing most errs. Thorstads study compared litracy aquisition by english and italian primary scool children, and found that th italians, ho had mastrd ther regulr orthografy by systmatic atention to fonics, acheved scors sevrl times betr than th english (se Mario Peis experience of both languajs described abov). Ther superiority was shown by a numbr of tests, perhaps th most revealng requiring th children to read and rite eit words of adult vocablry. Th results ar shown in *Table 5.3*. Over four times as many misreadngs and nearly eit times as many mispelngs ocurd in english as in italian. Obsrvations included th foloing: 'Th italian children spent most time in riting in th first year, and readng wat they had ritn. Ther wer no graded readng books . . . Ther was no remedial teachng.' (p. 529) 'Italian children take one year to acheve in readng and spelng wat takes english children thre to five years. Ther wer no tecnicl limits to watevr they myt want to read or spel. As they ar confidnt in ther skils, they aproach these tasks mor systmaticly and without th anxiety jenrated in th english children.' (p. 535) 'Th italian children used a fonlojicl stratejy in both [readng and riting].' (p. 536)

Th numbr of symbls (letrs) to be lernt in italian and english is virtuly th same, and th difrnce in achevemnt arises from th much gretr lernng load required in english, wher th use of th letrs has to be mastrd

Table 5.3: *Results of Thorstads anglo-italian 8-word test*

Word		% misred		% mispelt	
english	italian	english	italian	english	italian
cement	cemento	25	8	77	3
correct	corretto	33	0	62	17
literally	letteralmente	45	7	99	17
perceptible	percettibile	61	17	99	19
permits	permette	31	3	65	12
preparing	preparano	24	4	79	6
special	speciale	16	4	81	4
thermometer	termometro	28	17	83	6
No. of english errs per italian err		4.38		7.68	

word by word for thousnds of words, rathr than sound by sound for a few dozn sounds. Th lernng load in som othr riting systms is even gretr than in english, and th limitations on litracy corespondngly even starkr. Wile alfabets ar closed systms, with a smal, fixd numbr of symbls, chinese has an open systm. Ther ar sevrl tens of thousnds of caractrs (a larj dictionry may list around 50,000 — Lindqvist, 1991), but most ar outside th reprtoir of th avraj chinese, for hom 4,000 to 7,000 sufice in ordnry readng (Che Kan Leong, 1989). Altho many caractrs hav comn elemnts wich asist both lernng and readng, th time, memry load and complications involvd in acheving and maintainng even elementry litracy in chinese ar far gretr than required by regulr, closed systms. China, howevr, has taken two major steps to facilitate litracy aquisition. First, initial litracy skils ar taut in pin-yin (= 'spel sound'), a fonografic riting systm based on th roman alfabet, so that children alredy hav th necesry basic sycomotor skils befor they takl traditionl chinese caractrs. Secnd, in th 1950s and 1960s as many as 1,754 of th most comn caractrs wer simplifyd to aid litracy (Yue E Li and Upward, 1992).

Th pin-yin aproach, of givng beginrs basic litracy skils befor they face th ful dificltis of th adult riting systm, has been aplyd in english too, most recently thru th Initial Teachng Alfabet (ita), but using othr regulrized spelng systms too, always with striking success for initial litracy aquisition (Upward, 1992b). Th secnd aproach, of simplifyng th adult systm, has not recently been aplyd to english — Noah Websters spelng simplifications in America in th erly nineteenth century (Clark, 1965) wer th latest efectiv atemt (e.g., regulrizing *traveller* to *traveler* by analojy with *wanderer*, and *rigour* to *rigor* by analojy with *rigorous*), tho its benefits hav only sloly perclated across th Atlantic and hav been only eraticly adoptd in Canada and Australia. Both these aproachs to facilitating litracy in chinese ar relevnt to problms of litracy aquisition in english today.

Th valu of an initial teachng alfabet is also aparent in japnese. Th cor of th japnese riting systm consists of chinese caractrs, but they ar used in unpredictbly difrnt ways, and mastrng them is even mor dificlt than in chinese. Despite these complexitis, Japan has long claimd outstandng litracy standrds (Makita, 1968). These may not be entirely du to long ours of disiplind, concentrated memrization of th chinese caractrs, since japnese also uses som fortyeit sylabic symbls wich function fonograficly, each symbl regulrly representng th same sylabl. This systm is so straitforwrd that most children can alredy read and rite it befor they start scool. We may again reflect on th significnce of this 'hed start' in th lyt of John Downings findngs on th transfer of litracy skils from th i.t.a. to traditionl english orthografy (Downing, 1987). By his interpretation, th ke to th rapid, succesful aquisition of litracy skils in english is for children first to develop th basic sycomotor skils using a regulr fonografic riting systm, and only wen that is mastrd shud they confront th aditionl dificltis entaild by a complex adult riting systm such as that of english.

Mesajs for Teachrs: Th Need for Chanje

One of th insyts provided by th i.t.a. experimnts was that litracy aquisition in english can be esy, rapid and exiting. Provided spelng is regulr, lernng to read and rite givs an enormus stimulation to childrens powrs of self-expression and educationl morale in jenrl. Italian and many othr languajs send th same mesaj. Th presnt iregulr spelng of english by contrast severely discurajs larj numbrs of less able children, and causes al lernrs and users a lifetime of unecesry trubl. Those ho pronounce on educationl standrds, wethr teachrs or educationists, employrs or politicians, need to undrstand wy beginrs stumbl in english, wy even advanced students make frequent spelng mistakes, and how far short of its litracy potential th english-speakng world fals. Students shud not be denigrated as stupid or lazy, nor teachrs as incompetent: *it is th riting systm that is unsuitbl for lernrs, and not lernrs ho ar unsuitbl for th riting systm*. Mastrng a riting systm has no valu for its own sake — it is strictly a tool for comunication. If a tool is manifestly unsuitbl, being clumsy and awkwrd in th hands of most users, it is adaptd or replaced. Th same is normly tru of riting systms. We saw how chinese has taken steps both to help initial lernrs and to simplify th adult riting systm. Simlrly, most languajs with alfabetic riting systms hav from time to time modrnized ther spelngs too, so as betr to reflect curent pronunciation.

Table 5.4: Sound-valus of letrs in th classicl roman alfabet

Letr	Sound valu in latn (* = anomlus sound valus)
Vowls A/E/O	/a, e, o/, but long and short valus not difrentiated*.
B	/b/
C	Always /k/, nevr /s/; *Cicero* = /kikero/
D	/d/
F	/f/
G	Always /g/, nevr /dʒ/; *genius* = /genius/
H	Silent*: *honor* = /onor/
I (also J)	Long and short /i/. Also* I-glide /j/, pronounced as english consnantl Y.
(K)	Rarely used in latn, but pronounced like C as /k/*
L	/l/
M	/m/
N	/n/
P	/p/
Q + V (= U)	/kw/ (Q itself pronounced as C and K*)
R	/r/
S	Always /s/, nevr /z/.
T	/t/
V (also U)	Long and short /u/; also* W-glide.
X	/ks/ (/k/ as also C, K, Q*)
Y, Z, Ch, Ph, Rh, Th	Aditionl letrs & digrafs used in latn for translitrating greek

Thus, in 1947 duch simplifyd th endng -sch to -s, turnng for instnce th old form *nederlandsch* 'duch' into *nederlands* (Trouille, 1987); and in 1959 spanish alowd th silent initial p to be dropd from *psicología* to giv *sicología* (Smith, 1971). English by contrast has neglectd that esential task of modrnization for centuris, and pays th inevitbl price.

It shud be of intrest to teachrs to undrstand how th english riting systm has becom so confused. Th alfabet, inventd around 3,700 years ago (Hooker, 1990), evolvd thru fenician, greek and etruscn, befor th romans gave it most of th letr shapes we ar familir with in modrn english. In classicl latn times, around th year -100, it had th letrs givn in *Table 5.4*, with sound valus unambiguus exept for those astriskd. Th classicl roman alfabet was thus a mostly clear, simpl systm, orijnly with no digrafs like english ch, sh, th etc., and it has since lent itself fairly wel, with som aditions such as new letrs, digrafs and diacritics (accents), to th represntation of many othr languajs, one of th erliest being anglosaxn. Howevr, it did not distinguish certn sounds wich modrn english dos distinguish (e.g., long and short vowls), and it inheritd certn fonlojicl distinctions wich english ignors (e.g., c, k and q for variants of th sound /k/). Latn later lost som of its orijnl simplicity, wen for instnce th valu of th letr c split between /s/ befor e, i, y and th orijnl

Table 5.5: *How do u spel /k/ in english?*

	Do u spel /k/ as C, CC, CH, CQ, CQU, K, KK, Q or QU and wy?
C	*cat, arctic, arc, arcing*
CC	*soccer, hiccup, impeccable, account, occur, succumb, accursed*
CH	*chaos, school, technology, ache, monarch, stomach*
CK	*rock, rocky, chicken, hillock*
CQ	*acquaint, acquiesce, acquit*
CQU	*lacquer, racquet*
K	*king, weaken, yak*
KK	*trekking*
Q	*queen, quick, squeal*
QU	*quay, conquer, unique, mosque*

/k/ elsewher, so that th first sylabl of *Cicero* chanjed from /kɪk-/ to modrn english /sɪs-/. Th anglosaxns used th roman alfabet to create a workmanlike riting systm wich by and larj showd th pronunciation of words, indeed it is esir to lern to read old english than modrn english. Th invasion of french spelngs aftr 1066 efectivly destroyd that systm, and wat resultd was an unsystmatic hybrid to wich furthr elemnts wer unsystmaticly add from othr languajs, abov al greek, in evr incresing numbrs especialy from th fifteenth century onwrds. Around th seventeenth century many loose ends wer tidid up, as wen th form *bit* became standrd in place of mor complex variants such as *bytte*; but countless iregularitis remaind and som new ones wer even introduced, such as Samuel Johnsons *ache* for *ake*. Apart from Noah Websters abov-mentiond reforms in America, litl has now chanjed for two or thre hundred years, with th consequences for litracy alredy described.

Th extreme disordr of modrn english spelng is wel ilustrated by th difrnt posbilitis of spelng th sound /k/, as shown in *Table 5.5*. Som defendrs of th presnt spelng systm claim a redeemng featur in its alejd 'morfofonemic' stability. By this they mean that th root of a word maintains consistnt spelng even if its pronunciation chanjes, as wen (to quote an exampl givn by Chomsky) *courageous* preservs al th letrs of th base word *courage*, altho its vowl sounds ar radicly difrnt. Howevr *Table 5.6* shos how, in many instnces, english spelng dos not even maintain morfofonemic stability. For exampl, a rare instnce of intendd simplification, th removal of final κ from words like *frolick* in th nineteenth century, in fact produced a morfofonemic complication, in that it required κ to be insertd befor sufixs, as in *frolicked*. Th basic point of both *Table 5.5* and *5.6* is to sho how complex is th task facing lernrs and users of ritn english. Th variations in th spelng of /k/ ar esentialy unpredictbl, wich means that, despite recurent patrns givng som gidance,

Table 5.6: Morfofonemic variation involvng /k/ in english spelng

Ar /k/ spelngs morfofonemicly stable in english?	
C or CH?	*acrostic/hemistich*
C or CK?	*beacon/beckon, bloc/block, panic/panicked, hammock/havoc*
C or K?	*cat/kitten, cow/kine, curb/kerb, provocation/provoke, disc/disk, Celt/Kelt, sceptic/skeptic* (US)
C or QU?	*licorice/liquorice*
CH or K?	*autarchy/autarky, leuchaemia/leukaemia*
CK or QU?	*check* (US)/*cheque*
CK or CQU?	*lackey/lacquey, racket/racquet*
K or QU?	*embark/barque, mask/masque*

th spelng for each word containng th sound /k/ has to be lernt individuly. Yet /ᴋ/ is only one of forty or so sounds that make up th fonolojy of english, and th variations shown abov only concern spelng, i.e., th process of riting. Th process of readng involvs perhaps even mor complex variations, including for instnce, stress-asynmnt by th readr wich is not shown by th spelng at al, as wen *a present/to present* hav th same spelngs (Cut Spelng distinguishs *presnt/present*). Few othr languajs tolrate a riting systm that is remotely as unpredictbl as english.

Th most importnt mesaj for teachrs is that they shud not be satisfyd with th presnt spelng systm. Wenevr they observ lernrs havng dificlty, they wud do wel to ask wat is causing th dificlty. By noting and classifyng exampls of dificlty, teachrs wil both com to apreciate th problms of th systm betr and be betr able to help ther pupils. They wil becom aware that redundnt letrs giv rise to a majority of errs, and may decide to try spelng pronunciation as a device for helpng lernrs memrize dificlt spelngs (as sujestd by Drake and Ehri, 1984), or they may develop othr tecniqes of ther own.

Howevr, in th long term, ther can be no othr solution but to work for th modrnization, simplification and regulrization of th spelng systm itself. This is a matr hos ramifications mostly lie outside th scope of individul teachrs, tho they may hav som limitd oprtunitis for action; for instnce, teachrs may encuraj pupils to use regulr americn spelngs in prefrnce to iregulr british equivlnts (mor daringly, one formr teachr nown to th authr for many years delibratly taut *surprize* in prefrnce to *surprise*, but uncontrold individul initiativs of this kind wud be a recipe for even gretr caos). Mor jenrly, one initiativ teachrs cud take is to discuss among themselvs wat reformd spelngs they wud juj most useful for th lernng process, develop a consensus on prioritis, and put forwrd 'wantd lists' thru ther professionl bodis for considration by th apropriat authoritis. It was noticebl that th primary scool teachrs union in France thus suportd th 1990 french spelng reforms (Baddeley, 1993). For teachrs, mor than anyone, stand to gain imediatly from any esing of th task of litracy aquisition.

Th Cut Spelng in wich this chaptr is ritn is an exampl of th kind of experimntation and inovation that is now needd. Unlike som erlir proposals for th root and branch respelng of english from first principls, CS takes th presnt spelng as its startng point. Its procedur is chiefly th paring down of overelabrat traditionl spelngs by removing redundnt letrs, i.e., those that ber an unpredictbl relationship to th pronunciation. This not merely brings advantajs of econmy (riting becoms fastr and takes up less space), but it targets th most serius dificlty of conventionl english spelng. It is dificlt enuf wen non-standrd letrs ar used to represent sounds (such as th A in *any*, E in *pretty*, U in *busy*, etc.), but lernrs face a dubl dificlty with letrs wich do not represent sounds at al: in these cases, not merely must th corect sound valu of th letr and th corect letr for th sound be lernt, but so must th letrs position in th word. That is wy, in a word like *business*, th chief problm is not th aberant U, but th redundnt I. Teachrs wil find it helpful to identify how many of th problms ther pupils face arise from such redundncy, and considr wat tecniqes (e.g., spelng pronunciation) may be most helpful in overcomng them.

Aftr som decades wen it was rathr neglectd in education, english spelng is now receiving new atention, aroused by reports of declining litracy standrds. At th same time, reserch into readng processes is incresingly confirmng th importnce of fonics for th lernng process.[2] By th lojic of this chaptr, th contradictions between th dificlty of english spelng, th need for improved standrds of litracy, and th aplication of fonics (fonics only works proprly wen spelng represents pronunciation) shud be evidnt, and lead on to considration of ways of resolvng them. Th time may now be ripe for action, as it has perhaps nevr been befor, but as yet th necesry orgnizationl structurs do not exist. Th minute, but intrnationly based, Simplified Spelling Society, is only a jinjr group — it can ajitate for action but it canot itself introduce chanje.[3] A brodr groundswel of informd and influential opinion is needd. Perhaps a gretr undrstandng of th relationship between riting systms and litracy standrds, such as this chaptr has atemtd to create, wil help jenrate that groundswel.

Notes

1. For exampl, James A.H. Murray, first editr of th *Oxford English Dictionary*; W.W. Skeat, emnnt scolr of Old and Midl English and first presidnt of th

Simplified Spelling Society; Daniel Jones, Harold Orton (1948), as revisers of th *New Spelling* proposal for english spelng reform in its 6th edition, London: Sir Isaac Pitman and Sons, Ltd, for the Simplified Spelling Society.

2. For exampl, th work of Linnea Ehri (City University of New York) over many years; se also Vincent Connelly, University of St Andrews, doctoral thesis in progress.

3. Simplified Spelling Society, Secretary Bob Brown, 133 John Trundle Court, Barbican, London EC2Y 8DJ, Tel 071–628 5876, Fax 071–628 9147.

References

Aaron, P.G. (1989) 'Orthographic systems and developmental dyslexia: A reformulation of the syndrome', in Aaron, P.G. and Malatesha Joshi, R. (Eds) *Reading and Writing Disorders in Different Orthographic Systems*, Dordrecht, Kluwer.

Albrow, K.H. (1972) *The English Writing System: Notes Towards a Description*, Longman for the Schools Council, p. 3.

Allerup, P. (1993) 'IEA survey, findings' International Reading Conference, St Martin's College, Lancaster, September.

Baddeley, S. (1993) 'The 1990 French spelling reforms', *Journal of the Simplified Spelling Society*, 93, 2, p. 3.

Carney, E. (1994) *A Survey of English Spelling*, London, Routledge, p. xviii.

Centre for Educational Research and Innovation (CERI) (1992) *Adult Illiteracy and Economic Performance*, Paris, Organisation for Economic Cooperation and Development.

Che Kan Leong (1989) 'Reading and writing difficulties in a morphemic script', in Aaron, P.G. and Malatesha Joshi, R. (1989) (Eds) op. cit., p. 270.

Chomsky, N. and Halle, M. (1968) *The Sound Pattern of English*, New York, Harper and Row, p. 49.

Clark, J.W. (1965) 'American spelling', in Vallins, G.H. *Spelling*, 2nd ed. revised by Scragg, D.G., London, André Deutsch for 'The Language Library' series.

Coote, E. (1596) *The English School-maister*, London, Ralph Jackson and Robert Dexter.

Department for Education and the Welsh Office (1993) *English for Ages 5 to 16 (1993): Proposals of the Secretary of State for Education and the Secretary of State for Wales.*

Department of Education and Science (DES) (1988) *Report of the Committee of Inquiry into the Teaching of English Language* (The Kingman Report), London, HMSO, pp. 52, 56.

Department of Education and Science and the Welsh Office (1989) *English for Ages 5 to 16* (The Cox Report), par. 17.33.

Downing, J. (Ed) (1973a) *Comparative Reading: Cross-National Studies of Behavior and Processes in Reading and Writing*, New York, Macmillan.

Downing, J. (1973b) 'Is literacy acquisition easier in some languages than in others?', *Visible Language*, **7**, pp. 145–54.

Downing, J. (1987) 'The transfer of skills in language functions', *Journal of the Simplified Spelling Society*, **87**, 2, pp. 5–12.

Drake, D.A. and Ehri, L.C. (1984) 'Spelling acquisition: Effects of pronouncing words on memory for their spellings', *Cognition and Instruction*, 1, 3, Lawrence Erlbaum Associates, pp. 297–320.

Green, A. and Steedman, H. (1993) *Educational provision, educational attainment and the needs of industry: A review of research for Germany, France, Japan, the USA and Britain*, London, National Institute of Economic and Social Research.

Hart, J. (1570) *A Methode or Comfortable Beginning for all Unlearned, Whereby They May Bee Taught to Read English, In A Very Short Time, Vvith Pleasure* (The Epistle Dedicatorie, p. 2), London, Henrie Denham.

Henderson, L. (1984), in Henderson, L. (Ed) *Orthographies and Reading*, London, Lawrence Erlbaum Associates, pp. 11–24.

Hooker, J.T. (Ed) (1990) *Reading the Past*, London, British Museum Publications.

IEA (1992a) Warwick, Elley, B. (July 1992) *How in the World Do Students Read?*, International Association for the Evaluation of Educational Achievement.

IEA (1992b) Postlethwaite, T.N. and Ross, K.N. (November 1992) *Effective Schools in Reading: Implications for Educational Planners*, International Association for the Evaluation of Educational Achievement.

IEA (1993) Lundberg, I. and Linnakylä, P. (January 1993) *Teaching Reading Around the World*, International Association for the Evaluation of Educational Achievement.

Lindqvist, C. (1991) *China: Empire of the Written Symbol*, London, Harvill, p. 8.

Lloyd, S. (1992) *The Phonics Handbook*, Chigwell, Jolly Learning, p. 2.

Makita, K. (1968) 'The rarity of reading disability in Japanese children', *American Journal of Orthopsychiatry*, **38**, pp. 599–614, as quoted by Yule (1991) p. 28.

Martin, J.H. and Friedberg, A. (1986) *Writing to Read*, New York, Warner Books.

Michael, I. (1987) *The Teaching of English From The Sixteenth Century To 1870*, Cambridge, Cambridge University Press.

Moseley, D. (1989) 'How lack of confidence in spelling affects children's written expression', *Educational Psychology in Practice*, April.

Mulcaster, R. (1582) *The First Part of the Elementarie*, London, Thames Vautroullier.

Nolst Trenité, G. (1929), appendix to *Drop Your Foreign Accent: Engelsche Uitspraakoefeningen*, Haarlem, H D Tjeenk Willink and Zoon, pp. 117–21; also *Simplified Spelling Society Newsletter*, 42, 2, pp. 27–30.

Nyikos, J. (1987) 'A linguistic perspective of functional illiteracy: Toward an evaluative phoneme-grapheme analysis', in Embleton, S. (Ed) *The Fourteenth LACUS Forum 1987*, Lake Bluff, IL, Linguistic Association of Canada and the United States, p. 147.

PETERS, M.L. (1985) *Spelling Taught Or Caught? A New Look*, (2nd ed.) London, Routledge and Kegan Paul.

PITMAN, SIR J. and ST JOHN, J. (1969) *Alphabets and Reading*, London, Sir Isaac Pitman and Sons, Chapters 5 and 6, pp. 59–114.

ROSE, S. (1992) *The Making of Memory: From Molecules To Mind*, London, Bantam Press, p. 313.

SAMPSON, G. (1985) *Writing Systems*, London, Hutchinson, p. 204.

SMITH, C. (1971) *Collins Spanish-English English-Spanish Dictionary*, London and Glasgow, Collins, p. xxxiii.

SMITH, F. (1991) 'In the company of authors', *The Times Educational Supplement*, 23 August, p. 19.

STERLING, C. (1992) 'Introduction to the Psychology of Spelling', in STERLING, C.M. and ROBSON, C. (Eds) *Psychology, Spelling and Education*, Clevedon, Multilingual Matters, pp. 4, 6–8.

STEVENSON, H.W., STIGLER, J.W., LUCKER, G.W., LEE, S-Y HSU, CH-CH and KITAMARA, S. (1982) *Child Development*, **53**, pp. 1164–81.

STEVENSON, H.W., STIGLER, J.W., LUCKER, G.W., LEE, S-Y HSU, CH-CH and KITAMARA, S. (1985) *Child Development*, **56**, pp. 718–34.

STUBBS, M. (1980) *Language and Literacy: The Sociolinguistics of Reading and Writing*, London, Routledge and Kegan Paul, p. 43.

TARNOPOL, L. and TARNOPOL, M. (1976) *Reading Disabilities: An International Perspective*, Baltimore, MD, University Park Press.

TARNOPOL, L. and TARNOPOL, M. (1981) *Comparative Reading and Learning Difficulties*, Lexington, MA, Lexington Books.

THORSTAD, G. (1991) 'The effect of orthography on the acquisition of literacy skills', *British Journal of Psychology*, **82**, pp. 527–37.

TROUILLE, J.-M. (1987) 'Changes in the spelling of Dutch', *Journal of the Simplified Spelling Society*, 1987/2, pp. 14–16, par. 6.

UPWARD, C. (1992a) *Cut Spelling: A Handbook to the Simplification of Written English by Omission of Redundant Letters*, Birmingham, Simplified Spelling Society.

UPWARD, C. (1992b) 'Teaching literacy first, traditional English orthography second', in STERLING, C.M. and ROBSON, C. (Eds) op.cit., pp. 18–29.

UPWARD, C. (1992c) 'Is traditionl english spelng mor dificlt than jermn?', *Journal of Research in Reading*, **15**, 2, pp. 82–94.

VERNON, M. (1957) *Backwardness in Reading*, Cambridge, Cambridge University Press; also DOWNING, J. (1987), p. 9, par. 4.2.

YUE E LI and UPWARD, C. (1992) 'Review of the process of reform in the simplification of Chinese characters', *Journal of the Simplified Spelling Society*, 92/2, pp. 14–16.

YULE, V. (1991) *Orthography and Reading: Spelling and Society*, thesis submitted for the degree of Doctor of Philosophy, Faculty of Education, Monash University, Victoria, Australia, pp. 24–25.

Chapter 6

'Equal-Plus': A New Initial-teaching Orthography

N. Atkinson

Summary

A description is given of 'Equal-Plus', a new initial-teaching orthography currently being developed. This orthography bases its rationale on the sequence of competencies through which children are now known to pass in learning to read and spell. It makes use of such regularity as already exists in conventional English spelling and minimizes the need for 'unlearning'. Reference is made to pilot studies which show that the system is easy to learn. Evidence is given which suggests that its early use might facilitate reading and writing in conventional orthography.

Introduction

Children seem to recognize their first few written words through selective association (Gough, Juel and Griffith, 1992). They will select for a word some arbitrary visual attribute which distinguishes it from words previously noticed. For instance they may notice the shape 'R' at the beginning of a name (Razwana), the matching 'ee' in 'bee', the double hump at the beginning of 'Mum' or the tail on the end of 'donkey'.

The trouble is that reading by selective association, or 'visual-cue reading' as it sometimes called, rapidly increases in difficulty as more and more words are encountered until soon further progress can only be made with herculean effort. Typically, there is a deterioration in the ability to learn to read new words (e.g., Byrne, Freebody and Gates, 1992). Hence Bertelson (1986) describes this initial method of reading as 'non-productive'. In default of other strategies, children may persist with it for a long time; but to become skilled readers, they need to internalize the system by which elements of the written language (letters and letter sequences) are mapped onto elements of the spoken language (phonemes and phonemic sequences). Without transition to a type of reading which makes use of correspondences between symbols and sounds — a change to what is called by Gough, Juel and Griffith (1992) *cipher* reading, by Chall (1979, 1983) *Stage 1* reading (as opposed to *Stage 0* reading) and by Frith (1985) *alphabetic* reading — there is a real danger they will end up reading extremely poorly if at all.

How though is this transition best brought about? Ehri (1987) has elegantly demonstrated through a series of experiments the extreme implausibility of the argument that exposure to environmental print itself leads children to make letter–phoneme links (See Volume 1, Chapter 1). The dramatic differences which can be achieved through phonological-awareness training have been demonstrated by many investigators (e.g., Stuart and Masterson, 1992), and there has been much work showing how such training can be combined with the teaching of letter sounds (e.g., Bryant and Bradley, 1985; Byrne and Fielding-Barnsley, 1989; Byrne, 1992; Stuart, 1993) and how code-based programmes can be integrated with teaching to improve comprehension skills (e.g., Moran and Calfee, 1993). What has received relatively little recent attention however is the possibility of modifying the English orthography used by learners so as to make learning to read and write easier (see Chapter 5).

This is the aim of Equal-Plus, the new initial-teaching orthography the writer is currently devising. There are four subsidiary ambitions:

1.   to improve phonological awareness;
2.   to improve children's competence in matching written words and written-word elements with words and word elements in their spoken lexicon;
3.   to facilitate the learning of the main phonographic correspondences of our present spelling system; and
4.   to provide information about the general structure of this system.

Equal-Plus bases its rationale on the sequence of competences through which children are now known to pass in learning to read and spell (Read, 1971, 1975, 1986; Sterling, 1983; Cataldo and Ellis, 1990; Ehri, 1991; Schlagal, 1992; Treiman, 1993). Exploiting such regularities as already exist in traditional orthography (TO) (Fries, 1963; Venezky, 1970; Albrow, 1972; Linksz, 1973; Henry, 1988; Carney, 1994), Equal-Plus minimizes the need for 'unlearning'. Unlike the Initial Teaching Alphabet (i.t.a), it draws attention to these regularities. There is thus a real prospect that any early advantages it might have would be retained on transition to conventional orthography. Those of i.t.a tended to be lost (Warburton and Southgate, 1969).

Adults literate in English can read Equal-Plus (EP) at sight without any prior instruction. Here for instance is a specimen text taken from a well-known children's book written at the turn of the century:

Edith Nesbit (1906) *The Story of the Amu=let*, Lund+n, T Fish+r Unwin.

And now from the windo= ov a for we=ld cab the Kwe=n ov Babil+n beheld the wund+rs ov Lund+n. Bucking+m Palace she= thaut unintresting; Westminst+r Aby and the Houzes ov Parl+m+nt lit+l bet+r. But she= li=kt the Tow+r, and the Riv+r, and the ships fild her with wund+r and deli=t.

'But how badly u= ke=p yor sla=vs. How rechid and por and neglected tha= se=m', she= sed, az the cab rat+ld along the Mi=1 End Ro=d.

'Tha= arn't sla=vs; tha're werking pe=p+l', sed Ja=n.

'Ov corse tha're werking pe=p+l. That's wot sla=vs ar. Du: u= supo=z I do=n't no= a sla=v's fa=ce wen I= se= it? Wi= do=n't thair mast+rs se= tha're bet+r fed and bet+r clo=thd? Tel me= in thre= werds.'

No= wun ans+rd. The wa=j sist+m ov mod+rn Ingl+nd iz a lit+l dific+lt to expla=n in thre= werds e=v+n if u= und+rstand it — wich the childr+n did+n't.

'U='l hav a revo=lt of yor sla=vs if yor not careful', sed the Kwe=n.

'O= no=', sed Sirr+l; u= se= tha= hav vo=ts — that ma=ks al the difr+nce. Fath+r to=ld me= so=.'

'Wot iz this vo=t?' askt the Kwe=n. Iz it a charm? Wot du: tha= du: with it?'

'I= do=n't no=', sed the harasst Sirr+l; it's just a vo=t, that's al! Tha= do=n't du: enything p+rticu=l+r with it.'

'I= se=', sed the Kwe=n; 'a sort ov pla= thing. Wel, I wish that al the=z sla=vs ma= hav in thair hands this mo=m+nt thair fil ov thair fa=vrit me=t and drink.'

Inst+ntly al the pe=p+l in the Mi=l End Ro=d, and in al the uth+r stre=ts wair the por pe=p+l liv, found thair hands ful of things to e=t and drink. From the cab windo=s cud be= se=n pers+ns carrying evry ki=nd ov food, and bot+ls and cans az wel. Ro=st me=t, fowls, red lobst+rs, gra=t yelo=y crabs, fri=d fish, boild pork, be=f sta=k pudings, ba=kt uny+ns, mut+n pi=s;

mo=st ov the yung pe=p+l had oranjes and swe=ts and ca=k. It ma=d an enormus chanj in the l<u>oo</u>k of the Mi=l End Ro=d — bri=t+nd it up so= to spe=k, and bri=t+nd up mor than u= can imajin the fa<u>ce</u>s ov the pe=p+l.

'Ma=ks a difr+n<u>ce</u> duz+n't it?', sed the Kwe=n.

The Main Characteristics of Equal-Plus

Equal-Plus is greatly indebted to *Regularized English* (Wijk, 1959, 1969) and *Cut Spelling* (Upward, 1991) but is very different from both. Its main characteristics will probably be fairly clear from the extract. They can be set out very simply by making a few comparisons with Traditional Orthography (TO). We can concentrate first on stressed syllables.

Stressed Syllables

1. Within the set of words containing 'short vowel' sounds it is easy enough to identify a phonographically 'regular' subset. This can be arranged by onset, the initial consonant element if any, and rime, the sound which remains, in the form:

```
. . . . . . .
...   at   ...   it   ...   —   ...   —   ...
...   bat  ...   bit  ...   bet ...   —   ...   but
...   cat  ..    —    ...   —   ...   cot ...   cut
                                      . . . . . .   etc.
```

or alternatively can be arranged:

```
. . . . .   bat   cat
            bag   can
            ban   cad
                  cap   etc.
```

EP consistently represents these five vowel sounds by the letters <a, e, i, o, u> and it simplifies consonant representation so that for the most part, there is a one-to-one correspondence between consonant phonemes and consonant letters. For instance in the Nesbit text, TO <have, as, said, when, is, of, what, does, one> become EP <hav, az, sed, iz, ov, wot, duz, wun>. Other representations include <plad, bad; sez, hed,

frend; giv, siv, bild, mith; woz, cof, yot; cum, sum, ruf, blud, yung> for TO <plaid, bade; says, head, friend; give, sieve, build, myth; was, cough, yacht; come, some, rough, blood, young> and EP <sent, sel, jem, brij, ren, not, Fil> for TO <cent, cell, gem, bridge, wren, knot, Phil>.

The EP vowel spellings shown here are the ones most commonly used in TO for their respective sounds. They are also the ones used most frequently by young children in both their correct and incorrect spellings (Treiman, 1993). For children entering the *alphabetic* stage of spelling and reading, the consonant representations have a similar naturalness (Frith, 1985). At this crucial transition, preliminary studies show that the words generated by the specific augmentation of TO regularity illustrated are far more likely to be read correctly than their TO equivalents and that the spellings chosen are similarly more likely to be elicited than their TO equivalents. The effect sizes are large and do not seem to be influenced either by school or by accent.

In many accents, such as Received Pronunciation (RP) and General American, a distinction is made between the vowel sound in 'putt, but' and the vowel sound in 'put, push'. In EP, so as to reduce the possibility of confusion, instances of this second sound are given underlined letters:

<put, pull, push, cud (could), wud (would), shud (should), pul (pull), ful (full)>. The <oo> spelling of this sound is one which children find easy to learn. This is retained for all its TO instances and is also underlined:
<book, took, good, wood>.

2. The spelling paradigm for stressed syllables containing 'short' vowels is already fairly regular in traditional orthography. All that is needed is a little tidying up to make it user-friendly. In TO, the next most frequent pattern for stressed syllables is for obvious reasons often displayed in contrast to the first:

mat, mate	Tim, time	slop, slope	cub, cube
scrap, scrape	strip, stripe	cod, code	cut, cute etc.

(If we confine ourselves to single-syllable words, there are of course few pairs such as 'pet, Pete'.)

Token counts derived by aggregating the frequencies of running words (e.g., Dewey, 1950; Kučera and Francis, 1967; Reid, 1989) consistently show that the most frequent representation for what might be labelled 'letter-name long vowels' is vowel letter, consonant letter, e (or in polysyllables some other vowel letter). Unfortunately, in addition to using the convention exemplified above, TO also deploys a great range of tiresome vowel digraphs. Furthermore, 'letter-name long vowels' may be indicated with varying degrees of probability by particular consonant sequences (e.g., ld: cold, told; st: most, post).

Choice of representation in EP was guided by developmental studies of children's spelling (Read, 1986; Treiman, 1993). Initially, children tend to represent these vowel sounds by the letters which have names corresponding to them. They subsequently begin to add vowel letters which may or may not be correct as markers, so <cake> might be written first <cak> and then <caik> and <boat> first <bot> and then <bote>. Equal-plus uses the letters which would come naturally to young children and then adds an equal sign as a marker.

<may, made/maid, mate, way, wait/weight, wave, waved, pay, paid, pain/pane, great/grate> are thus written:
<ma=, ma=d, ma=t, wa=, wa=t, wa=v, wa=vd, pa=, pa=d, pa=n, gra=t>.

<see/sea, seen/scene, seat, me, meet/meat, these> are written:
<se=, se=n, se=t, me=, me=t, the=z>

<cry, cried, my, mine, might, pie, pine, pint> are written:
<cri=, cri=d, mi=, mi=n, mi=t, pi=, pi=n, pi=nt>

<no/know, known, go, goat, ghost, grow, grown/groan, bone, boast, most, though> are written:
<no=, no=n, go=, go=t, go=st, gro=, gro=n, bo=n, bo=st, mo=st, tho=>

<cute, cube> are written:
<cu=t, cu=b>

Pilot studies indicate that this convention is easy to learn. In only a few minutes, 7-year-old children with learning difficulties who had just learned to read and write phonologically regular consonant-vowel-consonant (CVC) words (cat, dog, tap, tip, top etc.) achieved a high degree of success reading and spelling words like the ones illustrated. It is anticipated that use of the 'equal' sign will facilitate perception of differences and similarities in the sound structure of words. Shifting the final consonant letter to the end of the word should increase use of information about its sound. Regularizing onset and rime units can be

Table 6.1: Stressed vowel sounds in Traditional Orthography

	Stressed Vowel Sounds
ar:	car, dark, charm, sharp, smart
or:	or, corn, pork, torch, short
au:	haunt, fraud, Paul, jaunt, taut
aw:	saw, raw, Jaws, drawn, crawl
er:	her, term, jerk, perch, stern
ur:	fur, burn, hurt, surf, burst
ir:	girl, first, third, skirt, birth
ou:	out, cloud, found, count, couch
ow:	now, cow, brown, owl, crowd
oi:	oil, boil, join, joint, moist
oy:	boy, toy, joy, Roy, Troy
air:	air, fair, chair, hair, stairs
are:	bare, care, dare, share, spare
ear:	ear, hear, dear, near, fear
eer:	deer, beer, jeer, peer, steer

expected to make these more salient and to facilitate use of the kind of analogy strategies discussed by Goswami and Bryant (1990). Decoding strategies in reading and encoding strategies in spelling should be much easier to establish.

There is a minor problem with the representation <u=>. For a number of words such as 'tube', there are differences between British and American pronunciations: Americans pronounce the vowel sound /u:/ while the British pronunciation tends to be /ju:/. By adopting <u:> for all spellings of /u:/ other than those represented in TO by the letters <oo>, significant discrepancies are avoided: the two signs <u=> and <u:> look very similar and the use for a few dozen words of one rather than the other should not create problems.

<oo> for /u:/ is a very simple spelling. It is learnt at such an early stage that it would be counter-productive not to use it in EP for words which in TO have this spelling for the sound e.g. <food, boot; groove, EP groov>. For other words such as <blue/blew, through/threw, grew, June, Judy, rude, true, truth, truly, tomb>, the representation <u:> accords better with the predominant TO representations and is probably preferable: <blu:, thru:, gru:, Ju:n, Ju:dy ru:d, tru:, tru:th, tru:ly tu:m>. <y> is used for the sound at the end of <Ju:dy, tru:ly>. In most accents, this sound closely approximates that of 'letter name long e'.

3. Traditional orthography has a number of other major representations for stressed vowel sounds. See Table 6.1. The TO representations in Table 6.1 are retained and supplemented in EP by:

a̱: gra̱ss, fa̱st, ba̱th, ca̱n't, da̱n<u>ce</u>

Two further units are used:

<u>war</u>:   <u>war</u>, <u>war</u>n, <u>war</u>d, <u>war</u>m, s<u>war</u>m
<u>al</u>:   <u>al</u>, b<u>al</u>, t<u>al</u>, w<u>al</u>, sm<u>al</u>

The spellings <ss> in <gra̱ss> and <<u>ce</u>> in <da̱n<u>ce</u>> will be noted. The possibility of consistently representing the sound /s/ by <s> and the sound /z/ by <z> was explored; but the arguments for retaining <s> for regular noun and verb inflections irrespective of whether they are voiced <sits, runs; cats, dogs> seemed overwhelming. This orthographic convention is learned very early (Atkinson, 1985). To violate it would cause great confusion to children who fail to voice certain letters owing to immaturity and would lead to unnecessary puzzlement in particular language communities. Most London children for example pronounce <paths> as /pɑːfs/ so spelling the final sound with the letter <z> would simply impose an additional burden. Similarly, it seemed sensible to make a clear distinction in the orthography between singular words and plural words. In addition to <s>, three other TO spellings of /s/ have therefore been retained: <ss>, <ce> and <se>. However, the last two are underlined to indicate that they represent single sounds. Hence children are discouraged from pronouncing <hor<u>se</u>> 'whores' or 'horsey', from imagining that <pen<u>ce</u>> means writing instruments <pens> and from thinking that <the prin<u>ce</u>> denotes more than one exotically titled personage (prin + s).

If words have vowel sounds which correspond to the ones above but have different TO spellings, these spellings are changed to accord with the predominant patterns so as to facilitate the learning of the major phonographic representations e.g:

<more, store, door, floor, court, four, oar, board> are written:
<mor, stor, dor, flor, cort, for, or, bord>

<caught, taught, ought, bought, talk, walk> are written:
<caut, taut, aut, baut, tauk, wauk>

<worm, word, work, earth, earn, learn> are written:
<werm, werd, werk, erth, ern, lern>

<bear, where, there/their, mayor> are written:
<bair, wair, thair, mair>

Table 6.2: *Representation of syllabic consonants in Nesbit text*

Words in TO	Words in EP	Words in TO	Words in EP
	<+n>		**<+m>**
London	Lund+n	Buckingham	Bucking+m
Babylon	Babil+n	system	sist+m
England	Ingl+nd	Parliament	Parl+m+nt
even	e=v+n		
children	childr+n		
didn't	did+n't		
difference	difr+n*ce*		
brightened	bri=t+nd		
moment	mo=m+nt		
doesn't	duz+n't		
onion	uny+n		
mutton	mut+n		

Words in TO	Words in EP	Words in TO	Words in EP
	<+l>		**<+r>**
little	lit+l	better	bet+r
rattled	rat+ld	river	riv+r
people	pe=p+l	Tower	Tow+r
difficult	dific+lt	wonder	wund+r
bottle	bot+l	master	mast+r
Cyril	Sirr+l	lobster	lobst+r
		particular	p+rticu=l+r

Some minor distinctions in pronunciation which might be made by the speakers of particular accents have been ignored. The aim is to link elements within written words to elements within spoken words in a manner which is generally useful to all speakers of English who are learning to read and write the language. There is no attempt to provide a phonetic transcription of any particular accent.

Unstressed Syllables

Two main simplifications are made to the representation of unstressed syllables.

1. When we say the word 'button', there is no vowel sound between the last two consonants. The peak of the final syllable is located in the final consonant which would phonetically be written [n̩] (Kreidner, 1989). Syllabic n, m, l and r are consistently represented in EP <+n, +m, +l, +r>. Examples from from the Nesbit text are given in Table 6.2. Young children typically omit vowel letters when they write words containing syllabic consonants. Spellings encountered recently included:

Table 6.3: Syllabic consonant representation as a source of uncertainty

Words in TO	Words in EP	Words in TO	Words in EP
	+n		**+m**
heaven	hev+n		
Devon	Dev+n	phantom	fant+m
seven	sev+n	bantam	bant+m
Dillon	Dil+n		
villain	vil+n		
vixen	vix+n		
Nixon	Nix+n		
lesson	less+n		
lessen	less+n		
dozen	duz+n		
cousin	cuz+n		

Words in TO	Words in EP	Words in TO	Words in EP
	+l		**+r**
kettle	ket+l	teacher	te=ch+r
metal	met+l	vicar	vic+r
model	mod+l	doctor	doct+r
waddle	wod+l	martyr	mart+r
symbol	simb+l	chauffeur	sho=f+r
mimble	mimb+l	mirror	mirr+r
chisel	chiz+l	Cheshire	Chesh+r
sizzle	siz+l	injure	inj+r
sandal	sand+l	Gloucester	Glost+r
handle	hand+l		
naval	na=v+l	metre*	me=t+r
navel	na=v+l	labour*	la=b+r
principle	prinsip+l	neighbour*	na=b+r
principal	prinsip+l		

Note: *British spellings

DOKTR <doctor, EP doct+r>, DINR <dinner, EP din+r>, JASN<Jason, EP Ja=s+n>, PARSL <parcel, EP pars+l>, BOTL <bottle, EP bot+l> and BATM<bottom, EP bot+m>.

At a later stage there is uncertainty about which vowel letter should be written and sometimes also uncertainty as to where the vowel letter should be placed in relation to the consonant letter. Words illustrative of the problems confronting learners of TO are shown in Table 6.3 together with their EP equivalents.

Equal-Plus attempts to postpone such uncertainties until the basic orthographic structures have been acquired. Transformation into EP seems to make words containing syllabic consonants considerably easier to read and write. In an informal preliminary investigation, it was found that children of 6 and 7 with learning difficulties who had just learned to read and write regular CVC words were able to read and write many of the EP words with less than five minutes practice using the <+n, +m, +l, +r> units. With a corresponding random selection of the TO words, the only success achieved by any child in a matched group was in reading <teacher> and <doctor>. There was a marked tendency for children in the TO group to place the stress of some of the words on the wrong syllable.

2. A number of sounds, of which /ʃ/ as in <ship, brush, station, pension> is the most obvious example, tend to have different spellings in stressed and unstressed syllables. It is important that some of the main spelling patterns of longer words receive early attention, for if children imagine that TO is a monosystemic representation of the sounds of the language, they are likely to experience considerable delay in learning to read and write words which are polysyllabic. The units <ti, si, ssi, ci> are therefore used in EP for the /s/ sound in words such as:

menti+n, pensi+n, missi+n, majici+n.

The consonant sound /ʒ/ heard at the beginning of <Zhivago>, at the end of <rouge>, in the middle of <treasure> and at the start of the third syllable of <occasionally> also needs to be represented from time to time. The choice of spelling is not easy because in TO no one pattern predominates. Perhaps it might be best to have a special unit sion for words such as:

vision, television, confu=sion, conclu:sion, perswa=sion, inva=sion

<su> could then be used for words which already contain these letters such as:

mesu+r

and <zh> could be used for what remains such as:

ru:zh.

One further representation is needed, a special unit for the ending <ture> which is fairly frequent in the texts young children read and write. This is written <ture>:

picture, na=ture, cre=ture, fu=ture, adventure, torture, arkitecture

The inventory for unstressed syllables can now be completed. Schwa vowels, e.g., the sounds represented by the <a> in <attend, EP atend> and the <u> in <support, EP suport>, are almost invariably represented by the same letters which are used in their TO spellings unless they are covered by the <+n, +m, +l, +r> convention.

Messages for Teachers

Equal-Plus attempts to alleviate some of the burdens which an unreformed orthography places on those who are learning to read and write English. Its central features are a very simple method of representing 'letter-name long vowels' and a very simple method of representing syllabic consonants. These provide a wide range of potential teaching strategies.

These features could be used on their own. A system which radically simplifies English orthography would still remain. Scarcely any unlearning would be required: scarcely a single letter in a single word would need to be changed on transfer to traditional orthography. By extending cursive ligatures, to represent the equal sign, by drawing a line across ligatures to represent the plus sign and by putting a dot over ligatures for <u:> it would be easy to write all words in joined writing:

ta=k, ta=king, ta=k+n, Parl+m+nt, cu=t, su:t, di=lu:t

EP could be used in many other ways. Children could use it in their writing for words they found difficult to spell. Teachers could use for it for showing how the same sounds are represented differently in contrasting sets of words or for showing how TO sometimes represents different sounds, e.g., those corresponding to the tense marker <ed>, with the same letters so as to give easily identifiable units of meaning. The plus system could be extended to all 'schwa' or 'neutral vowels'. It could be restricted to words children found difficult. But behind EP and all its potential variants is a single idea: the notion that the main features of English orthography should be taught first and minor details taught later. Take a particular word by way of example. <Me=t> is sufficient to identify a word in the child's spoken lexicon. Having already learnt many of the basic structures of English orthography, children can learn through subsequent word study the particular letter which is used as a marker.

They might for instance be told a story about the netball or football team of *Ea*st Acton School being taken to the s*ea*side as a special tr*ea*t by their t*ea*cher. The t*ea*m could have a m*ea*l on the b*ea*ch. They might *ea*t m*ea*t and b*ea*ns and p*ea*s and then f*ea*st on p*ea*ches and cr*ea*m. *Ea*ch child might then be given either t*ea* or ice cr*ea*m. Further incidents could easily be contrived. Children who were usually n*ea*t and tidy might get their cl*ea*n j*ea*ns dirty. Someone else might make a s*ea*t out of discarded clothes and be bitten by fl*ea*s. In this way, a number of words with a particular sound could be memorably associated with a particular letter sequence. One spelling would tend to reinforce another.

Other sound–symbol correspondences might be taught very differently. For instance, older children might be given an historical explanation of the <o> spelling in <money, month, son> (Scragg, 1974). The different TO realizations of <+n>, <darken, action, magician>, might be approached through units of meaning.

What is important is that all children acquire at an early stage a basic sound–symbol structure on which they can build. A disturbing outcome of the research into i.t.a. was the strong aptitude x treatment interactions. Downing (1967) summarized very fairly the results of his own early researches:

> The improvements in t.o. reading are most noticeable generally among the high achievers — those who 'will learn anyway and, therefore, do not really need educational innovations' according to some British educators. The slower learning children do begin to show some benefit from i.t.a at the end of the third year, but the poorest 10 per cent show negligible improvement in test results. (Downing, 1967, p. 293)

Equal-Plus is much simpler than i.t.a and, unlike i.t.a, it deliberately foregrounds TO regularities. It is anticipated that its effects on 'slow learners' or those with specific learning difficulties could usually be shown in a few weeks and its effect on high achievers in a few hours. The response of young children with learning difficulties has been highly encouraging but substantial classroom-based research, formal and informal, is now needed with a wider population. For this, there are two main requirements.

First, it is necessary to specify particular orthographic domains so that the effects of specific transformations on the reading and spelling of words having particular characteristics can be determined. For teachers who are used to recording the content, method and outcomes of their teaching, this strategy will appear fairly natural. It is also highly important. Equal-plus is not a cut and dried system. Many details will no doubt be improved by modification. One needs to know which orthographic transformations are beneficial and to seek open-mindedly viable alternatives for those which are not.

Second, careful attention needs to paid to the possible effects of teaching method. In the research reported by Downing and Jones (1966) — commended by Warburton (Warburton and Southgate, 1969, p. 207) as 'the most efficiently designed research that has been carried out [into the effects of i.t.a.] and hence the most convincing' — five out of the twelve teachers said that they used phonic methods earlier with the i.t.a class than with the TO class. There were no differences in the opposite direction. Studies consistently show that code-emphasizing approaches produce reading attainments which are superior to those associated with other approaches (Chall, 1979, 1983; Perfetti, 1991). As Warburton comments, 'There is no doubt that the t.o. children grew in inferior phonic soil' (Warburton and Southgate, 1969, p. 260). It is important that the effects of medium and method are not confounded. For those conducting large-scale research, calculating through analysis of variance separate effect sizes for each would be one possible strategy for avoiding this.

An alternative — generally much more accessible to schools and preferable in many ways — is to have matched groups or subjects taught by a code-based approach in TO and EP. This possibility is feasible even within a single classroom. However if the children are sometimes taught in withdrawal groups, control of factors influencing outcomes will probably be easier. Classroom materials can then remain entirely in TO. The EP withdrawal groups can make extensive use of TO texts with interlinear EP transcriptions so that the potentialities of EP as a phonographic code are fully exploited. They can be encouraged to explore ways in which their speech maps onto TO. Thus transfer to traditional orthography, instead of being left to the end of the intervention, can be made an integral part of most of the reading and writing lessons.

Whether such experiments are formal or informal, their results should lead to valuable reflection on both medium and method. To achieve substantial improvements in standards of literacy, we may need to change both.

Conclusion

Equal-Plus offers new ideas for teaching children the main structures of the English writing system. It accords well with what is known about the successive competences involved in learning to read and write. There seems a real prospect that its use will improve children's orthographic understanding and that the development of both word recognition and spelling will be facilitated. This possibility, which would enable teachers to give greater emphasis to higher-order reading comprehension skills and to the discourse-level skills needed for different kinds of writing, is susceptible to immediate investigation within the classroom.

References

ALBROW, K.H. (1972) *The English Writing System: Notes Towards a Description*, London, Longman.

ATKINSON, N. (1985) 'Phonographic Knowledge and the Spelling Attainment of Children Aged 6 to 9', Unpublished M.Ed (Ed Pych) dissertation, University of Manchester.

BERTELSON, P. (1986) 'The onset of literacy: Liminal remarks', *Cognition*, **24**, pp. 1–30.

BRYANT, P.E. and BRADLEY, L. (1985) *Children's Reading Problems*, Oxford, Basil Blackwell.

BYRNE, B. (1992) 'Studies in the acquisition procedure for reading: rationale, hypotheses and data', in GOUGH, P.B., EHRI, L.C. and TREIMAN, R. (Eds) *Reading Acquisition*, Hillsdale, NJ, Lawrence Erlbaum Associates.

BYRNE, B. and FIELDING-BARNSLEY, R. (1989) 'Phonemic awareness and letter-sound knowledge in the child's acquisition of the alphabetic principle', *Journal of Educational Psychology*, **81**, 3, pp. 313–21.

BYRNE, B., FREEBODY, P. and GATES, A. (1992) 'Longitudinal data on the relations of word-reading strategies to comprehension, reading time and phonemic awareness', *Reading Research Quarterly*, **27**, 2, pp. 141–51.

CARNEY, E. (1994) *A Survey of English Spelling*, London, Routledge.

CATALDO, S. and ELLIS, N. (1990) 'Learning to spell, learning to read', in PUMFREY, P.D. and ELLIOTT, C.D. (Eds) *Children's Difficulties in Reading, Spelling and Writing*, London, Falmer Press.

CHALL, J.S. (1979) 'The great debate: Ten years later with a modest proposal for reading stages', in RESNICK, L.G. and WEAVER, P.A. (Eds) *Theory and Practice of Early Reading* (Vol. 1), Hillsdale, NJ, Lawrence Erlbaum Associates, pp. 29–56.

CHALL, J.S. (1983) *Stages of Reading Development*, New York, McGraw Hill.

DEWEY, G. (1950) *Relativ* Frequency of English Speech Sounds*, Cambridge, MA, Harvard University Press.

DOWNING, J. (1967) *Evaluating the Initial Teaching Alphabet*, London, Cassell.

DOWNING, J. and JONES, B. (1966) 'Some problems in evaluating i.t.a.: A second experiment', *Educational Research*, **8**, 1, pp. 100–14.

EHRI, L.C. (1987) 'Learning to read and spell words', *Journal of Reading Behavior*, **19**, pp. 5–31.

EHRI, L.C. (1991) 'The development of reading and spelling in children: an overview', in SNOWLING, M. and THOMSON, M. (Eds) *Dyslexia: Integrating Theory and Practice*, London, Whurr Publishers Ltd.

FRIES, C.C. (1963) *Linguistics and Reading*, New York, Holt, Rinehart and Winston.

FRITH, U. (1985) 'Beneath the surface of developmental dyslexia', in PATTERSON, K.E., MARSHALL, J.C. and COLTHEART, M. (Eds) *Surface Dyslexia: Neuropsychological and Cognitive Studies of Phonological Dyslexia*, London, Routledge and Kegan Paul.

GOUGH, P.B., JUEL, C. and GRIFFIN, P.L. (1992) 'Reading, spelling and the orthographic cipher', in GOUGH, P.B., EHRI, L.C. and TREIMAN, R. (Eds) *Reading Acquisition*, Hillsdale, NJ, Lawrence Erlbaum Associates.

GOSWAMI, U. and BRYANT, P. (1990) *Phonological Skills and Learning to Read*, Hove, East Sussex, Lawrence Erlbaum Associates.

HENRY, M.K. (1988) 'Beyond phonics: Integrated decoding and spelling instruction based on word origin and structure', *Annals of Dyslexia*, **38**, pp. 258–75.

KUČERA, H. and FRANCIS, N.W. (1967) *Computational Analysis of Present-day American English*, Providence, RI, Brown University Press.

KREIDLER, C.W. (1989) *The Pronunciation of English*, Oxford, Basil Blackwell.

LINKSZ, A. (1973) *On Writing, Reading and Dyslexia*, New York, Grune and Stratton.

MORAN, C. and CALFEE, R. (1993) 'Comprehending orthography: Social construction of letter-sound systems in monolingual and bilingual programs', *Reading and Writing: An Interdisciplinary Journal*, **5**, pp. 205–25.

NESBIT, E. (1906) *The Story of the Amulet*, London, T. Fisher Unwin.

PERFETTI, C. (1991) 'The psychology, pedagogy and politics of reading', *Psychological Science*, **2**, pp. 70–6.

READ, C. (1971) 'Pre-school children's knowledge of English phonology', *Harvard Educational Review*, **40**, pp. 1–34.

READ, C. (1975) *Children's Categorization of Speech Sounds in English*, (NCTE Research Report No. 17), Urbana, IL, National Council of Teachers of English.

READ, C. (1986) *Children's Creative Spelling*, London, Routledge and Kegan Paul.

REID, D. (1989) *Word for Word: The Top 2,000 Words Used by 7 and 8 Year Olds*, Wisbech, Cambridgeshire, Learning Development Aids.

SCHLAGAL, R.C. (1992) 'Patterns of orthographic development into the intermediate grades', in TEMPLETON, S. and BEAR, D.R. (Eds) *Development of Orthographic Knowledge and the Foundations of Literacy*, Hillsdale, NJ, Lawrence Erlbaum Associates.

SCRAGG, D.G. (1974) *A History of English Spelling*, Manchester, Manchester University Press.

STUART, M. (1993) 'Learning to read: A longitudinal study', *Education 3–13*, **21**, 1, pp. 19–25.

STUART, M. and MASTERSON, J. (1992) 'Patterns of reading and spelling in 10-year-old children related to prereading phonological abilities', *Journal of Experimental Child Psychology*, **54**, 2, pp. 168–89.

STERLING, C.M. (1983) 'Spelling errors in context', *British Journal of Psychology*, **74**, pp. 353–64.

TREIMAN, R. (1993) *Beginning to Spell*, New York, Oxford University Press.

UPWARD, C. (1991) *Cut Spelling*, Birmingham, Simplified Spelling Society.

VENEZKY, R. (1970) *The Structure of English Orthography*, The Hague, Mouton.

WARBURTON, F.W. and SOUTHGATE, V. (1969) *i.t.a.: An Independent Evaluation*, London, John Murray and W. and R. Chambers.

WIJK, A. (1959) *Regularized English*, (Acta Universitatis Stockholmiensis VII), Stockholm, Almqvist and Wiksell.

WIJK, A. (1969) 'Regularized English. The only practicable solution of the English spelling reform problem', in HAAS, W. (Ed) *Alphabets for English*, Manchester, Manchester University Press.

Note

* Dewey was an advocate of spelling reform. This is his own spelling and is followed by Harvard University Press on the spine, on the title page and throughout the book.

Part 2

Assessment

Defining the Reading Domain: Is a Curriculum Definition Sufficient to Establish a Standard?

T. Christie

Summary

The nature of the reading domain is discussed from the assessment point of view and a model is proposed which includes a range of contexts of performance, each pitched at a defined level of maturity. This is the differentiation by task approach to the assessment of reading in the National Curriculum. Empirical data from twenty-five teachers in Northern Ireland are reported to show that teachers who produce high-quality assessment with the tasks tailored to the individual child, are also teachers whose class average-reading scores tend to be high. The implications for teaching and testing are discussed.

Introduction

The assessment of reading is an almost universal practice in schools (Gipps and Goldstein, 1983) and yet we have learned very little from all this activity. Large questions remain unanswered at both national and classroom levels. Have reading standards deteriorated (Turner, 1990)? What is the best teaching approach for this non-reader? When Vincent and de la Mare (1986) came to revise the individually administered Neale test, they could not find any systematic account of the diagnostic expertise which they believed that teachers must have developed in using the test. There is no point in assessing reading unless the test generates usable, and useful, results. Clearly the issue of utility, the guiding principle of test construction, is a real one in relation to the assessment of reading.

The issue has been sharpened by the introduction of National Curriculum Assessment, itself an uneasy compromise between competing approaches to the improvement of teaching and learning. The Task Group on Assessment and Testing advocated formative assessment as the major engine of curriculum change (DES, 1988). It took the view that direct assessment of pupils by their teacher would sensitize the teacher to what the pupils had made of the teacher's intentions and create a feedback loop for the improvement of performance of both parties. If national-assessment instruments were developed as tools for teachers to use in obtaining this feedback, every classroom teacher would become a potential action researcher and the quality of education would be raised. But there is a competing model for educational improvement. The publication of league tables of school performance combined with greater freedom of parental choice of schools puts the parent, rather than the teacher, in the position of action researcher and brings the evaluative potential of National Curriculum Assessment to the fore. The improvement of teaching and learning by closing down underachieving schools and weeding out ineffective teachers calls for a very different kind of assessment tool. If schools are to be evaluated by the performance of their pupils, it does not make sense to involve teachers too deeply in the determination of levels of attainment.

The tension between formative and evaluative functions of assessment is not confined to Britain. In the United States it is described as the tension between instructional assessment (Wiggins, 1989) and accountability assessment (Mehrens, 1992). Nor is it simply a debate about purposes. If fitness for purpose is to inform the design of assessment, these competing approaches lead to entirely different specifications for effective reading tests.

Defining the Reading Domain

The problem of assessing reading is to determine along which dimension assessment should take place. Some means must be found of honouring the multiplicity of contexts in which reading is demanded, the range of strategies and competences that the reader may bring to bear and the efforts of teachers to extend that range to ever more reading contexts and ever more children while keeping this complex interplay within bounds. Figure 7.1 schematizes these three factors. If only one is chosen any variation in the other two is essentially ignored. It certainly goes unrecorded. All observations which vary along other than the chosen dimension are treated for measurement purposes as repetitions of the main dimension (Cattell, 1966).

Figure 7.1:   Potential dimensions in the measurement of reading

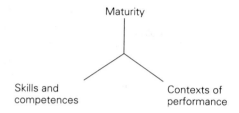

Each of the main dimensions in Figure 7.1 is itself an amalgam of potentially independent dimensions. The reading context could readily be subdivided into the linguistic difficulty of the text, the genre to which it belongs, the purpose for which it is being read, the format in which the reader's response is to be recorded and the rater's stance, whether participant or remote, but all of these variables can be subsumed as elements of the context of performance. Contexts of performance vary along a dimension of task authenticity.

Table 7.1:   From state intervention to the revised code, 1862, page 259

Reading	Standard I	Narrative monosyllables
	Standard II	One of the narratives next in order after monosyllables in an elementary reading book used in the school
	Standard III	A short paragraph from an elementary reading book used in the school
	Standard IV	A short paragraph from a more advanced reading book used in the school
	Standard V	A few lines of poetry from a reading book used in the first class of the school
	Standard VI	A short ordinary paragraph in a newspaper, or other modern narrative

The earliest attempts at large-scale reading assessment were based on authentic classroom tasks. These were under teacher control even though this was 'high stakes' testing — salaries depended upon the outcome. As the summary statements of the State Intervention to the Revised Code of 1862 indicate (see Table 7.1), reading was to be assessed by reference to a range of every day reading tasks distinguished largely by the nature of the texts involved. The 'standards' can be conceptualized as a set of cells moving diagonally upwards across the context-maturity facet of Figure 7.1.

Unfortunately, while this early attempt to define the reading domain paid due attention to a diversity of texts, the skills and competences to be assessed were largely confined to recitation. The specification of performance was not informed by an analysis of the reading construct.

The first National Curriculum in England failed to specify comprehension as a component of reading skill. Generations of 'barking at print' ensued.

The dimension of reading competences in Figure 7.1 became the focus of early psychometric tests of reading (Burt, 1921; Vernon, 1938; Schonell and Schonell, 1942). These made little effort to describe the complexity of contexts in which reading takes place. In accordance with the abilities model, an opposite reductionist tendency held sway. The attempt was to identify the kernel, the single, pure representative sample of the activity, which would predict its various manifestations. Operational definitions of reading skills and competences became entirely circular, being provided only by the tests themselves. There was no discourse model against which to test construct validity (Spolsky, 1990). Tests which fractionate reading into skills create a considerable distance between the real performance and the various subtests of the instrument. Only the expert user is likely to appreciate the effect on construct validity of selecting one skill from the whole. As a result, although these early psychometric tests have four or five subtests a potential profile of competences was frequently sacrificed in practice to a single surrogate measure of the maturity dimension, the graded word-reading list.

The measurement model of the time, classical true score theory (see Cronbach *et al.*, 1972, Chapter 2) was but poorly responsive to multifaceted accounts of learning and to the fact that individual children may follow different routes to comparable levels of attainment. The use of classical true score theory to evaluate tests of educational achievement was almost a category error. It treated achievement as a linear function of one or more abilities. These claims for the predictive validity of surrogate measures robbed the maturity dimension of its central pedagogical importance. The key questions, what develops, in what order if any, and why, were not addressed.

Figure 7.1 sets out the three dimensions of the reading-assessment domain as essentially orthogonal to each other. While some contexts of performance will occur with greater frequency than others as the child develops, it is essentially the case that any context of performance could occur at any level of maturity. Similarly, although any context may make salient demands on one or another competence — the idea of 'primary traits' which underlies the writing domain in the American National Assessment of Educational Progress — all competences have potential in all contexts. Young children are just as much engaged with the complexities of the reading process as their older counterparts (Chittenden, 1983). Finally, there are those who would claim that there are no linear hierarchies in children's development of understanding as they mature (Noss *et al.*, 1989). The context-maturity facet of Figure 7.1 respects that position as a starting point in defining the reading domain.

Models such as Figure 7.1 have to be evaluated both in terms of how closely they represent reality and also in terms of the extent to which they meet the utilitarian purposes for which they are designed. The Torch tests (Mossenson *et al.*, 1987) carry all the hallmarks of Figure 7.1 as a representation of reality. Eleven distinct types of skill (the competence dimension) are identified, ranging from copying complete sentences verbatim from the text to inferring emotion from a few scattered clues and the writer's tone. Furthermore there is a range of texts (the context dimension) for different degrees of maturity in reading. However, the performance context is much diminished, just as in 1862, by the use of only one mode of response, a variant of the cloze test. Heap's (1980) analysis of extraneous test-related rather than reading-related problems associated with assessment concludes that only diversity in format can prevent cumulative and invalid deficit for some children. The 'instrument effect', which reliance on a single mode of response invites, creates an artificial concordance between all skills and all contexts.

Instrument effect in the Torch scale is open to further reinforcement through the use of the Rasch (1960) model to select items for the test. The Rasch model assumes a single dimension underlying the test (maturity in Figure 7.1) and further requires that all test items relate to the dimension in precisely the same way. Thus the inclusion of an item, and hence the operational characteristics of the dimension, are crucially dependent upon the characteristics of all other items in the test. Should an item not behave in the same way as the generality of other items, say it has a markedly higher correlation with the total score, then that item will be rejected as part of the scale. A Rasch scale therefore automatically excludes any task which is likely to create differentiation *within* the reading performance of the individual child. It is precisely this within child differentiation which leads to different readers accessing text in different ways, the essence of Clay's (1988) 'Reading Recovery Program'. An essential diagnostic element is taken out of the test at the point of reading scale construction. Within child differentiation is as potent a threat to the integrity of a Rasch scale as it is to internal consistency as a measure of reliability (Stanley, 1971).

Item homogeneity is the main Rasch criterion. It is a method of reading-test construction designed to differentiate readers, not reading. In the case of the Torch scales, which are very long, covering seven years of educational progress, an admirable heterogeneity of text and of skill demand is elided through a single item type towards a single global score of reading ability. In the interests of manageability — the utilitarian purpose — the multifaceted model of Figure 7.1 is collapsed into a single maturity dimension.

Choosing a Measurement Model

A single dimension, the testing objective of the 1920s, is disastrous from the pedagogical point of view. How can teachers respond to such a score? It is a single number and all the teacher can endeavour to do is to make it larger. In these circumstances teaching to the test is the only sensible strategy but, as Goodhart's Law demonstrates in economics, attempts to manipulate a predictive variable, rather than to manipulate the performance that the variable predicts, immediately destroy the set of relationships which lent the variable predictive validity in the first place. The mini-economy of many classrooms echoes our national economic plight. Ritualistic behaviour is rife.

If a one-dimensional model is ineffectual, a three-dimensional model would be unmanageable. It would be far from clear how to interpret scores in terms of a way forward for the child or class. We are left then with a choice between competing two-dimensional models as guides to test construction. Three different bases of argument all point to the context-maturity facet as that guide. Alexander *et al.*, (1991) systematize over 300 articles on the usage of knowledge terminology in studies of learning. Following Flavell (1987), they analyse metacognitive knowledge into three major elements. 'Self-knowledge', how individuals perceive themselves as thinkers and learners, grows from knowledge of one's own and others' task performance. 'Task-knowledge', how individuals categorize the types of task that they encounter, grows from experience of tackling them. 'Strategic knowledge', the awareness that different procedures or processes may have to be initiated to permit more effective learning or thinking, grows from the other two types of knowledge (pp. 328–9 *passim*). The promotion of such metacognition of the printed text and its pleasures is every teacher's goal. It is promoted through encounters with authentic tasks.

Henning and Cascaller (1992) provide pragmatic grounds for selecting the context-maturity facet. Their empirical study of the American 'Educational Testing Service' (ETS) Test of English as a Foreign Language found such strong interactions between tested communicative competences and the social register and pragmatic functions of the contexts of communication in which they were tested that the researchers conclude that any test of communicative competence would be better to specify contexts of performance to ensure validity of assessment (p. 21). More expert readers (these were potential university students) use task analysis to make strategic decisions about how to approach a communicative task. As a result authentic tasks cannot be used to provide direct assessment of separate and distinct skills. The phenomenon is now well attested in language testing even at the level of the individual item (Alderson, 1989). The pragmatic issue is whether, in the face of a profusion of competing and contradictory language models, each suggesting a different partitioning of the competence dimension, there is point in teasing out how any individual has responded to any item which is not itself an authentic task.

The third consideration is both ethical and educational. Messick (1989) has argued for the past decade that the evaluation of both the intended and the unintended consequences of any testing is integral to the validation of test interpretation and use. Task-driven performance assessment promises authentic and direct appraisals of educational achievement leading to positive consequences for teaching and learning. Construct-driven assessment on the other hand must be held responsible in part for Cato *et al.*'s (1992) finding that teachers lacked awareness of the different language demands of areas of the curriculum and had difficulty in articulating both their methods and the view of language which underlay their choice of method (p. 10). In fact their classroom practice itself often reflected a greater variety of techniques than they had specified in either questionnaire or interview (p. 25). It is an unintended consequence of our current approaches to the testing of reading that it deskills teachers in thinking about the teaching of reading. That is the real test bias (Frederiksen, 1984).

National Curriculum assessment offers the opportunity to redress the balance. The definition of reading is atheoretical, eclectic rather than focused, and describes a set of weak progressions — some, more, a lot more — without analysing how they can be brought about. The utility of Figure 7.1 is its implicit guidance that we test that curriculum, not through a set of internally consistent competence constructs, but through authentic tasks, each free-standing and exemplifying a Statement of Attainment, that is through context-dependent task performance. Whether the Statements of Attainment are pitched at the right level of specificity, or even the right level of attainment, whether they are too many or too few, whether the aggregation rules make sense, is thereby rendered almost irrelevant in the short-term. These are all empirical questions capable of empirical resolution against an educational criterion; their efficacy in guiding teaching endeavour.

Educational Effects of the Model in Action

The Centre for Formative Assessment Studies (CFAS) in its pioneering work on the assessment of end of Key Stage 1 assessment in England and Wales (SEAC, 1990) developed the idea of a separate task to exemplify each Statement of Attainment. The consequent problem of manageability (there were 228 Statements of Attainment) was tackled by giving priority to informal teacher judgment. The teacher decided which tasks were well within the capacity of the child and only formally tested the area of proximal development (Moll, 1992): the teacher set only those tasks which were a potential challenge to the individual child. External statistical monitoring was used to validate the teacher's choice of task and the outcome of the task itself validated the teacher's judgment of the child's level. In essence the task was used to confirm the teacher's everyday classroom observation and such confirmation was forthcoming in over 90 per cent of some 3,000 judgments made of reading. A modified form of the procedure in which the teacher's judgment of entry point had to be confirmed by all tasks at the appropriate level was adopted subsequently for use in all Key Stage 1 assessments of reading in England and Wales.

CFAS was later approached by the Northern Ireland Schools Examination and Assessment Council (NISEAC) to supply a reading test along these lines for its end of Key Stage 1 assessment which occurs at age 8. The data which follow refer to the trial of that reading test.

Method

The test is in four major parts, each a set of reading tasks presented as a pupil reading book with table of contents and index as appropriate to the reading level. Levels 2 and 3 are in the same book with a defined break point between levels 2 and 3. Levels 1 and 4 are in separate books. In addition there is a separate reading-aloud passage which can be used to determine whether borderline children should start at level 1 or go straight to the level 2 and 3 book. There are thus five possible starting points which are under teacher control. The exit point is determined by the child's performance but there is again an element of teacher decision as to whether the child should proceed. This interactive approach to the testing of reading was completely new to the twenty-five teachers from eleven primary schools who took part in the trial. They had a two-hour introductory session on how to use the test structure and on the scoring of outcomes. In the following eight schooldays they tested between six and thirty-four children each, yielding a total pupil sample of 492 children for whom individual task outcomes are available.

From these data two variables of immediate interest have been derived: the outcome level for each child and an index of assessment quality for each teacher. Outcome levels have been assigned using the n–1 rule, that is the child is awarded a level providing that attainment is demonstrated in all or all but one of the tasks at a level. There is a task for each Statement of Attainment (SoA). However not all teachers completed all appropriate assessments of a child. Where no level outcome has been established the child has been assigned to the level immediately below the level assessed if there was attainment of one or more SoA at the level assessed and to two levels below the level assessed if there was no positive attainment at the level assessed.

Assessment quality is on a three-point scale, with one penalty point subtracted from the three point maximum for each of the following circumstances.

- −1 if no level is established for the child;
- −1 if the child establishes a level but the teacher fails to confirm the level although confirmation is possible, e.g., if a child completes all level 2 tasks successfully and is not then given the opportunity to attempt level 3. If the child attained level 2 with one missing attainment (the n–1 rule) that was taken as an indication that level 3 was not yet possible and the point was not deducted. If the child attained all level 4 SoA, the point was not deducted as there were no level 5 tasks available to use as confirmation.
- −1 if the child was taken two levels beyond his or her achieved level, e.g., a child who attains level 1 should be tested at level 2 but if level 2 is not attained should not be tested at level 3.

Assessment quality has been scored for each child individually and then averaged over the pupils in a class to produce a teacher-assessment quality score.

Results

This was the first trial of the test, so the items were untried. To what extent then did they reflect the expected structure of the context-maturity facet? According to the National Curriculum there are a series of contexts of performance for reading at each level but the scoring rules assume that there will be complete mastery of all the contexts of performance at a level before the next level of maturity is also attained. The alternative view would have very different levels of maturity in different contexts of performance. These are referred to as 'strands' in the National Curriculum documentation.

A total of 380 children were tested at two or more levels of maturity. In only twenty cases did this untried test produce inconsistent results with a higher level attained while a lower level remained incomplete. In every case of inconsistency, level 3 with four tasks was achieved while level 2 with five contexts of performance remained incomplete. The index of level consistency is .95, sufficiently high to allow for the exploration of assessment quality. The index of level consistency indicates the strength of the maturity axis of the context-maturity facet.

The context of performance axis is much less well defined in the test. There were forty-seven cases of positive attainment at two adjacent levels of the test without either level being achieved, forty-five of those involving levels 2 and 3. As such cases arise from deficient assessment strategies on the part of the teachers concerned, their frequency is an underestimate of the potential for this occurrence and cannot in itself be taken as evidence of the strength or weakness of the contexts of performance axis. However examination of these forty-five cases provided only weak evidence for two strands. In most cases the outcome appeared to arise from random errors on the children's part.

Teachers adopted one or other of two strategies in conducting the trial. Ten teachers used just one or two test levels and selected children to fit the test. From the point of view of assessment quality this was a poor strategy, yielding an accurate assessment of only 27 per cent of the ninety-seven children tested in this way. The alternative strategy involved complete classroom groups with the test form used tailored to the level of the individual child. This approach, adopted by fifteen teachers, yielded accurate assessments of 53 per cent of the 395 children involved. Within this group of teachers, however, assessment quality varied a great deal (mean = 2.29; s.d. = .27) from 36 per cent totally accurate assessments to 77 per cent totally accurate assessments. When teacher-assessment quality was correlated with the mean reading level of the class (mean = 2.07; s.d. = .44) a significant positive relationship was found (r = .48 with 13 d.f; p < .05). This relationship is much stronger than the relationship between reading level and the accuracy of assessment of the individual child (r = .30; d.f. = 490; p < .01) and cannot be attributed in its entirety to an artefact of the method of computing assessment quality.

Furthermore the class advantage in mean-reading level was not won by either homogenizing or differentiating the class group. The correlation between the within-class standard deviation (mean = 0.81; s.d. = 0.14) and assessment quality was essentially zero (r = .08 with 13 d.f.; n.s.).

Messages for Teachers

The implications for teachers are fourfold. Firstly, it should be recollected that this was the very first trial of these tasks and yet they fell neatly into their assigned levels. The National Curriculum may look like an eclectic set of Statements of Attainment but these SoA do delineate stages in reading acquisition with some accuracy. Using the SoA as a guide, it is possible for teachers to devise appropriate reading tasks for each stage and to be clear about where to go from where each young reader is at.

Secondly, being clear about what to do next depends on an accurate picture of where the young reader has reached. Using a uniform test which measures only one or other of the two dimensions, maturity or context of performance, will not provide the information. Teachers who addressed only the contexts of performance at a single level of maturity learned only that the children were not where the teacher had thought they were. Years of use of tests which measure levels of maturity in a single context of performance have proved equally uninformative.

Thirdly and most importantly, teachers who were sensitive to individual pupil performance, challenging the child without setting tasks totally outwith the child's current capacity, taught classes with higher-average levels of reading performance. Correlation does not imply causation so it cannot be said that accurate assessment of current performance causes progress. Rather what is being argued here is that tests should be constructed in such a way that the assessment skills required of teachers should be at least a subset of the professional skills of good teachers of reading.

Finally, accurate assessment is not associated with any exaggerated differentiation of the reading capacities of the children in a class nor with classes where all children are kept at the same stage of reading acquisition. In Northern Ireland at age 8 all of the first four levels of reading maturity are to be found in the average classroom. Some children just take a long time to get to level 2.

Conclusion

The fundamental problem in reading-test construction is that so little is known for certain about what is to be measured and that is, in part, because of the way that reading has been conventionally measured. From its earliest days, reading assessment has polarized the reading process. A series of unnecessary oppositions has been created between the reader and the text, ability and achievement, prediction and performance, a single capacity versus congeries of relatively independent competences or Armstong's (1990) specific objection to National Curriculum assessment as opposing the measurement of outcomes to the essential intersubjectivity of education. They manifest themselves in the distinction between construct-driven and task-driven test construction but have a deeply pragmatic root.

It is manifestly obvious that to measure reading requires a sample of reading performance. The choice is therefore between an exploration of the performance in context and the prediction of performance from surrogate activity. A full performance assessment is complex, time consuming and much influenced by the manner, mode and focus of exploration (Resnick and Resnick, 1991; Linn *et al.*, 1991). It is an interpretative act. It places the teacher at the heart of an interactive process, listening, probing and only incidentally counting as the child engages with the text. Performance prediction on the other hand can be quick (see Ballard's (1920) One Minute Reading Test), reasonably objective and readily standardized but unrepresentative of the complexity of the reading process. Ironically the logistic advantages of the predictive approach have proved paramount in schools and school systems. Ease of management of reading-test administration has taken precedence over pedagogical utility in informing the management of reading acquisition.

References

ALDERSON, J.C. (1989) 'Cognition and Reading: cognitive levels as embodied in test questions', *Reading in a Foreign Language*, **5**, 2, pp. 253–70.

ALEXANDER, P.A., SCHALLERT, D.L. and HARE, V.C. (1991) 'Coming to terms: How researchers in learning and literacy talk about knowledge', *Review of Educational Research*, **61**, 3, pp. 315–43.

ARMSTRONG, M. (1990) 'Does the National Curriculum rest on a mistake?', in EVERTON, T., MAYNE, P. and WHITE, S. (Eds) *Effective Learning: Into the New ERA*, London, Jessica Kingsley.

BALLARD, T.B. (1920) *Mental Tests*, London, University of London Press.

BURT, C. (1921) *Mental and Scholastic Tests*, London, Staples Press.

CATO, V., FERNANDES, C., GORMAN, T., KISPAL, A. and WHITE, J. (1992) *The Teaching of Initial Literacy — How do teachers do it?*, Slough, NFER.

CATTELL, R.B. (1966) 'The Data Box: its ordering of total resources in terms of possible relational systems', in CATTELL, R.B. (Ed) *Handbook of Multivariate Experimental Psychology*, Chicago, Rand McNally.

CHITTENDEN, E.A. (1983) 'Styles, reading strategies and test performance: a follow-up study of beginning readers' (Research Report, RR-83–31), Princeton, NJ, Educational Testing Service.

CLAY, M.M. (1985) *The Early Detection of Reading Difficulties*, London, Heinemann.

CRONBACH, L.J., GLESER, G.C., RAJARATNAM, N. and NANDA, H. (1972) *The Dependability of Behavioural Measurements: Theory of Generalisability for Scores and Profiles*, New York, Wiley.

DEPARTMENT OF EDUCATION AND SCIENCE AND THE WELSH OFFICE (1988) *National Curriculum Task Group on Assessment and Testing: a report*, London, DES.

FLAVELL, J.H. (1987) 'Speculation about the nature and development of meta-cognition', in WEINERT, F.E. and KLUWE, R.H. (Eds) *Metacognition, Motivation and Understanding*, Hillsdale, NJ, Erlbaum.

FREDERIKSEN, N. (1984) 'The real test bias: Influences of testing on teaching and learning', *American Psychologist*, **39**, pp. 193–202.

GIPPS, C. and GOLDSTEIN, H. (1983) *Monitoring Children*, London, Heinemann Educational.

HEAP, J.L. (1980) 'What counts as reading: limits to certainty in assessment', *Curriculum Inquiry*, **10**, 3, pp. 265–91.

HENNING, G. and CASCALLER, E. (1992) 'A preliminary study of the nature of communicative competence', (TOEFL Research Report 36), Princeton, NJ, Educational Testing Service.

LINN, R., BAKER, E. and DUNBAR, S. (1991) 'Complex performance based assessment: expectations and validation criteria', *Educational Researcher*, **20**, 8, pp. 15–21.

MEHRENS, W.A. (1992) 'Using performance assessment for accountability purposes', *Educational Measurement: Issues and Practice*, **11**, 1, pp. 3–9.

MESSICK, S.J. (1989) 'Validity', in LINN, R. (Ed) *Educational Measurement*, 3rd ed., New York, Macmillan.

MOLL, L.C. (Ed) (1992) *Vygotsky and Education: Instructional implications and applications of sociohistorical psychology*, Cambridge, Cambridge University Press.

MOSSENSON, L., HILL, P. and MASTERS, G. (1987) *Torch Tests of Reading Comprehension: Manual*, Melbourne, Australian Council for Educational Research.

NOSS, R., GOLDSTEIN, H. and HOYES, C. (1989) 'Graded assessment and learning hierarchies in mathematics', *British Educational Research Journal*, **15**, pp. 109–20.

RASCH, G. (1960) *Probablistic Models for Some Intelligence and Attainment Tests*, Copenhagen, The Danish Institute for Educational Research.

RESNICK, L. and RESNICK, D. (1991) 'Assessing the thinking curriculum', in GIFFORD, B. and O'CONNOR, M. (Eds) *Future Assessments*, Boston, Kluwer Academic.

SCHONELL, F.J. and SCHONELL, F.E. (1942) *Schonell Reading Tests*, Edinburgh, Oliver and Boyd.

SCHOOLS EXAMINATION AND ASSESSMENT COUNCIL (1991) *The Pilot Study of Standard Assessment Tasks for Key Stage One: a report by the STAIR consortium*, London, SEAC.

SPOLSKY, B. (1990) 'Introduction to a colloquium: The scope and form of a theory of second language learning', *TESOL Quarterly*, **24**, 4, pp. 609–16.

STANLEY, J.C. (1971) 'Reliability', in THORNDIKE, R.G. (Ed) *Educational Measurement*, 2nd ed., Boston, American Council for Educational Research.

TURNER, M. (1990) *Sponsored Reading Failure*, Warlingham, IPSET.

VERNON, P.E. (1938) *Burt (rearranged) Word Reading Test*, London, Hodder and Stoughton Educational.

VINCENT, D. and DE LA MARE, M. (1986) 'Developing a new individual reading test', in VINCENT, D., PUGH, A.K. and BROOKS, G. (Eds) *Assessing Reading: Proceedings of the UKRA Colloquium on the Testing and Assessment of Reading*, London, Macmillan Education.

WIGGINS, G. (1989) 'A true test: towards more authentic and equitable assessment', *Phi Delta Kappan*, **79**, pp. 703–13.

Chapter 8

A Framework for Literacy Assessment

P. Smith

Summary

This chapter introduces the broad principles and approaches to reading assessments in Australian settings. The history of profiling in Australia, the UK and in the USA is outlined. A description is given of the Victorian Reading Development Scales used to monitor the literacy progress of children over years 1–10. Data from the trials on over 5,000 pupils over four years are discussed and an outline is provided of how practising teachers use the profile framework to organize reading-assessment activities in the classroom.

Introduction

The philosophy at the heart of any assessment system should be the promotion of students' learning. This means that assessment goes hand in hand with teaching and learning and should not be an afterthought. Because of such an integration, assessment should provide information on what may happen next in the learning and also information about current, and previous, learning. With this philosophy in mind it is possible to develop central principles of assessment.

Principles of Assessment

1. Assessments should describe the skills, attitudes and concepts that the student has developed. These should be related to the curriculum and the instructional objectives. That is, the assessment should be criterion-referenced. This leads to a description of what the student can do rather than a comparison with other students. Both teacher and student need a clear description of the performances expected.

2. Assessments should enable the teacher, the parents and the student, where appropriate, to analyse the learning, or lack of it, taking place. This formative, rather than diagnostic, approach makes recommendations of further action possible.

3. Assessments should be agreed upon by two or more teachers working together. This moderation is a process of bringing individual judgments in line with general standards. Sharing experiences and judgments of students' achievements with other teachers can help develop and maintain a common understanding of what could be judged as a standard or appropriate performance.

4. Assessment should fit within an overall plan of the development and progress of the student. Thus each assessment task should reflect the expected progress and development of the student. Criterion-referenced assessment can be used to describe the development and progress of students in terms of tasks performed, skills developed, attitudes exhibited, aspirations displayed and knowledge acquired. Various standards or criteria for each of these characteristics can be identified and organized in order of increasing sophistication. When assessment tasks are set for students, their performance can be compared with these standards.

5. Assessments should allow for uncertainty in observations. There is always room for some error in a test score and notions such as the reliability of a test have been defined in order to allow for uncertainties. Replacing tests with other forms of assessment does not necessarily increase the accuracy. Thus assessments need to be graded in judgment to allow for uncertainty, and assessors need to allow for error in their judgments.

6. Assessments should describe the students' progress in a fair, relevant and accurate manner and should have the same meaning for different teachers, parents and students. The assessment information should be both interpretable and communicative.

Method

The rest of this chapter describes the developing and refining of an assessment approach involving student profiles. The assessment information is interpreted in terms of the task, the group and the individual. The Victorian Literacy Profiles project, a practical example involving 5,000 students in the Victorian education system, demonstrates how an education system or region can apply the assessment principles outlined at the beginning of this chapter.

How the Scales Were Developed

When developing the profiles-assessment system, teachers in workshop settings were asked to group areas of language development into the major skills of reading, writing, listening and speaking. Initially, they focused their attention on each of these skills, on broad educational reading and writing goals and on areas of learning or topics identified by the teachers. For each topic, steps indicating progress were identified as the outcomes of instruction. These steps were also defined as the desirable attributes of students after instruction in each topic.

This approach combined the identification of topics, the outcomes associated with each goal and a range of methods for gathering information or evidence of achievement for each goal. Information-gathering methods were called assessment methods. These methods in turn were matched with the desirable student attributes for each goal or topic. The evidence of achievement of an outcome that was gathered by each assessment method was then written into a corresponding matrix cell. Each piece of evidence was called a 'performance indicator'. More than thirty of these matrices were developed through teacher workshops. Table 8.1 shows one such matrix, illustrating the goal of developing an approach to new words.

In the example in Table 8.1, teachers listed the outcomes, or student attributes, and the assessment methods as follows:

Outcomes, or student attributes:

- seeking help from others;
- using visual cues;
- using auditory or graphophonic cues; and
- using semantic and syntactic cues.

Assessment methods:

- direct observation and anecdotal records;
- listening to oral reading; and
- conferencing with students.

Teachers used the matrices as guides for observation in the classroom. They collected samples of students' work, records of observations, and other evidence of outcomes. These were moderated at subsequent teachers' workshops. An average of six matrices were developed at each workshop. The total set of matrices presented teachers not only with a detailed observation schedule, but also with a large number of indicators.

Table 8.1:   *Matrix worksheet: Approach to unknown words*

	MILESTONES			
Assessment techniques	Asks others	Uses visual cues	Uses auditory cues	Uses context cues
Observation and anecdotal records	asks adults/ peers what a word is	moves eye between words and pictures	reuses words already heard in stories, wall stories or oral reading activities	rereads sentence when unable to read a word
	asks adults/ peers what a word means	substitutes a similarly shaped word for the unknown word	uses first sound of a word when attempting a new word	expresses that it was the context that gave clues for the word
			attempts to sound parts of words	queries meaning of sentence when unable to read word
Running records	asks adults/ peers for meaning and pronunciation of a word	uses appropriate substitutions, e.g., house/ home		
Parent–teacher conference	asks parent for meaning and pronunciation of words	states the picture helped to read the text	states a word is known because it sounds right	rereads sentence when unable to read a word
				explains that it was the context that gave clues for the word

Teachers in twenty-two schools observed and recorded the reading behaviours of 332 students using a set of matrices. To determine whether a behaviour was being exhibited, a rating scale was used to indicate the confidence level of the observer. The number '0' was used to indicate that the behaviour described by the indicator was not observed, '2' was used if the observer was sure that the behaviour was exhibited, and '1' was used if the observer was not convinced that the behaviour was part of a student's reading performance.

Indicators of Reading Development

The indicators were checked for accuracy and mapped onto an underlying development scale using item-response theory for rating scales

Table 8.2: *A sample spread of behaviour indicators for assessing 'reading development'*

Attributes-level Indicators

- Supports an argument or opinion on the text by reference to evidence presented in a variety of sources.
- Discusses and writes about an author's bias and technique.
- Discusses the styles used by different authors.
- Uses narrative and expository texts appropriately.
- Expresses and supports an opinion on whether an author's view is valid.
- Uses a known text as a model for own writing.
- Can find the main idea in a passage.
- Follows written instructions.
- Uses context as a basis for predicting the meaning of unfamiliar words.
- Can retell a story with approximately the same sequence of events.
- Can locate own name and other familiar words in a short text.
- Turns one page at a time from the front to the back of the book.
- Holds the book the right way up.

(Andrich, 1978). Some interesting results were obtained. For instance, the indicators describing behaviour outside the teachers' direct observation were found to have erratic rating patterns. There were indicators of students' behaviour at home, their borrowing of books from public libraries and their reading activities outside the classroom. These indicators were excluded from the development scale. Table 8.2 presents a selection of the indicators from the development scale.

Of course, the examples in Table 8.2 are not an exhaustive or systematic list of all the observable behaviours for assessing reading development. These indicators were selected from the calibrated list spread over the full range of behaviours. A long checklist of indicators did not help either the monitoring or the analysis of the students' reading development. It was also clear that these indicators were very closely placed on the continuum and thus were difficult to distinguish from one another. Further, because the reading behaviour depended on the context, content and purpose of the reading task, the relative positions of adjacent indicators could be unstable.

The full list of indicators was examined for patterns that might be useful for summarizing them into bands or groups, a process that was similar to the aggregation of indicators in language-acquisition scales such as the Australian Second Language Proficiency Rating Scale (ASLPR) (Ingram, 1984). Several reading progressions, such as those illustrated in Table 8.2, were identified in the list of calibrated indicators. All of these progressions could be empirically shown to fit into the overall development of reading behaviour. The difficulty was to put them into useable form. Progressions seemed to be related to underlying factors, such as: attitudinal behaviour, the influence of reading on writing, role-playing, retelling behaviour, reactions to reading materials, analysis and interpretation, social or interactive roles in reading behaviour, word-approach skills, and types of reading materials chosen.

Formation of 'Bands'

Not all of the progressions could be traced all the way through the list of indicators from bottom to top. Thus bands were formed by marking approximately equal intervals on the underlying scale. The indicators between the equally spaced points on the scale formed the descriptive bands. The apparent underlying factors were used to ensure that each band contained a diverse and logically consistent set of indicators. A reading band represented a very broad outline of reading behaviour rather than describing a discrete point of development. While seven bands were initially developed (Griffin, 1990), they did not represent anything other than apparent groupings of development indicators. They did not represent expected achievement levels for specific years or grades. The bands were labelled from A to G. Band A was set at the earliest developmental level in order to avoid the association of value with development and to enable the scale to be extended later with other band levels as work progressed with teachers at more advanced levels. The bands were also cumulative, in that a student developing behaviours at band E would be likely to have established behaviours at lower bands and perhaps have established behaviours at higher bands (see appendix to this chapter for descriptions of reading behaviour in each band).

Drafts of the reading bands were taken to schools for discussion with teachers, consultants, academics and others. They were asked to edit the reading bands so that they felt comfortable with their format and content. Modifications involved moving descriptors, editing their expression, adding new important indicators in the appropriate places or deleting those that did not add to the overall description. After the drafts had been revised by the various experts, further drafts of reading bands were prepared for field trials. Additional advice from teachers on recording and monitoring procedures led to another rating scale modelled on the levels identified in *Reading On* (Victorian Ministry of Education, 1985) and later in the *Growth Points* (Victorian Ministry of Education, 1988). The recognized development levels in that text were identified as beginning, developing and established. Teachers' familiarity with these terms and with the global, holistic, impression monitoring outlined in the Victorian reading text meant that familiar terms could be

Table 8.3: Expected and unexpected rating patterns for students with different backgrounds

Name	A	B	C	Band D	E	F	G
David	3	3	3	3	2	2	2
Renee	3	3	3	3	2	2	1
Fiona	3	3	3	3	2	2	1
Shane	3	3	3	3	2	2	1
Scott	3	3	3	3	2	2	1
Maria	3	3	3	3	2	2	1
Michael	3	3	3	3	1	2	1
Henry	3	3	3	2	2	1	1
Stewart	3	3	3	3	1	1	1
Rebecca	3	3	3	2	1	1	1
Rosanna	3	3	3	3	1	1	1
Cassy	3	3	3	3	1	1	0
Janelle	3	3	3	3	1	1	0
Nicole	2	2	3	1	1	1	1*
Katy	2	1	1	1	0	1	1*
Kelly	2	2	1	1	0	0	0
Rosie	2	1	1	1	0	0	0*
Christine	2	1	1	1	0	0	0*
Pavolla	3	0	0	0	0	0	0*
Petra	2	0	0	0	0	0	0*
Stephen	0	1	1	0	0	0	0**

Notes: * Non-English speaking background
** Integration student

used for each band. A term was added for insufficient evidence of a particular behaviour within a band, giving a four-point scale.

    0 — no evidence
    1 — beginning
    2 — developing
    3 — established.

In a pilot study of the bands, students were rated using the four-point scale. The set of ratings for a sample class is shown in Table 8.3.

Unexpected rating patterns emerged from some class groups. When the class results were analysed using a Rasch rating-scale model, some students were identified as developing in ways dissimilar to the rest of the class (Andrich, 1978). These analyses are outlined elsewhere (Griffin and Jones, 1988). In the set of ratings in Table 8.3, those marked with asterisks were identified as misfitting the underlying development scale. Upon discussion with the class teacher, these results were attributed to students with non-English-speaking backgrounds or with specific learning difficulties. A more detailed discussion of these is presented elsewhere (Griffin, 1989).

Field Trials

The reading bands received extensive trials. *The Victorian 100 school study* (Rowe and Griffin, 1988), provided a formal opportunity to trial the reading bands as a monitoring and reporting instrument for gathering data on students' reading development in the following ways:

- Teachers' ratings were used for the reading bands.
- The Test of Reading Comprehension (TORCH) (Mossensen, L., Hill, P. and Masters, G., 1987) was administered.
- ACER Primary Reading survey Test form AA (ACER, 1972) was used for year 1 students because the TORCH test does not apply to this level.

The study provided the opportunity to examine the concurrent validity of the reading scale, the internal consistency of the teachers', ratings, and the relationships between the ratings and test scores at various levels of aggregation. Data on reading development was gathered on over 5,000 students covering years 1, 3, 5, 7 and 9.

Messages for Teachers

The analyses in Figure 8.1 shows that the bands are far from a stepwise sequence of development. Different patterns of growth illustrate that development is not linearly defined by the reading and writing bands. The shaded regions in the figures are divided into two parts. The lower and upper shaded areas of each 'box' illustrate the regions with the highest probability that a teacher will rate the bahaviours of a student as 'beginning' or 'developing' (a rating of 1 or 2 respectively) for each band level. Regions with the highest probability of a rating of 'no evidence' or 'established' (a rating of 0 or 3 respectively) for the behaviours of a student for each band level below and above the shaded regions respectively. The regions indicate the 'expected' rating pattern for a student, given an overall estimate of the student's reading or writing development.

Development is estimated numerically by a student's total rating score over all the bands, and the student's 'expected' rating pattern assumes a predictable progression. A scale is shown on the left-hand side of each of the figures. Each shows evenly spaced units and is defined by item response theory analysis. Each scale represents the development of reading or writing behaviour. Each also represents the

Figure 8.1: *Reading bands and regions of most probable development*

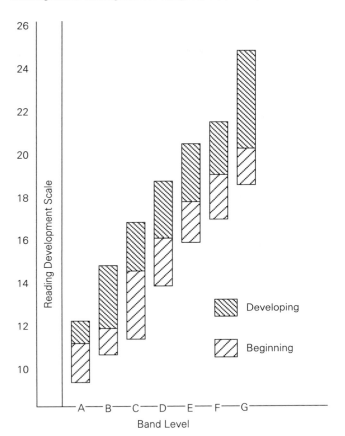

total score for a student, obtained by adding the teacher's rating for the student over all the reading or writing bands. Note that increments of 1 in the total score do not represent even increments in reading development. Nevertheless, the figures show how a student's total score can be used to identify the student's 'expected' behaviour for each of the bands. A ruler held horizontally across the bands at a point on the scale that represents a student's total score will show how each band is likely to be represented in the student's reading or writing behaviour.

More importantly, Figure 8.1 shows the most probable progression patterns in reading development. Since the boxes for the bands overlap, it is unlikely that a student will fully establish any particular band level of behaviour before beginning to exhibit behaviours from the next band. An individual should therefore exhibit a broad range of behaviours at any one time. It is expected that a student will exhibit behaviours covering about three bands at any one time. The frequency with which behaviours are exhibited will also vary. The identification of a specific development level defined by a single descriptive indicator (or a single band level or score) would, in all likelihood, be inaccurate. For a student with a total reading score of 11, for example, the most likely rating pattern assigned to the student would be 3, 3, 2, 1, 1, 1, 0. Note that this differs from reading profiles of 3, 3, 2, 2, 1, 0, 0 for a second student and 3, 3, 3, 2, 0, 0, 0 for a third student. In the first case, the student is developing at band C and beginning to show indications of reading behaviour for bands D, E and F. If the instructional target level is defined as the developmental level, then the instructional target range for this student would be activities associated with band C. In the second case, the student is developing at bands C and D and would require a broader instructional programme. The third student is developing at band D and would require a higher level of instruction.

Conclusion

The reading-development scales illustrate that it is possible to design an assessment and reporting system that is based on direct observation and which harnesses and makes explicit the formative and intuitive assessment of classroom teachers. Throughout the development of these scales, group-moderation procedures were central to identifying the appropriate reading behaviours, defining these for the descriptors in the reading bands and choosing exemplar materials and assessment tasks relevant to each band in the reading progressions. In addition, teachers' judgments were statistically moderated by comparing the teachers' ratings with the students' scores on a reference test. Details of this study are reported elsewhere (Griffin, 1989).

By involving teachers in an action research process it was possible to build an empirical base consisting of teachers' observations, which were used to define the growth of literacy in children. (The Writing Bands have not been discussed in this article although they were developed by use of a similar process.) The resulting reporting framework makes communication possible between teachers and parents, between teachers and the school system and between teachers and teachers. The bands will enable descriptive reports to be written for employers. In fact, the bands provide a common framework so that student growth and development can be monitored and the information gained can be communicated in a variety of ways without changing standard interpretation of assessment data and without taking away a school's right to develop a curriculum to fit local needs.

Acknowledgment

The content of this chapter is based on research conducted by the author in conjunction with Professor Patrick Griffen for the Assessment Research Centre, at RMIT. Patrick Griffen's contribution to, and comments on, earlier drafts are gratefully acknowledged.

Appendix: Literacy Profiles — Reading Bands

Band G: Reads materials of varying complexity, e.g., manuals, articles, Shakespeare etc. Interprets simple maps, tables and graphs in the context of evidence presented. Makes generalizations, summaries, conclusions from reading materials. Reads widely for interest, to learn or for pleasure. Reads at different speeds, using scanning, skim reading or careful reading as appropriate. Makes informed choices about reading materials. Can use a variety of resources to locate reading. Supports argument or opinion on text by reference to evidence presented in a variety of sources. Compares information from different sources. Extracts and connects embedded ideas from complex sentences and paragraphs. Can analyse the cohesiveness of text as a whole. Discussion shows an ability to identify opposing points of view and main and supporting arguments in text. Discusses and writes about authors; bias and technique. Displays critical opinion and analysis in written reports of reading materials.

Band F: Discusses author's intent for the reader. Makes links between arguments and ideas in text with personal experience. Discusses styles used by different authors. Forms generalizations about a range of genre including myth, short story etc. Offers reasons for the mood of the text. Writing and discussions show varied interpretations of text. Offers critical opinion or analysis of reading passages in discussion. Verbally justifies appraisal of a text. Can select passages or phrases to answer questions without careful reading of whole text. Formulates research topics and questions and finds information required from reading materials. Uses narrative and expository texts appropriately. Reads aloud with fluency and expression. Expands on and synthesizes information from a range of texts in written work. Maps out plots, procedures and character developments in novels and other texts. Varies reading strategies according to purposes for reading and nature of text. Makes connections between texts, recognizing linking themes and values.

Band E: Improvises on a range of texts in role-play. Writing shows meaning inferred in the text. Explains a piece of literature and describes settings. Expresses and supports a view on whether an author's point of view is valid. Discusses implied motives of characters in the text. Makes comments and expresses feelings about characters. Rewrites text in own words. Uses known text as model for own writing. Can record authors' implied messages. Uses a range of books and print materials as information sources for written work. Reads to others with few inappropriate pauses. Uses suffixes, prefixes, and meaning of word parts to interpret new words. Can use directories such as a table of contents or index telephone and street directories to locate information in multiple sources.

Band D: Discusses different types of reading materials. Reads materials with a wide variety of styles and topics. Selects books to read for a purpose. Discusses materials read at home. Can find main idea in a passage. Tells a variety of audiences about a book. Recommends books to others. Uses vocabulary and sentence structure from reading materials in written work as well as in conversations. Themes from reading appear in art work. Substitutes words with similar meaning when reading aloud. Begins to self-correct using knowledge of language structure and sound–symbol relationships. Uses knowledge of language structure and/or sound symbol to make sense of a word or phrase. Follows written instructions. Reads often. Reads silently for extended periods.

Band C: Rereads a paragraph or sentence to establish meaning. Uses context as the basis of predicting meaning of unfamiliar words. Reads aloud showing understanding of purpose of punctuation marks. Uses picture cues to make appropriate substitutions. Uses pictures to help read a text. Concentrates on reading for lengthy periods. Writing and art work reflect understanding of text. Reads, retells, discusses and expresses opinions on literature. Seeks recommendations for books to read. Chooses more than one type of book. Can find where another reader is up to in a reading passage. Recalls events and characters directly from text. Chooses to read when given free choice.

Band B: Takes risks when reading. Selects own books to read. Verbally describes connection among events in texts. Writes, role-plays and/or draws in response to a story or other form of writing etc. (e.g., poem, message). Creates ending when the text is left open. Asks others for help with meaning and pronunciation of words. Recounts in writing, drama or art work, or retells using language expressions from reading sources. Consistently reads familiar words and symbols within a text. Predicts words. Matches known clusters of letters to clusters in unknown words. Uses words in environment when reading and writing. Shows knowledge of sound–symbol relationships when writing. Reads books with simple repetitive language patterns. Uses pictures for clues to meanings of text. Can recognize words within other words. Uses features and format of books in reading. Retells with approximate sequence.

Band A: Holds book the right way up. Turns pages from the front to the back. Can point to the beginning and end of sentences, and distinguish between upper and lower-case letters. Can turn to the start and end of books. Responds to literature (smiles, claps, listens intently). Joins in familiar stories. Locates words, lines, spaces, letters. Refers to letters by name. Can locate own name and other familiar words in a short text. Identifies known familiar words in other contexts. Chooses books as free-time activity. Shows preference for particular books.

References

ANDRICH, D. (1978) 'Application of a psychometric rating model to ordered categories which are scored with successive integers', *Applied Psychological Measurement*, **2**, pp. 581–94.

AUSTRALIAN COUNCIL FOR EDUCATIONAL RESEARCH (ACER) (1984) *Primary Reading Survey Test*, ACER, Hawthorn, Victoria.

BOOMER, G. (1987) 'Organising the nation for literacy', Opening address to the Australian Reading Association, Sydney, July.

BOOMER, G. (1988) 'Standards and literacy: Two hundred years towards literacy: Where to from here?', in *Directions: Literacy*, Victoria State Board of Education Annual Lecture, June, pp. 10–16.

GOODMAN, K.S. and GOODMAN, Y.M. (1979) 'Learning to read is natural', in RESNICK, L.B. and WEAVER, P.A. (Eds) *Theory and Practice of Early Reading*, Hillsdale, NJ, Earlbaum, Vol. 1, pp. 137–54.

GRIFFIN, P. (1990) 'Profiling literacy development, monitoring the accumulation of reading skills', *Australian Journal of Education*, **34**, 3, pp. 290–311.

GRIFFIN, P. (1991) *The Development of Language Development Profiles in English as a Second Language*, Melbourne, Phillip Institute of Technology, Mimeo.

GRIFFIN, P.E. and JONES, C. (1988) 'Assessing the development of reading behaviour: A report of the reading bands', paper presented at the Annual Conference of the Australian Association for Research in Education, University of New England, Armidale, November.

INGRAM, D. (1984) *The Australian Second Language Proficiency Rating Scales*, Canberra, AGPS.

MOSSENSEN, L., HILL, P. and MASTERS, G. (1987) *Test of Reading Comprehension* (TORCH), Australian Council for Educational Research, Melbourne.

OECD (1986) *New Information Technology and Reading*, Centre for Educational Research and Innovation, Paris, Organisation for Economic Co-operation and Development.

ROWE, K. and GRIFFIN, P. (1988) *The Victorian 100 School Study*, Melbourne, Victorian Ministry of Education.

VICTORIAN MINISTRY OF EDUCATION (1985) *Reading On*, Melbourne, Curriculum Branch, Victorian Ministry of Education.

VICTORIAN MINISTRY OF EDUCATION (1988) *Growth Points*, Melbourne, Curriculum Branch, Victorian Ministry of Education.

Chapter 9

Reading Standards at Key Stage 1 in Schools in England and Wales: Aspiration and Evidence

P. Pumfrey

Summary

This chapter presents a study investigating the reliability and validity of KS1 SAT reading-assessment scores and the individually administered word-reading tests of the British Ability Scales and the Differential Ability Scales. The former had been standardized on a nationally representative sample of British pupils in 1976; the latter on a representative sample of American pupils in 1989. The results cast doubts on the reliability, validity and utility of the NC SATs in assessing standards and progress in reading.

Introduction

Reading matters. It is an amplifier of human potential. The ability to read opens up to the individual the thoughts and feelings of other minds, past and present, here and in other countries, through the medium of text. Not to be able to read in our society is to be disadvantaged and marginalized both culturally and economically. Parents have no doubts concerning the importance of reading. Teachers and schools are expected by society to ensure that children become literate in the fullest sense of the word. How can we determine whether standards in reading are stable or changing for better or worse?

Context

In 1989, an HMI report on *Standards in Education* made the following points concerning standards in primary schools.

> In maintained primary schools, standards in basic language work are generally sound in that most pupils are taught the early stages of reading and writing systematically. *Indeed, there are discernible improvements in both the quality and range of written work* [my emphasis] due partly to the influence of the National Writing Project . . . Unfortunately there is still far too little stimulation and challenge for pupils to read more widely once fluency has been established. (DES, 1989, par. 9)

Despite this reservation, at that time reading standards during the early stages of education did not appear to be a cause of serious concern. Indeed, in view of the relationships between all aspects of literacy, one would have difficulty in understanding how the *general* standard of pupils' writing could increase if their general standard of reading was not doing so in tandem. Despite this, it is also possible that increasing means on reading test scores can be associated with an increasing number and proportion of pupils with low reading attainments.

To a government that had held power for the previous eleven years and is, in considerable measure, accountable to the electorate for standards in the state educational system, 1990 marked the beginning of a period of growing disquiet concerning the implementation of the National Curriculum in general and concerning the teaching and assessment of reading in particular. That disquiet continues in 1995.

In 1990, on the basis of standardized reading tests results collected on successive cohorts by some LEAs over many years, the possibility was raised that reading standards might be falling. Senior educational psychologists from nine education authorities released to the *Times Educational Supplement* anonymous confidential data based on the test scores of nearly 400,000 7-year-old pupils. It was asserted that, over a period of years, there had been a statistically and educationally significant decline in the mean reading-test scores of successive cohorts.

The psychologists met to discuss their concern on 22 June 1990. Of nine authorities represented, eight seemed to show a decline. The ninth is a small authority which re-standardises its test each year, but believes, nevertheless, that there is no decline . . . It remains the case, though, that conclusive evidence of a *single* authority without such a decline has yet to appear (Turner, 1990a).

Commenting that 'The issue is too important for the facts to be locked away in a drawer', John MacGregor, the then Secretary of State for Education, demanded to see the data. In fact, the evidence from Croydon LEA was already in the public domain. On 6 July their chief inspector is reported as confirming that the mean reading-test scores of

7-year-old pupils in the Borough had declined since 1985. A week later, four out of eleven educational authorities contacted by the *Times Educational Supplement* were reported as having reading-test results which suggested a drop in reading standards among 7 year-old-pupils (Castle, 1990).

In September 1990, the Independent Primary and Secondary Education Trust, formerly the Education Unit at the Institute for Economic Affairs, published a booklet describing the findings (Turner, 1990b). The report claims that there is clear evidence that hundreds of thousands of children in nine LEAs south of a line from the Mersey to the Wash are subject to a sharply downward trend in reading attainments at the ages of 7 or 8. It is also claimed that there had been a 50 per cent increase in the number of pupils who can be described as 'very poor readers'. This unwelcome claim resulted in a severe decline in the standard of public discussion of this claim and of the evidence bearing on it.

To any government, an assertion headlined 'Reading standards fall!' is a potential political disaster. It arouses public interest and concern equivalent to 'The Titanic has sunk!'. The speed with which the then Secretary of State for Education despatched HMI to investigate, and simultaneously involved the NFER in a complementary survey of reading attainments in the autumn of 1990, underlined the extreme political sensitivity of the issue. HMI produced a report by the end of the year (December, 1990) based on 3,000 inspection visits, involving 120 primary schools where HMI observed the teaching and learning of reading in 470 classes and listened to over 2,000 pupils read aloud. The pupils were in National Curriculum Years R, 1, 2, 3 and 6. Pupils' reading fluency, accuracy and understanding were judged using HMI techniques (Rose, 1992). This inspection provided part of the evidence on which HMI's judgments were made concerning reading standards and the effectiveness with which reading was being taught in their published report (DES, 1991d). The widespread availability of standardized reading-test results in primary schools was not apparently used to moderate HMI's conclusions concerning reading standards.

> The evidence from such testing cannot contribute to a reliable national picture of reading standards; or the direction in which they are moving or if they are moving at all. (ibid., par. 7)

Even when classroom observations and hearing children read are carried out by highly experienced professionals such as HMI, are we not, once again, being invited to give too much weight to empirically unsupported, somewhat subjective assessments concerning reading standards?

At the same time as the HMI carried out its survey, the School Examinations and Assessment Council (SEAC) was asked to carry out a survey of the arrangements made by LEAs for monitoring reading standards. The NFER undertook this work and concentrated on NC Year 2 assessment practices. Their report entitled *An Enquiry into LEA Evidence on Standards of Reading of Seven Year Old Children* makes interesting reading (Catto and Whetton, 1991). All 116 LEAs in England and Wales were approached. Thirty-six had not carried out LEA-wide testing of reading since 1981. Two LEAs refused to take part in the study. Ninety-five LEAs provided information. Of these, since 1981, fifty-nine had carried out authority-wide testing of reading in some years during the period up to 1990. The instruments used are considered critically and a number of weaknesses identified. A central, albeit highly controversial, assertion made was that 'The tests reflect outdated and narrow conceptions of reading, and certainly do not match the processes of reading defined in English Attainment Target 2 of the National Curriculum' (ibid., p. 22).

The standardizations of the tests were criticized, but for the purposes of large-scale monitoring of reading attainments, it was considered that technical deficiencies were not so great as to invalidate their use for this purpose.

> Some of the tests are now very old and the content of these often includes words which would be difficult for modern children. This alone could account for a decline in scores. For these reasons it would not be advisable to use any of the tests as measures of reading as defined by the National Curriculum. They are not appropriate or adequate for this purpose (ibid., p. 22).

The report concludes:

> The attempt to discern a national picture of pupils' performance from disparate methods of assessment highlights the need to have national assessment procedures with agreement as to the forms in which test results will be analysed and reported, together with a statutory obligation to make data publicly available. (ibid., p. 168)

Early in 1991, the House of Commons Select Committee on education, science and arts undertook an examination of the evidence and issues raised by the reading standards controversy. In their subsequent report, it was stated: 'We conclude that the claim that reading standards have fallen in recent years has not been proved beyond reasonable doubts' (par. 12).

The Government responded to the Select Committee's report noting the above point. The Government further commented: 'The national interest requires that standards of reading should rise in pace with society's ever more demanding needs for literacy; it is not enough that standards should not be falling. All schools should strive to match the standards of the best, and LEAs should ensure that reading standards in their area are kept under control'.

How might this be done? It was intended that the National Curriculum assessment arrangements based on 'clear national targets for pupils' reading attainments across the full age range for compulsory education' would be the way forward. This leads to the central role of Standard Assessment Tasks (SATs). It also raises the question as to whether reading SATs can provide in one measure the variety of information teachers and parents require in order to monitor and enhance children's reading attainments and progress in reading.

The basis of the SAT approach to the assessment of reading standards and progress is clearly somewhat different from that underpinning the use of standardized word-reading tests such as the British Ability Scales (BAS) and the Differential Ability Scales (DAS). One of the major emphases of the reading-assessment procedures developed for National Curriculum reading SATs has been the importance of ensuring that the assessment materials are as 'naturalistic' as possible, in book form and with a story content that is culturally familiar. Such requirements are based on the assumption that children's reading is predominantly context-dependent, and that, if faced with anything unfamiliar in either form or content, children will underperform.

In part, as a consequence of this view concerning the development of reading, normative word-reading tests have been severely criticized during the last decade. Their form and content were said by some critics to be of little utility to teachers and parents in relation to the assessment of standards and progress in reading of individual pupils and groups. Many of the criticisms have been shown to be invalid.

An extensive review of research into the early stages of learning to read, supported by the US Office of Educational Research and the Reading Research and Education Centre at the Centre for the Study of Reading based at the University of Illinois, Urbana-Champaign, underlines this point. In skilled reading, *generalizability* and *automaticity* of reading skills are of the essence. '. . . the ability to read words, quickly, accurately, and effortlessly, is critical to skillful reading comprehension — in the obvious ways and in a number of more subtle ones . . . unless the processes involved in individual word recognition operate properly, nothing in the system can either' (Adams, 1990, p. 3). Context cues alone are insufficient to optimize reading development and improve reading attainments and progress.

Testing a pupil's ability to read decontextualized words, as in word-recognition tests such as the BAS and the DAS, is not necessarily a pedagogic sin; it is much more likely to represent an educational virtue. A test of decontextualized word reading does not have the same 'face validity' (often referred to as 'ecological validity') as reading SATs in that the former does not reflect real-world reading tasks. Despite this, word-reading tests can efficiently provide valid empirical information about standards and progress of individuals and groups in the decoding skills that underpin reading comprehension. (The pedagogy whereby automaticity in early reading can be best achieved is a separate issue from that concerning the respective uses and limitations of the reading SATs and decontextualized word-reading tests).

Aspirations

Concern about pupils' educational standards in general and reading attainments in particular, are matters of perennial interest. In England and Wales, the implementation of the Education Reform Act 1988 established a National Curriculum. Its prime purpose was to raise educational standards. Each individual pupil's attainments and progress were to be regularly monitored at the end of the four Key Stages into which the curriculum was divided. Key Stage 1 covers the chronological age range from 5:00 to 7:06 years. These pupils were the first to whom National Curriculum English was taught, reading standards assessed and subsequently reported in national league tables covering all local education authorities (DES, 1991c; DfE, 1992).

English is one of three 'core' subjects in the National Curriculum. Within English, 'reading' is one of four components. In theory, the Standard Assessment Tasks provided common assessment procedures whereby valid evidence concerning standards and progress in reading can be systematically, comprehensively and annually collected for every pupil attending state schools at the end of each Key Stage. The form, content, administration, scoring and reporting of National Curriculum English Profile Component 2 'reading' of KS1 SATs have been clearly presented. Each year they have been modified in response to criticisms (SEAC, 1991, 1992, 1993).

The Parents' Charter makes explicit parents' rights and responsibilities in relation to the education of their children.

> The Government's plans are designed to ensure that you have all the information you need to keep track of your child's progress, keep in touch with his or her school and compare all local schools. (DES, 1991a)

> The point of the new tests is to give you and the teachers an exact [sic] picture of what your child has learned. Knowing how your child measures up against *national* standards will give you the best idea of his or her real progress. (DES, 1991b, p. 2)

On the one hand, these intentions and claims reassure us that the Government, the then Department of Education and Science and the current Department for Education are concerned with accuracy when measuring children's real progress against national standards. On the other hand, it is possible that the confident tenor of the above claim is inversely proportional to its validity, given the SAT-based assessment procedure that was to be used.

Put simply, on the evidence currently available, the claims for the quality of the information provided by the reading SATs probably contravenes the Trades Descriptions Act. With reference to the procedures to be adopted for the assessment of reading standards, for the Government, through its agents the School Examinations and Assessment Council and its successor body the School Curriculum and Assessment Authority, to make a mistake is forgivable. To make a mistake because of inadequate consultation, is less forgivable. To refuse to reconsider a mistake made because of lack of consultation, would be unforgivable.

In order to allay the many hostilities that had been aroused by the massive workloads placed on teachers as a consequence of change upon change to the National Curriculum, Sir Ron Dearing was brought in by the Government. In a speech given in May 1993, to teachers in the West Midlands, he is reported as saying 'When you hear a class teacher with thirty-five KS1 children just coming up to the age of seven saying you have to complete 10,391 standard assessments, you realize what is involved'. SATs at KS 1 are complex and time-demanding. They have been severely criticized by teachers and research workers (NUT, 1991; Pumfrey and Elliott, 1991; Smithson, 1991; Bennett *et al.*, 1992; Pumfrey, 1992; Sainsbury *et al.*, 1992; NUT and the School of Education, University of Leeds, 1993).

This study, carried out in collaboration with Drs C.D. Elliott and

S. Tyler, investigated the reliability and validity of the Key Stage 1 SAT reading scores in relation to pupils' scores on two individually administered word-reading tests. These were the *British Ability Scales* and the *Differential Ability Scales* (Elliott, 1983; 1990). The former had been standardized on a nationally representative sample of British pupils in 1976; the latter had been standardized on a representative sample of American pupils in 1989.

We were interested in two related questions. The first was whether there had been any changes in the word-reading attainments of a representative sample of English children over fifteen years. The second was to compare children's scores on two word-reading tests and on the NC En PC2 Reading SATS at KS 1.

Evidence of a decline in mean word-reading test attainments in the sample at this age level was not identified on the BAS at Key Stage 1. However, a comparison with the more recently standardized American DAS results suggests that complacency is not appropriate. The results also cast doubts on the reliability, validity and utility of the National Curriculum SATs in assessing standards and progress in reading.

Reference is made to two ongoing studies at the University of Manchester School of Education following up and extending the above research into reading standards, Standard Assessment Tasks and the National Curriculum.

Method

A socio-economically stratified nationally representative sample of Year 2 pupils was drawn from the schools within a large local education authority. All members of the sample had completed their SAT reading assessment in June 1991 (N = 209). The SAT assessment procedure and discussion culminated in a crude four-point ranking of groups: Working towards level 1 (W), levels 1, 2 and 3 and above.

Results

In the following November, each pupil completed the word-reading tests of the BAS and the DAS. Order of presentation and sex of the subjects were counterbalanced in the administrations. Thirteen qualified, experienced teachers and an educational psychologist, all having been trained in the administration of the tests, collected the data from twelve schools.

Sample
N = 209:   107 boys,   102 girls
Year 3:   age range   87–99 months
• 71 children in 4 schools with advantaged catchment area
• 60 children in 4 schools with mixed catchment area
• 78 children in 4 schools with disadvantaged catchment area

Table 9.1 summarizes the composition of the nationally representative sample of pupils. Pupils' scores on the National Curriculum English tests were compared with the the national figures for the four grades. The national figures for 1991 presented by the Department of Education and Science showed 71 per cent of pupils at level 2 or above and 21 per cent at level 3. For the whole of the LEA from which the current sample was identified, the overall percentages were 77 per cent at level 2 or above and 26 per cent at level 3, respectively, i.e., somewhat higher SAT reading scores than the national averages.

In contrast, for the nationally representative selected sample within the LEA, there were 70 per cent pupils at level 2 or above and 19 per cent at level 3. This approximates the national figures. It is necessary to keep in mind that the errors of measurement associated with the SAT scores are not as yet known. The assumption is that they are likely to be considerable.

The importance of word-reading abilities and test scores in relation to the development of literacy, has been referred to in the 'Context' section above. The sample's scores on the BAS and DAS were compared using analysis of variance. This demonstrated that the main effects of order of presentation and sex were not statistically significant, although the girls' mean scores were slightly higher. The first order interaction combining the effects of order and sex was also non-significant.

By comparing the mean scores of the sample on the BAS and the DAS with the normative data obtained in 1976 and 1989 respectively (see Table 9.2), two interesting comparisons can be made. First, it is possible to see whether standards on the BAS have changed over a period of fifteen years. It is also possible to compare the performance of this sample of English pupils with the scores of American pupils on the more recently standardized DAS word-reading test.

Three points deserve consideration. The first is that the mean scores of pupils on the BAS has not altered significantly from that obtained by the standardization sample in 1976. However, a second point is of considerable relevance to the issue of reading standards in England. There

Table 9.2: Total sample results on BAS and DAS

Total Sample
• BAS Word-reading mean = 100.2
s.d. = 18.0
• DAS Word-reading mean = 98.5
s.d. = 18.2
t = 4.45   df = 208   p < .001

Table 9.3: Total sample: SAT, BAS and DAS intercorrelations

Total Sample		
	Correlations	
	BAS	DAS
SAT	.67	.66
BAS		.95

appears to be an increase in the standard deviation of the scores on the BAS, assuming our sample to be nationally representative. It is likely that, even though the mean scores have remained stable, there has been a increased *spread* of scores over time. Thus the presence of more high-scoring pupils would counterbalance the increase in lower-scoring pupils. In summary, the number and proportion of pupils with low word-reading attainment test scores may have increased despite the apparently stable mean score. The third point concerns the comparison of the sample's scores on the DAS and the American standardization sample results. A small but statistically significant mean-score difference was identified. The standard deviation of DAS scores for the English sample was similar to that obtained on the BAS. There can be no grounds for complacency over standards of word-reading skills at KS 1.

The reliabilities and validities of the BAS and the DAS are well-established. The correlations between pupils' SAT reading scores, BAS word-reading test and DAS word-reading test scores are presented as Table 9.3. These figures support the high reliabilities and concurrent validity of the BAS and the DAS. The reading SAT score includes reading accuracy scores based on particular words correctly read by the pupil in the context of a short story. The semantic and syntactic complexities of the stories differ markedly (Morris, 1992). These and other unquantified sources of error variance exist between the stories from which the teacher is allowed to select. There are also other components of reading that contribute towards the reading SAT result. It is highly likely that, partly as a consequence of uncontrolled and unquantified sources of error variance, the SAT reading assessment is likely to be of much lower reliability that that of the BAS and DAS. In addition, the

Table 9.4: *BAS scores and socio-economic status of school intake*

	BAS Standard Scores			
	Mean	s.d.	Range	RA Range
Advantaged schools	108.1	12.6	78–135	6:0–14:00
Mixed schools	103.5	19.3	69–135	5:5–14:05
Disadvantaged schools	90.4	16.8	66–135	5:0–11:10

restricted four-point range of the reading SAT tends to reduce the covariance with other measures having a much wider degree of interindividual variance. In view of such criticisms, can the reading SAT results provide the quality of information that the government has suggested is expected?

Varied aspects of reading are tapped somewhat unsystematically and, in parts, subjectively using reading SATs at KS1. It is argued that these reading skills require the pupil to have internalized and automated the processing of a number of words that permeate pupils' textual materials and are encountered and read with great frequency. Limitation in the child's working memory requires automatization in the processing of the surface features of text as a necessary but not sufficient condition for the meanings within the text to be efficiently and rapidly constructed. Pupils who are in the early stages of learning to read may well have to invest considerable conscious effort in using the grapho-phonic and/or syntactic aspects of text, in contrast to competent readers who do not. The capacity of working memory is limited. Reading words out of context is a valid index of generalizability of an important skill underpinning efficient reading.

Turning to the BAS scores of the sample, their relationship to the socio-economic status of the school intake is shown in Table 9.4. The above pattern of BAS scores has been replicated in many other studies using other reading tests in other cultures and at other times (Pumfrey, 1990; Lake, 1992; Lewis, 1992). On average, the higher the socio-economic status of the catchment area of the school, the higher the pupils' mean BAS scores. Why this should be the case and what the findings indicate in relation to raising reading standards, will continue to be highly controversial. What is clear from the data is the very considerable range of interindividual differences on BAS scores *within* each school. Whatever it is that enables some pupils to learn more rapidly than others, it is to be found in pupils in *all* schools irrespective of the material advantages or otherwise of their intakes; but it is not *equally* present in all schools.

Table 9.5: Reading SAT levels across three categories of school

	SAT Levels (per cent)		
Level	Advantaged schools	Mixed schools	Disadvantaged schools
Approaching level 1	0	2	4
Level 1	22	25	36
Level 2	55	40	56
Level 3	23	34	4

Table 9.6: Range of BAS word-reading scores at each SAT level

	BAS Word-reading Scores			
	Mean	s.d.	Range	RA Range
Approaching level 1	67.8	2.9	66–72	5:0–6:02
Level 1	86.2	13.7	66–120	5:0–9:06
Level 2	101.5	14.0	69–135	5:7–12:09
Level 3	120.1	10.2	99–135	7:7–14:05

A similar pattern (see Table 9.5) is reflected in the percentage of pupils at each of the four reading SAT levels across the three categories of school.

The most challenging results were those in which the means, standard deviations and reading-age ranges of BAS word-reading test scores were compared across each of the four levels of reading attainment identified by the SAT reading-assessment procedure. These results are set out as Table 9.6. A SAT level 1 reading assessment can be attained by pupils having a BAS reading age range of from between 5:00 to 9:06 years. A SAT level 2 reading assessment can be obtained with a BAS word-reading test reading-age range of between 5:07 to 12:09 years.

Subsequent work on reading comprehension test scores and SAT NCEn 2 Reading levels indicates a similar overlap (Davies and Brember, in press).

It is contended that SATs do not provide the quality of *summative* information from which standards and progress in the reading attainments of individuals and groups can be validly assessed. They cannot inform us whether or not the National Curriculum English programme is affecting reading attainments. For summative purposes, the evidence presented here suggests strongly that well-constructed and standardized normative reading tests have much more to commend them than SAT reading assessments.

Table 9.7: Range of reading-comprehension test scores at each SAT level for 1991

	Sample	Level 1	Level 2	Level 3
n=	176	35	106	35
Reading score	5–39	5–27	17–35	24–39
Reading age	–6–10.75	–6–7.05	–6–9.25	6.75–10.75
Comprehension	60–131	60–100	81–125	91–131

Notes: –6 indicates a reading age below the cut off point of 6.
N = 176 (5 randomly selected schools)

Table 9.8: Range of reading-comprehension test scores at each SAT level for 1992

	Sample	Level 1	Level 2	Level 3
n=	171	27	88	56
Reading score	1–37	1–32	10–32	18–37
Reading age	–6–10.00	–6–8.05	–6–8.05	–6–10.0
Comprehension	40–131	40–105	69–115	85–131

Notes: –6 indicates a reading age below the cut off point of 6.
N = 171 (5 randomly selected schools)

The early development of pupils' reading abilities is, in large measure, dependent on a mastery of the alphabetic principle. It represents a foundation without which other aspects of reading are unlikely to develop. Automaticity is important, overlearning is essential and mastery matters. Technically sound instruments, such as the BAS and the DAS word-reading tests, based on the accurate decoding of decontextualized words, represent a more valid foundation for summative assessment of standards and progress than do SAT reading assessments. The latter are incapable of delivering the information their proponents promise.

The study involving BAS, DAS and reading SATs was replicated in 1992, albeit under more difficult circumstances. The results are being analysed. Initial indications are that they show considerable stability in relation to the word-reading test results from the previous year (Pumfrey, 1993).

Other work at the University of Manchester compares reading SAT levels with scores from a standardized test of reading comprehension, the NFER Primary Reading Test. The findings cast further doubt on the quality of the information provided by the reading SATs at KS 1, insofar as summative assessment is concerned. Preliminary results from the 1991 and 1992 cohorts (see Table 9.7 and Table 9.8) based on 176 and 171 pupils attending five randomly selected schools within an LEA make the point (Davies, 1993).

In presenting these preliminary analyses, the limitations in the sampling, data and analyses are acknowledged. Despite these weaknesses, the argument that SATs are of utility in summative assessments at Key Stage 1, enabling standards and progress in reading to be gauged for the individual, the school, the LEA and the nation, is open to serious question.

Messages for Teachers

The assessment of children's reading standards, attitudes towards reading and their progress in the early stages of learning to read can provide valid indices of the effectiveness of an educational system. Monitoring both cognitive and affective aspects of reading development requires a simultaneous consideration of the objectives of the reading programme, the curricula, resources and methods whereby these objectives will be achieved and the assessment of pupils' progress towards the stated objectives.

'Whatever exists, exists in some quantity and can, in principle, be measured.' Thus spoke Thorndike, one of the pioneers of applied psychology and expert in educational measurement. More importantly, the measurement of children's inter and intra-individual differences in reading products and underlying processes can be undertaken to the advantage of all concerned.

In the nineteenth century, Lord Kelvin had earlier stated an important principle. It is pertinent to virtually any field, including that of reading. 'When you can measure what you are speaking about and express it in numbers, you know something about it; but when you cannot measure it, when you cannot express it in numbers, your knowledge is of a meagre and unsatisfactory kind.' Sadly, measurement and numbers can also be used as a smoke-screen to hide our lack of understanding of the reading process and its development.

In December 1992, Professor Stuart Sutherland, Her Majesty's chief inspector of Schools in England and Wales and head of the Office for Standards in Education (OFSTED) commented on the management of education as follows. 'If you can't measure it, you can't manage it.'

The informed use of reading tests and assessment techniques can contribute towards improving the reading attainments and progress of pupils. Despite the limitations of testing and assessment, they are essential if the educational system is to demonstrate its accountability. Unfortunately, the value of reading tests is frequently under or overvalued by users. This can be a consequence of a restricted appreciation of their conceptual bases, available sources, technical strengths and weaknesses and their legitimate uses. It can also derive from limitations in our conceptualization of the reading process and its development.

Before using *any* form of reading-assessment procedure, ask, and answer, the following four questions. Dependent on how adequate you and your colleagues consider your answers to be, decisions can be made whether to:

- use the test or technique;
- modify it, justifying any modification made;
- reject its use, making clear your reasons for so doing; or
- defer a decision.

The final option enables one to explore the question and the basis of one's answer in greater depth.

1. For what individual and/or institutional decision-making purposes will the information that I collect be used?

In relation to reading-assessment results, one major distinction is whether the information obtained is to be used for institutional decision-making purposes or for individual decision-making purposes. The former typically concerns the assessment of groups of pupils. The data can be anonymous. The focus is on interindividual differences in reading-test scores. These can be used to produce 'league tables' comparing trends in national reading standards and also standards over time in a school or a class, the comparison of groups of pupils such as boys and girls, and in selection procedures. In contrast, individual decision-making is oriented towards the identified individual student's particular pattern of intra-individual differences, and to the instructional implications of the patterns identified.

2. Does the assessment technique provide valid indices of reading standards and progress?

In England and Wales, National Curriculum English includes expressive skills, such as oracy and writing (including spelling), and receptive skills, such as listening and reading. Their developmental interrelationships are complex.

There are many methods of assessing children's reading attainments, attitudes towards reading and progress in reading. It is important that teachers understand the relative strengths and weakness of the following assessment procedures in relation to the stated objectives of the reading programme:

- observational procedures;
- informal reading inventories;
- normative assessments; and
- criterion-referenced assessments.

In 1991, *The Parent's Charter* stated 'The Government's plans are designed to ensure that you have all the information you need to keep track of your child's progress, keep in touch with his or her school, and compare all local schools.' Standard Assessment Tasks and teacher assessments have been developed by the Schools Examination and Assessment Council on an inadequate theoretical and empirical basis. In contrast, there exists a well-developed theory of normative reading-test construction.

The comparison of the results of a NCEn2 (reading) Standard Assessment Task and that of the BAS and DAS word-reading test results highlights the important differences between an apparently simple test of word reading constructed according to an explicit theory of test construction and that of a SAT constructed on much more subjective and less explicit criteria. The underlying assumptions concerning the nature of the phenomenon being tested should be made explicit by advocates of any reading test or assessment technique.

The ten-point scale of reading attainments on which the SAT NCEn2 (reading) level is based is inadequate. It cannot allow the valid inter and intra-individual discriminations on which differentiation of the curriculum depends. The claim that SATs can provide 'formative, summative, evaluative and informative' assessments concerning both standards and progress in reading of individuals and groups at KS1 is highly questionable.

3.   Is the collection of these data a worthwhile use of pupils' and my time?

'The point of the new tests is to give you and the teachers an exact picture of what your child has learned. Knowing how your child measures up against *national* standards will give you the best idea of his or her real progress' (DES, 1991, p. 2).

An understanding of the nature of reliabilities and validities and their interrelationships is essential if a user is to understand the merits of a reading test or assessment technique. The means of assessing NCEn2 (reading) SAT appears to be changed each year. This makes comparisons across years virtually meaningless. An inordinate amount of teacher time has been swallowed up in obtaining information on reading at

KS1 using SATS. Many teachers assert that this time could have been more constructively used in teaching their pupils.

4.   As part of my continuing professional development, what ideas do I need to follow up in order to enhance my understanding of the development and assessment of children's reading skills?

Teachers have both an individual and a collective professional responsibility to conceptualize and control the development of reading to the benefit of all their pupils. In discharging this responsibility, never forget the uniqueness of the individual pupil. Remember that generalizations deriving from the reading attainments and progress of groups frequently 'decay' when one is concerned with understanding the individual pupil's instructional needs.

As one component of the broader field of literacy, an ongoing awareness of current research into the nature of reading and its development is essential. This should be matched by an enhanced understanding of the technicalities involved in reading-test construction, the assessment of both reading standards and progress, and the interpretation of the results obtained.

When it comes to the assessment of cognitive, affective and motivational aspects of reading development, beware the bureaucratic 'tail' attempting to wag the pedagogic 'dog'. Above all, members of the teaching profession must develop their professional expertise and use their critical acumen in this and in all other curricular fields.

Conclusion

On 29 May 1992, a report in the *Times Educational Supplement* was headed 'Scots SATs abandoned'. Apparently the Government proposed dropping national tests for 8 and 11-year-olds following widespread objections from parents and teachers. 'In a consultation paper issued by the Scottish Office yesterday, it was conceded that criticism had led to the Government reviewing its position.' A more efficient and cost effective strategy involving the use of teacher assessment linked to Confirmatory Threshold Testing, as in Scotland, could provide the formative information on reading development that teachers require.

Theoretically based empirically grounded systematic observation, assessment and testing are important professional skills whereby children's reading attainments and progress can be appraised. The three major complementary approaches involve systematic observations by experienced members of HMI (Rose, 1992), the use of objective reading tests and, currently, the National Curriculum reading SATs approach. In relation to *summative* assessment of standards and progress, normative (and domain-referenced mastery) objective reading tests have important roles that have largely been neglected to date. The history of efficient national monitoring of reading standards based on standardized objective reading tests organized by the then Ministry of Education that was operative here for many years, has either been forgotten, ignored or dismissed (Pumfrey, 1992).

In the Autumn of 1991, the results of the National Curriculum KS 1 assessment in England were published in the form of 'league tables' for English, mathematics, science and reading (NC En Profile Component 2). The process was repeated in 1992 (DfE, 1992). Based on the SATs reading results, the percentages of KS 1 pupils at levels 2 and 3 have increased. This has been claimed by the Government as an indication of an improvement in reading standards and a vindication of its curricular policies and assessment procedures. In view of the inherent instabilities within the reading SATs procedures and the changes in content and procedure that have taken place between 1991 and 1992, this claim is suspect.

Despite unprecedented expenditure,including a flood of publications, SEAC has not met its brief in connection with the core NC Profile Component of Reading. If valid information on standards and progress is required, the form and content of SATs require drastic amendment. On the basis of the information collected at KS 1 using reading SATs, we cannot know whether reading standards of the individual, the school, the LEA, or the national cohort are stable, rising or falling.

References

ADAMS, M.J. (1990) *Beginning to Read: Thinking and Learning About Print*, Cambridge, MA, MIT Press.

BENNETT, S.N., WRAGG, E.C., CARRE, C.G. and CARTER, D.S.G. (1992) 'A longitudinal study of primary teachers' perceived competence in, and concerns about, National Curriculum implementation', *Research Papers in Education*, **7**, 1, pp. 53–78.

CASTLE, M. (1990) 'One in three confirms a decline', *Times Educational Supplement*, 6 July, p. 6.

CATTO, V. and WHETTON, C. (1991) *An Enquiry into LEA Evidence on Standards of Reading in Seven Year Old Children*, Slough, NFER.

DAVIES, J. (1993) 'Children's reading attainments in 1991 and 1992: a comparison of SATs and standardised reading test results', Unpublished research in progress, School of Education, University of Manchester.

DAVIES, J. and BREMBER, I. (in press) 'The first Standard Assessment Task in Reading at KS 1: What does it tell us'?

DEPARTMENT FOR EDUCATION (DfE) (1992) *Testing 7 Year Olds in 1992: Results of the National Curriculum Assessment in England*, London, HMSO.

DEPARTMENT OF EDUCATION AND SCIENCE (DES) (1989) *Standards in Education: 1987–1988*, The Annual Report of HM Senior Chief Inspector of Schools based on the work of HMI in England, London, HMSO.

DEPARTMENT OF EDUCATION AND SCIENCE (1991a) *The Parents' Charter: You and Your Child's Education*, London, HMSO.

DEPARTMENT OF EDUCATION AND SCIENCE (1991b) *How is Your Child Doing at School? A Parents' Guide to Testing*, London, Central Office of Information for HMSO.

DEPARTMENT OF EDUCATION AND SCIENCE (1991c) *Testing 7 Year Olds in 1991: Results of the National Curriculum Assessment in England*, London, HMSO.

DEPARTMENT OF EDUCATION AND SCIENCE (1991d) *The Teaching and Learning of Reading. A Report by HMI: Autumn, 1990*, London, HMSO.

ELLIOTT, C.D. (1983) *The British Ability Scales. Manual 2*, Windsor, NFER-Nelson.

ELLIOTT, C.D. (1990) *The Differential Ability Scales*, New York, The Psychological Corporation.

GORMAN, T. and FERNANDES, C. (1992) *Reading in Recession*, Slough, NFER.

LAKE, M. (1992) 'Social background and academic performance: evidence from Buckinghamshire', in PUMFREY, P.D. (Ed) *Reading Standards: Issues and Evidence*, Division of Educational and Child Psychology of the British Psychological Society, Leicester, pp. 17–32.

LEWIS, J. (1992) 'Reading Comprehension, Attitudes to Reading and Locus of Control Belief', A cross-cultural study, Unpublished Ph.D thesis, School of Education, University of Manchester.

MORRIS, J. (1992) 'Texts for Reading Assessment', Paper presented at the 29th. Annual Conference of the United Kingdom Reading Association, University of Exeter School of Education.

NATIONAL UNION OF TEACHERS (NUT) (1991) *Miss, The Rabbit Ate The 'Floating' Apple: The Case Against SATs*, London, NUT.

NATIONAL UNION OF TEACHERS AND THE SCHOOL OF EDUCATION, UNIVERSITY OF LEEDS (1993) *Testing and Assessing 6 and 7 year Olds: The Evaluation of the 1992 Key Stage 1 National Curriculum Assessment. Final Report*, London, NUT.

PUMFREY, P.D. (1990) 'The reading attainments and examination results of British West Indian pupils: Challenges of, and responses to, underachievement', in PUMFREY, P.D. and VERMA, G.K. (Eds) *Race Relations and Urban Education: Contexts and Promising Practices*, London, Falmer Press, pp. 231–58.

PUMFREY, P.D. (Ed) (1992) *Reading Standards: Issues and Evidence*, Division of Educational and Child Psychology of the British Psychological Society, Leicester.

PUMFREY, P.D. (1993) 'Reading Standards: Standardised objective tests and Standard Assessment Task results', Unpublished research in progress.

PUMFREY, P.D. and ELLIOTT, C.D. (1991) 'National reading standards and Standard Assessment Tasks: An Educational House of Cards?, *Educational Psychology in Practice*, **7**, pp. 74–80.

REGO, L.M.L.B. (1991) 'The role of early linguistic awareness in children's reading and spelling', Unpublished Ph.D thesis, Department of Experimental Psychology, University of Oxford.

ROSE, A.J. (1992) 'The Teaching of Reading in Primary schools: Quality and Standards. An HMI Perspective', in PUMFREY, P.D. (Ed) (1992) *Reading Standards: Issues and Evidence*, Division of Educational and Child Psychology of the British Psychological Society, Leicester, pp. 13–16.

SAINSBURY, M., WHETTON, C., ASHBY, J., SCHAGEN, I. and SIZMUR, S. (1992) *National Curriculum Assessment at Key Stage 1 in the Core Subjects: 1992 Evaluation*, London, SEAC.

SCHOOL EXAMINATIONS AND ASSESSMENT COUNCIL (SEAC) (1991) *Assessment Handbook English: En 2 Reading: En 3/4/5 Writing. Standard Assessment Task Key Stage 1*, London, HMSO on behalf of the Secretaries of State for Education and for Wales.

SCHOOL EXAMINATIONS AND ASSESSMENT COUNCIL (SEAC) (1992) *Assessment Handbook English: En 2 Reading: En 3/4/5 Writing. Standard Assessment Task Key Stage 1*, London, HMSO on behalf of the Secretaries of State for Education and for Wales.

SCHOOL EXAMINATIONS AND ASSESSMENT COUNCIL (SEAC) (1993) *Assessment Handbook English: En 2 Reading: En 3/4/5 Writing. Standard Assessment Task Key Stage 1*, London, HMSO on behalf of the Secretaries of State for Education and for Wales.

SMITHSON, M.J. (1991) *And the Infant SAT on the Flaw: An Initial Look At Reading in the Standard Assessment Tasks for Key Stage 1*, Lewes, East Sussex Learning Support Service.

TURNER, M. (1990a) 'A closed book?', *Times Educational Supplement*, 20 July 1993, p. 12.

TURNER, M. (1990b) *Sponsored Reading Failure*, Warlingham, IPSET.

TURNER, M. (1992a) 'Organized inferiority? Reading and the National Curriculum', *Education Section Review*, **16**, 1, pp. 23–25.

Chapter 10

Teachers as Participants in the National Reading Examinations

E. Meiselles

Summary

In response to some of the criticisms against recent national examinations in reading, lsrael's Ministry of Education has embarked upon two conceptual changes in the design of new examinations. The first is that the new national examination will be in the form of a communicative language test and the second, that the school teachers will participate in determining the standards and the content outline of future examinations. Teachers' questionnaires and the analysis of responses are the basis for the advocated changes. It is concluded that the traditional multiple-choice standardized tests have had a negative effect on the teaching of reading.

Introduction

Israel's 1990 public examination was designed to re-establish the reading ability of the fifth-year junior school children and identify those who had not mastered, as yet, the basic reading skills expected. Children's level of competency was determined by a commissioned panel of 'experts' who composed and validated the standardized test. The proposed paper consisted primarily of short-graded reading passages followed by closed-ended questions, which required the selection of a 'correct' response out of the four alternatives offered for most questions. Students failing to choose any three or more correct answers out of the first fifteen criterion-referenced questions were deemed incompetent readers, regardless of their overall raw score in the whole sixty questions test. Indeed, in many cases the total scores of the so-called underachievers exceeded those of their 'competent' counterparts, which challenges the assumed predictive validity of the latest public examination (Nevo, 1992).

A further study of the public examination recently administered, also reveals: firstly, a very narrow cross-curricular repertoire of short reading texts depicting by and large, descriptive genre characteristics; and secondly, abrupt switches from one topic to another, which means that any attempt to maintain a reasonable communicative sense between the writer, the reader and the message (text) was, to say the least, accidental. Indeed, more than half of the reading passages offered are between one and three sentences long. These sharp changes therefore require irregular refocusing, which is communicatively unreal and very exhausting.

The main criticism however, has been directed at the test's heuristic implications that reading is a collection of staged skills which can be passively tested. All the reader needs to do is identify the required skill and guess the correct alternative. In other words, literary competency has been redirected to the control of routinized content-related skills, with little or no reference to structurally related strategies of unfolding meaning and identifying genre characteristics for communicative purposes (Valencia and Pearson, 1987). After all, public-accountability examinations, argues Cohen (1987), dictate in most cases what aspects of, and how any subject is taught. Whether we like it or not, what is eventually taught and what is tested are intimately related.

The Ministry of Education and Culture in Israel has recently embarked on the participation of teachers in the construction of the next public reading examination in Summer 1994. The aims were twofold:

- to narrow the widening gap between the more progressive teaching approaches encouraged in recent years in the literacy classroom and the demands of the traditional public examinations and the presentation of their scores; and
- to reinstate the diminishing role of teachers as assessors for formative purposes, and reduce by default, the overemphasis on summative assessment.

The reason for this shift and the partial outcomes of the proposed venture are considered.

Traditional Testing and Curricular Misalignment

The two key assumptions underlying most standardized testing technology and practice, are *decomposability* and *decontextualization*. These assumptions were compatible with the routinized skill goals of the past and with the psychological theories of the first part of this century. They are however, incompatible with what we know today about the nature of human cognition and learning (Johnston, 1990). Psychological theories of the 1920s assumed that thought could best be described as a collection of independent pieces of knowledge. This decomposability assumption can be clearly recognized in the behaviourist work of psychologists such as Edward Thorndike and Burrhus Skinner, which has had a profound influence on the instruction and testing of reading.

Decontextualization, the second major assumption built into standardized tests, asserts that each component of a complex skill is a fixed entity that will take the same form wherever it is used. If students know how to distinguish a fact from an opinion for example, they can do so under all conditions. It makes sense to select key critical-thinking skills for decontextualized practice in schools; but this assumption no longer appears valid. Developments in the epistemology and philosophy of science show that there is no absolute line between fact and theory, data and interpretation (Lakatos, 1978).

Consequently, most of the current standardized tests are severely wanting and they are tuned to a curriculum of the past. Even in school districts with an official policy against teaching for tests, considerable attention in the press or elsewhere to the test scores causes teachers to readapt their teaching and match their curriculum to the national tests (Leinhardt and Seewald, 1981). Furthermore, the public accountability systems of assessment for the purpose of reallocating funds had centred on summative rather than formative evaluation.

Public-testing practice remained essentially unchanged from the era in which it was considered enough for schools to teach the mastery of routine skills by reading predictable texts (Fuhrma, 1988). Yet empirical evidence has shown that:

- children cannot understand what they read without making inferences and using information that goes beyond the written text.
- facts acquired without structure and rationale disappear quickly.

To gauge the extent to which the decomposition and decontextualization assumptions permeate today's achievement tests, Shavelson and Stern (1981) for example, examined the standardized-test batteries widely used in educational assessment as part of mandated testing programs. They found that reading-comprehension tests generally present short passages, together with multiple short questions. In asking for bits of information rather than interpretation of an extended passage, these tests reflect the decomposability assumption, treating knowledge and skills as accumulations of isolated pieces of information and not as coherent, interactive systems. In addition, these tests encourage quick finding of answers rather than reflective interpretation, allowing each examinee an average of five to six minutes to read a series of brief passages and answer five to eight questions per passage. Although the tests require a degree of textual interpretation, their isolated questions rarely examine how students interrelate parts of the text and do not require justifications that support their interpretations. In other words, the nature of the questions and the speed with which they must be answered do not invite the kind of reflection and elaboration demanded by the newer communicative approaches to reading.

In summary, these tests tacitly convey a definition of reading as pursuing short passages to answer other people's questions. Furthermore, their format suggests that the answers to these questions are already known by the person asking them. Under such circumstances, reading comprehension appears to be a matter of finding predetermined answers. We need a much wider cross-curricular repertoire of reading texts depicting different genre characteristics. The reader should ultimately demonstrate the use within the context of the immediate text and beyond it, employing for example, the rhetorics of persuading, arguing, reporting etc. Applebee (1978) notes for instance, that first-year junior pupils can be taught to handle skilfully narrative characteristics and at the age of 10 they can sustain a structured argument, express opinions, compare and contrast, and even persuade (Stein and Glen, 1979) (see also Chapters 7 and 8 in this volume).

Messages for Teachers

In response to the recent changes in the teaching of reading and the traditional approach to testing, a 'dynamic model of formative assessment' designed to complement the communicative-process approach to the teaching of meaningful reading had been suggested (Champion and Brown, 1985). Their heuristic model is based on the Vygotskian concept of the 'proximal development zone' — the area of further advancement to be accomplished by employing cues of reflective interpretation, the justification for it and its eventual re-application beyond the text's framework. This nonlinear process approach to literacy must, in their view, be progressively enriched by:

- prior world knowledge such as, exposure to information, rhetorical characteristics and expressive cues, related to the texts in question and beyond them; and
- applying what is read and/or written to other areas of knowledge and to different communicative situations across the curriculum.

The 'dynamic model of formative assessment' should therefore address its efforts to those strategies of unfolding meaning and using it in differently related communicative circumstances. Readers are thus expected, in other words, to demonstrate their comprehension by responding to a given text in varied situations. This redeployment and re-application of communicative characteristics and skills be it in writing or orally, is a more valid approach to assessing reading than the closed-ended multiple-choice questions traditionally used (see for example Calfee, 1987).

Guided by the growing evidence that Israel's teachers are by and large, more attuned to the recent changes in teaching methods and testing of reading, than the so-called public-examination experts, the chairman of the Pedagogic Institute formed an *ad hoc* steering committee.[1] Also invited to participate was a representative body consisting of more than fifty teachers from varied disciplines and different schools across the country, in order to compose the next public reading-cum-writing examination due to take place in Summer 1994. This select group of teachers is responsible for the collection of varied and relevant reading passages of interest to their fifth-grade students. They are also requested to suggest valid ways of testing their students' reading ability in communicative terms with particular reference to:

- a wider cross-curricular repertoire of different types of texts; and
- a wider range of testable strategies akin with unfolding meaning and using it in differently related communicative situations.

Several examples of questions attempting to test reading in communicative terms along the lines advocated above, are presented below:

1. The reader is asked to act as a policeman reporting a theft which took place on the beach, as eventfully described in the reading passage proposed.
2. The reader is encouraged to write a thank you letter to a lifeguard on behalf of a boy whose life was saved by the lifeguard, as vividly described in the poem.

3. The reader is invited to defend the choice of travelling by a private car instead of a train to a Summer resort, by reconsidering the advantages and disadvantages of different means of transportation as reported in the local newspaper.
4. The reader is requested to anticipated the problem of weightlessness on the moon's surface, and give a personal account of this imaginary experience.
5. The reader is requested to outline the effect of freezing water in a sealed bottle with reference to:

   - the purpose of the experiment;
   - the materials used; and
   - the outcome of the experiment.

6. The reader is encouraged to persuade the incoming tourists to the Holyland to visit the Sea of Galilee as a significant historical site.

In the sample presented above the texts are varied and like many other types of writing from different sources, submitted for pre-test selection and review, they comprise writing assignments designed to demonstrate both functional understanding and communicative applicability.

Conclusion

It is still too early as yet, to assess the validity of the proposed interpretation of the communicative approach to testing. What is quite certain however, is that the traditional standardized tests are not only inadequate, but they continue to have a negative effect on the teaching of reading. The departure from the traditional decomposability and decontextualization concepts in teaching and testing, has been gradual and one-sided. The shift from teaching reading as separate staged skills to an interactive communication, has not found its fullest expression in testing reading. Consequently, the gap between teaching and testing has not narrowed. The testing model reviewed above has been designed to reduce this conceptual mismatch between teaching and testing. The principles of a 'dynamic model of formative assessment' have been employed and integrated with the strategies of unfolding meaning and using it in differently related communicative situations.

Notes

1. All school teachers in Israel are encouraged to take a one-year fully paid sabbatical every six years, for an advanced course in education. Furthermore, regular in-service teacher training is remuneratively attractive.

References

APPLEBEE, A.N. (1978) *The Child's Concept of a Story*, Chicago, IL, University of Chicago Press.

CALFEE, R.C. (1987) 'Assessing school reading', *The Reading Teachers*, **6**, 3, pp. 20–8.

CHAMPION, J.C. and BROWN, A.L. (1985) 'Dynamic assessment: One approach and some initial data', *Technical Report No. 361*, Urbana, IL, Center for the Study of Reading.

COHEN, S.A. (1987) 'Instructional alignment: Searching for a magic bullet', *Educational Research*, **16**, 8, pp. 16–20.

FARR, R. and CAREY, R.F. (1986) *Reading: What Can Be Measured?*, Newark, DE, International Reading Association.

FUHRMAN, S. (1988) 'Educational indicators: An overview', *Phi Delta Kappa*, **69**, 7, pp. 486–7.

JOHNSTON, P. (1990) 'Assessing the process and the process of assessment in the language of arts', in SQUIRE, J. (Ed) *The Dynamics of Language Learning*, Urbana, IL, NCTE.

LAKATOS, I. (1978) 'The methodology of scientific research programs', *Philosophical Papers*, **1**, New York, Cambridge University Press.

LEINHARDT, G. and SEEWALD, A.M. (1981) 'Overlap: What's tested, what's taught?', *Journal of Educational Measurement*, **18**, 2, pp. 85–96.

NEVO, D. (1992) *Useful Assessment: Assessing Educational Projects*, Tel Aviv, Masada Publications.

PEARSON, P.D. (1986) 'Twenty years of research in reading comprehension', in TAFFY, E.R. (Ed) *The Context of school-Based Literacy*, New York, Random House.

SHAVELSON, R. and STERN, P. (1981) 'Research on teachers' pedagogical thoughts, judgements, decisions and behavior', *Review Research*, **41**, 3, pp. 455–98.

SPIRO, R.J. and MEYERS, A. (1984) 'Individual differences and underlying cognitive processes', in PEARSON, P.D. (Ed) *Handbook of Reading Research*, New York, Loughlan.

STEIN, N.L. and GLAN, C. (1979) 'An analysis of story comprehension in elementary school children', in FREEDLE, R. (Ed) *New Directions in Discourse Analysis*, Norwood, NJ, Ablex Publishing.

VALENCIA, S.W. and PEARSON, P.D. (1987) 'Reading assessment: Time for a change', *The Reading Teacher*, **40**, 2, pp. 726–32.

Chapter 11

A Comparison of Teacher Strategies, Aims and Activities in Two Countries Participating in the IEA Reading-literacy Study

V. Froese

Summary

This chapter compares and discusses teacher strategies, aims and activities in two jurisdictions, British Columbia in Canada and the USA in the International Association for the Evaluation of Educational Achievement (IEA) Reading-literacy Study. British Columbia espouses a child-centred literacy curriculum, whereas the majority of states in the USA use material-centred reading approaches, known as basal readers. Aspects of teaching as well as student achievement are compared for the 9 year-old populations across the two systems. There is evidence of important differences in the material-centred and the pupil-centred jurisdictions with respect to teachers' aims, strategies and activities. However, the answer to 'but who did best?' is not simple. Indications are that similar test achievement can be obtained by quite different educational curricula.

Introduction

The purpose of this chapter is to compare and discuss teacher strategies, aims, and activities in two jurisdictions participating in the IEA Reading-literacy Study: British Columbia in Canada and the United States. These two jurisdictions are of particular interest since British Columbia (BC) espouses a child-centred literacy curriculum whereas the majority of states in the USA use material-centred reading approaches known as basal readers. Because of space limitations only the younger age groups

(Population A) are considered here. Before specifically addressing the strategies, aims, and activities it is necessary to consider the context in which the information was gathered.

Overview of IEA Reading-literacy Study

In 1986 the International Association for the Evaluation of Educational Achievement (IEA) initiated this literacy study and an international steering committee first met in Washington, DC in 1988. A tentative blueprint was mapped out by representatives from thirty-five participating systems (countries in most cases). Warwick Elley was appointed chairperson of the steering committee and an International Coordination Centre under the direction of Neville Postlethwaite was established in Hamburg, Germany to facilitate the study. The steering committee was responsible for item development, for questionnaire development, for pilot testing (1989–90), and for the final selection of items.

The actual test administration for the IEA Reading-literacy study was completed in 1990 in the southern hemisphere and in 1991 in the northern hemisphere. The goals of the study were as follows:

1. to produce valid international measures of reading literacy;
2. to identify the proportion of students reaching various levels of literacy;
3. to show the frequency and use of reading literacy;
4. to identify factors influencing literacy in students, teachers, and schools; and
5. to establish a 1991–2 database for future comparisons.

Although initially it was intended to assess literacy in the general sense this was abandoned due to complexity and cost for the more focused 'reading literacy' which was defined as 'the ability to understand and use those written language forms required by society and/or valued by the individual' and the focus was on materials commonly found in the home, school, community, and workplace in all countries.

Students to be included were generally 9 and 14-year-olds but the sample was defined as 'all students attending on a full-time basis at the grade level in which most students aged 9:00–9:11 years (or 14:00–14:11 years) were enrolled during the first week of the eighth month of the school year'. The younger age group was referred to as Population A and marked the end of primary school, and the older group known as Population B marked the end of compulsory schooling in most countries. Due to the nature of the definition about half the participating systems tested in grades three and eight (including BC), the other half at grades four and nine (including the USA), and one system at grades five and ten (New Zealand). All told some 93,039 students in 4,353 schools at Population A and 117,020 students in 4,720 schools at Population B participated in the study. Teachers numbered 4,992 at Pop. A and 5,526 at Pop. B level. More specifically BC tested in 157 schools in Pop. A and 197 in Pop. B; the USA tested 165 in Pop. A and 165 in Pop. B.

The systems participating in the IEA reading-literacy countries were: Belgium, Botswana, Canada (BC), Cyprus, Denmark, Finland, France, Germany, Greece, Hong Kong, Hungary, Iceland, Indonesia, Iceland, Italy, Ireland, The Netherlands, New Zealand, Nigeria, Norway, The Philippines, Portugal, Singapore, Slovenia, Spain, Sweden, Switzerland, Thailand, Trinidad and Tobago, The United States, Venezuela, and Zimbabwe.

Method

The Instruments

Reading-literacy tests were developed for both Populations A and B. For Population A, a word-recognition test with forty matching items was included as well as a number of narrative, expository, and document passages with accompanying multiple-choice, short-answer, and long-answer responses. Population B had narrative, expository, and document items but no word-recognition component. Each group had two testing sessions, approximately seventy-five minutes for the younger age group and about eighty-five minutes for the older group. A student questionnaire was untimed and paced by the teacher. The questionnaire included personal information and interests, details about home, about reading habits, about homework, and about the reading instruction they were receiving.

The classroom teacher completed a teacher questionnaire which included information about the teacher's educational training, about the class being tested, about teaching activities, about aims of reading instruction, about the classroom and school library, and about school organization. Additionally a school principal's questionnaire was administered to document the principal's training, community resources, facts about the school library, instructional time, and about the principal's role.

Finally, a national case-study questionnaire was completed to provide information about the cost of schooling, the structure of the school system, student enrolment, the reading curriculum, gender statistics, teacher training, and so on. Some of this information was used to devise a Composite Development Index (CDI) which was later used to interpret reading-literacy outcomes.

Unique Features of the IEA Literacy Study

Since it had been approximately twenty years since the last large-scale international literacy study had been undertaken by Thorndike (1973), it was natural to expect that curricula in the various countries might have changed as well. As a result considerable debate surrounded the content of the instruments to be used. Particularly evident was the realization that the teaching of literacy had progressed in some countries from an exclusively bottom–up (i.e., skills) approach to a modified top–down (i.e., meaning-based) approach. The final result, after much debate, was a fair compromise. Some of the unique features of the resulting instrument follow.

1. Common passages
   Three common passages (Temperature, Marmot, Shark) were embedded in the Population A and the Population B tests to give some indications of growth in ability to answer comprehension questions between age groups. In fact, an approximate 24 per cent growth was observed in the five-year age difference of the two groups.
2. Passage length
   Since there is some indication that reading behaviour changes with sustained reading it was agreed that both short and long passages would be included. Long passages were defined as those requiring more than two minutes to read, and because of space and time limitations only two were included at each age level. In Pop. A passages ranged from about forty to over 700 words, in Pop. B from about 150 to over 1,000.
3. Question types
   Since considerable criticism has been expressed over an exclusive reliance on multiple-choice questions, other response modes were included. These included two types of open-ended items — some required word responses to be written, others required several sentences. Other items required students to respond in a variety of ways to directions.

4. Text type

   Three types of text were presented: narrative, expository, and document. Narrative text was defined as continuous text in which the writer's aim is to tell a story — whether fact or fiction. Expository text was continuous text designed to describe, explain or otherwise convey information or opinion to the reader. And documents were structured information displays presented in the form of charts, tables, maps, graphs, lists or sets of instruction.

5. Passage content

   Because reading literacy was defined as the ability to understand and use those written-language forms required by society and/or valued by individuals, it was decided to include a balance of passages based on the themes of home, school, and society/work. For Pop. A there were passages about animals, pets, family, school timetable, and a postcard. At the Pop. B level there were passages about animals, job vacancies, bus schedules, humour, and medicine directions.

6. Participation

   The IEA reading-literacy study was one of the largest of its kind, it involved thirty-two school systems from around the world. Most systems represented countries but some like Germany (West) and Germany (East) were the result of political changes during the course of the study. Others were different because they represented only parts of countries: Belgium (French) and Canada (BC). In the latter case, only the Province of British Columbia, one of ten provinces in Canada, participated in the study. Twenty-one language groups were involved including nine countries that tested in English: Canada (BC), Botswana, Ireland, New Zealand, The Philippines, Singapore, Trinidad and Tobago, The United States, and Zimbabwe.

7. Statistical Analysis

   Extensive pilot testing preceded the selection of passages and items. Passages were back-translated to assure accuracy. Pilot testing allowed the selection of items that performed similarly across translations in the twenty-one different languages that were involved. A statistical scaling technique known as the Rasch procedure was used to produce scales for each domain with a mean of 500 and a standard deviation of 100. This allows the comparisons of scores on a common scale across countries, regardless of the language of testing. Probability sampling was under the direction of an international sampling coordinator to assure that fair sampling procedures were followed in all countries.

8. Student, teacher, school information
    The extensive information gathered about students, teachers, and schools (described earlier in this chapter) allows a variety of in-depth analysis of factors that affect achievement. It is possible, for example, to look at teaching strategies that lead to high achievement; to examine which school and community attributes are related to achievement; to see how aims of instruction affect achievement; and so on. From the student's perspective it is possible to examine how aspects of the school and home environment affect achievement. The data also gives insight into the frequency and use of reading literacy in today's world.

Results

Student-centred vs Material-centred Instruction

At the outset it was stated that this chapter intended to look at results from the IEA reading-literacy study from the perspective of two jurisdictions with contrasting curricular approaches. British Columbia espouses a child-centred curriculum whereas a majority of the United States use the material-centred reading approaches known as basal readers.

While it is difficult to pin down exact numbers, a study of 10,000 elementary teachers in the USA in the 1970s found that 94 per cent of them relied on basal materials (Education Product Information Exchange, 1977); a later estimate was 90 per cent (Goodman, Shannon, Freeman and Murphy, 1988). Essentially these basal or reading series consist of a graded set of textbooks for each of the elementary grades and accompanying workbooks, a teacher's manual which provides instructions as to what the teacher should do in each lesson, and various supporting materials (i.e., charts, big books, tapes, etc.), and testing materials which closely emulate the instructional materials. Instruction based on such materials has dominated reading instruction in the United States for over fifty years.

In British Columbia many teachers used similar materials until recently, but by 1991 only 5.3 per cent reported using them. Some 23 per cent indicated using a literature-based or Whole Language approach, and 56.6 per cent indicated that they used eclectic approaches. A Royal Commission on Education (1987–8) conducted an extensive review of BC schools and its report *A Legacy for Learners* made eighty-three recommendations dealing with a wide range of topics, including curriculum, assessment, reporting, and learning. Three key points about learning were intended to shape the programme:

1. Learning requires the active participation of the learner.
2. People learn in a variety of ways and at different rates.
3. Learning is both an individual and a social process. (BC Ministry of Education, 1989).

The publication also stated five goals of the primary programme:

*   aesthetic and artistic development;
*   emotional and social development;
*   intellectual development;
*   physical development; and
*   social responsibility.

One paragraph simply describes what was intended:

> **Teachers** plan learning experiences based on the guiding principles of the program. **They** observe the *learner* carefully within the context of daily learning. **They** talk with the *student* in conversations and conferences and listen to what the *child* is saying about his or her learning. **They** examine collections of each *student's* work. **Teachers** encourage *students* to represent their ideas in many different ways, including painting, role playing, writing, constructing, manipulating objects, etc. Through these processes **teachers**, over time, begin to get a picture of what the *student* can do and can make informed decisions about future learning [my emphases]. (BC Ministry of Education, 1989, p. 4)

Even from this brief description the reader can see that the two systems are quite different in terms of who makes the decisions. In the basal programmes most decisions have been made by the 'experts' guiding the material development and are incorporated into the directions provided for the teacher and student. In the BC curriculum the classroom teacher is expected to make the decisions based on contextualized observation in real learning situations.

The IEA reading-literacy study in 1991 provided an opportunity to observe how teachers in the contrasting systems saw their roles (i.e., reading aims), what types of classroom exercises they favoured (i.e., reading activities), and what sort of methods they preferred (i.e., reading strategies).

Teacher Strategies, Aims and Activities

The teacher questionnaire provides considerable information about the teachers' educational training, the class being tested, teaching procedures, the classroom library, and school organization. Further, the study makes it possible to examine the connection of these various attributes with achievement on the reading portion of the test. Because of space constraints, this chapter considers only the teachers' aims, instructional strategies, and assigned reading activities.

1. Aims
   Teachers were asked to rank their top five aims of reading instruction of twelve items presented. Note that because not every teacher ranked all items only relative differences should be considered in Figures 11.1 and 11.2.
2. Instructional strategies
   Teachers were asked to indicate how often they used each of the thirteen instructional strategies when teaching reading. Choices were almost every day, about once or twice per week, about once per month, or almost never. The findings are presented in Figures 11.3 and 11.4.
3. Reading activities
   Teachers were asked to mark how often students were typically involved in a list of twenty-eight reading activities. Again frequencies were described as almost daily, about once or twice per week, about once per month, or almost never. Data are presented in Figures 11.5, 11.6, and 11.7.

To establish a sense of importance of the various aims, strategies, and activities, a half dozen doctoral students in a reading-education programme at the University of British Columbia were asked to rate them as to whether they involved high, middle, or low levels of cognitive activities. Figures 1–7 present comparisons for the two jurisdictions (BC and USA) grouped by level (high, middle, low). The reader may wish to impose some other order on these items, but it was felt to be a useful way of considering them.

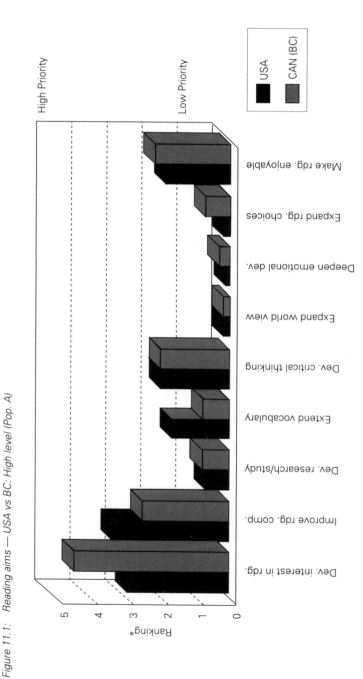

Figure 11.1: Reading aims — USA vs BC: High level (Pop. A)

Note: *1 = low priotity 5 = high priority
Dev. = Development, rdg. = reading, comp. = comprehension

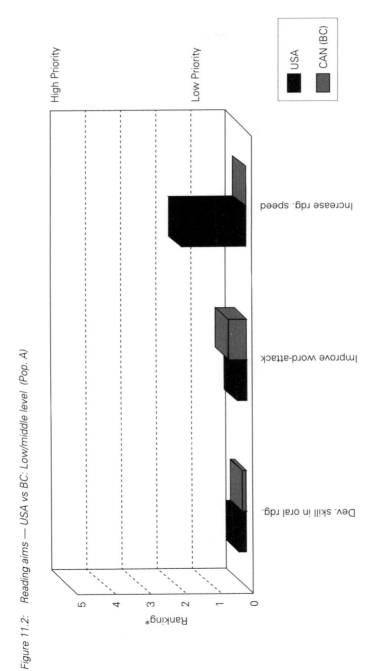

Figure 11.2: Reading aims — USA vs BC: Low/middle level (Pop. A)

Note: *1 = low priority 5 = high priority

Since it is instructive to determine how students in the two jurisdictions performed on the literacy test it was necessary to complete a supplementary growth study (Froese and Conry, 1993) since grade-three students were tested in BC (average age 8.9), grade-four students in the USA (average age 10.0), and grade-five students in New Zealand (average age 10.0). Figures 11.8, 11.9 and 11.10 illustrate the international-standard scores achieved (mean = 500, sd = 100) in the various domains on the literacy test by BC students, American students, and for added interest two other countries testing in English: New Zealand and Ireland. It should be remembered, however, that the growth study was conducted in 1993, exactly two years after the original IEA study.

Messages for Teachers

As can be seen from Figure 11.1, when considering those aims considered to be 'high' cognitively, five of nine aims are ranked more highly by BC teachers. These are:

- develop interest in reading;
- develop research and study skills;
- deepen emotional understanding;
- expand reading choices; and
- make reading enjoyable.

BC and US teachers are virtually tied on developing critical thinking and expanding world view. The US teachers rank improving reading comprehension and extending vocabulary more highly. In Figure 11.2, in the 'low/medium' level activities, only one, improving word-attack, is rated higher by BC teachers, the others are rated higher by US teachers. Why the differences? An understanding of basal series makes the finding fairly apparent. The typical pattern suggested in the manuals is to introduce a story by focusing on vocabulary that is intended to be 'new', to read the selection silently, answer comprehension questions from the manual or workbook, and discuss the selection (and have students read orally selected passages) and correct the questions. The student-centred curriculum in contrast integrates the language activities with the learning of other content, whether science, social studies, or literature. It emphasizes the heuristic function of language, but also stresses the making of choices, and the social nature of learning.

Figures 11.3 and 11.4 focus on reading strategies. Again, when

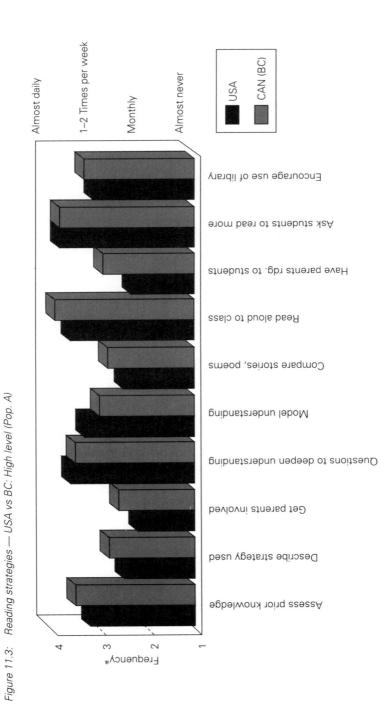

Figure 11.3: Reading strategies — USA vs BC: High level (Pop. A)

Note: *1 = almost never; 2 = monthly; 3 = 1–2 times/wk; 4 = almost daily

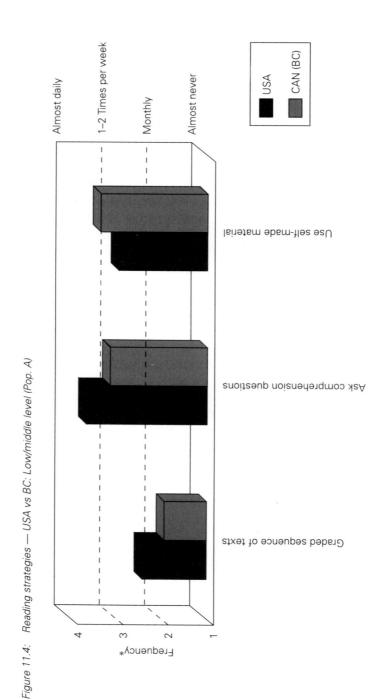

Figure 11.4: Reading strategies — USA vs BC: Low/middle level (Pop. A)

Note: *1 = almost never; 2 = monthly; 3 = 1–2 times/wk; 4 = almost daily

considering the 'high-level' strategies, seven of ten are used more frequently by BC teachers; of the three 'low/middle' strategies two favour the US teachers. As can be seen from Figure 11.3, BC teachers frequently assess prior knowledge, describe strategies used, get parents involved, compare stories and poems, read aloud to class, have parents reading to students, and encourage use of the library. The US teachers favour questioning to deepen understanding and to model understanding — both again closely related to the basal methodology. It is particularly interesting to note the importance placed on involving the parents by the BC teachers. Also, the strategies appear to reflect the wider range of materials read, the adaptation of strategies to reading different materials, and use of reading for learning. Figure 11.4 indicates that the US teachers use graded sequence of texts and ask comprehension questions more frequently whereas BC teachers use self-made materials more frequently. This appears to reflect the different methodologies quite plainly.

The next set of figures, Figures 11.5, 11.6 and 11.7, give an indication of the types of activities teachers indicate that they use in the classroom. Ten of the fifteen 'high-level' activities are used more frequently by BC teachers. These include silent reading in class, independent reading, discussing books, incidental vocabulary development, reading plays or dramas, drawing in response to reading, reading other students' writing, making predictions, having students lead discussions, and writing responses to reading. US teachers use summarization, making generalizations and inferences, and reading in the subject areas more frequently. To some extent the latter are more routinized and reflect a more structured common set of readings, while the former indicate a range of individually selected materials which have been individually selected by students. Figure 11.6 indicates that of the nine 'middle-level' activities, seven are used more frequently by BC teachers: oral reading in groups, teacher reading to class, reading games, dramatizing stories, diagramming stories, studying the style and structure of materials, and comparing pictures and text. US teachers use writing comprehension answers more frequently. Of the 'low-level' activities listed in Figure 11.7, the US teachers use three of five more frequently; that is, word-attack, oral reading, and vocabulary lists. It is almost ironic that letter–sound relationships are given more attention by the BC teachers when the basal-reader methodology typically stresses phonics. It may be that vocabulary control actually reduces the necessity to apply the very skills that are intended to be learned.

After pointing out the above differences it is common to be asked: But who did better? This naturally depends on which criteria one uses,

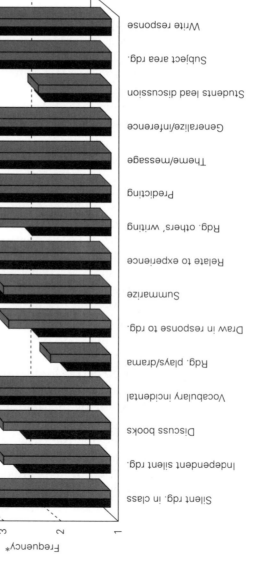

Figure 11.5: Reading activities — USA vs BC: High level (Pop. A)

Note: *1 = almost never; 2 = monthly; 3 = 1–2 times/wk; 4 = almost daily

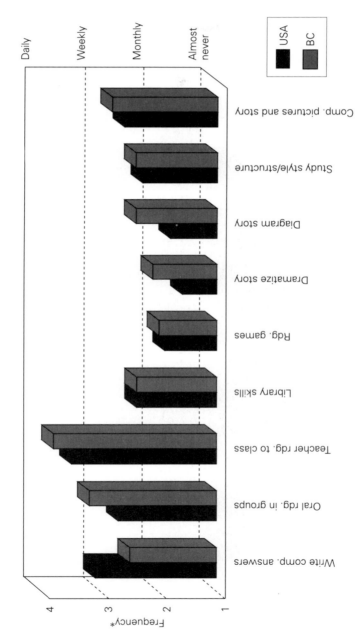

Figure 11.6: Reading activities — USA vs BC: Middle level (Pop. A)

*Note: *1 = almost never; 2 = monthly; 3 = 1–2 times/wk; 4 = almost daily

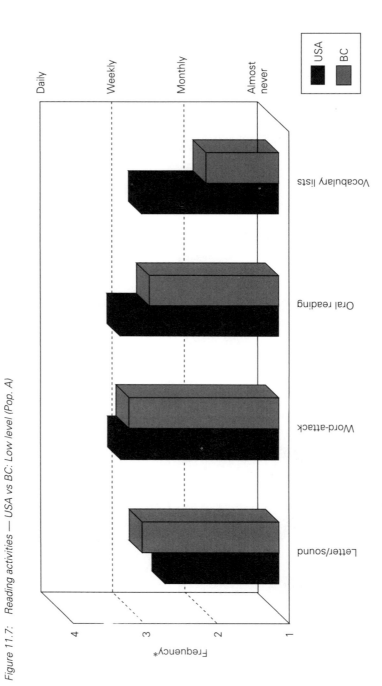

Figure 11.7: Reading activities — USA vs BC: Low level (Pop. A)

Note: *1 = almost never; 2 = monthly; 3 = 1–2 times/wk; 4 = almost daily

or what one values. Figures 11.8–11.10 provide some brief comparative-achievement information for the three domains tested-document, expository, and narrative. In general BC students and US students performed very similarly when comparing grade-four students on the international standard scale. Both jurisdictions performed slightly better than Ireland, a country also testing in English, and when comparing BC grade-five students with New Zealand grade-five students the former achieved significantly higher levels.

Figure 11.11 indicates the growth of achievement of BC students from grade three to grade ten when responding to the same passages. Steady growth is seen until grade eight, then plateauing occurs partly because students are topping out on the measures used. Growth of about 13 per cent is experienced between grades three and four on the narrative, expository, and document items when considering international standard scores. This is a radical contrast to the growth found by Elley (1992) of about 5 per cent. The growth between grades four and five tapers off considerably to 5.5 per cent for narrative, 4.5 per cent for expository, and 5.6 per cent for document items. The answer to 'But who did better?' is not simple. In fact indications are that similar achievement can be obtained by quite different educational curricula. However, insofar as the data on teachers' aims, strategies, and activities reflect their methodologies, there is evidence of important difference in the material-centred and the student-centred jurisdictions contrasted in this report.

Conclusion

The reader may find further information about the IEA reading-literacy study in publications by Elley (1992), Postlethwaite and Ross (1992), and by Lundberg and Linnakylä (1993). It is important to note, however, that comparisons in these publications are made across countries regardless of the age or grade level of the students. As indicated by the BC growth study, and by previous data found in a Swedish study, grade level is a significant determinant of achievement and should not be overlooked when making comparisons among countries. As indicated in a recent article (Stahl, Higginson and King, 1993), we need to be cautious about 'misinterpreting or misrepresenting cross-national or cross-cultural findings, and judging the results of a nation's literacy assessment as an Olympic event in a worldwide game of pedagogy'.

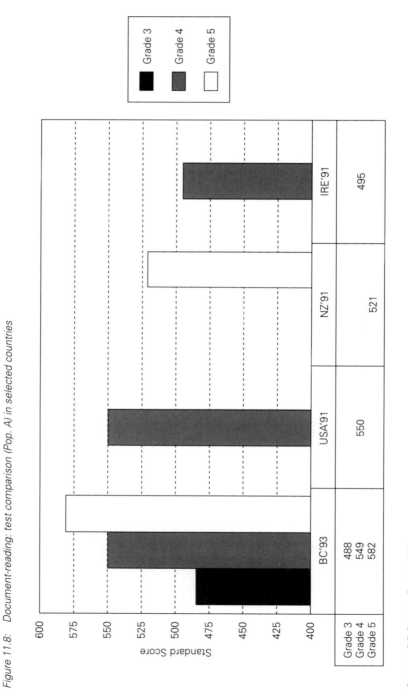

Figure 11.8: Document-reading: test comparison (Pop. A) in selected countries

Source: BC Growth Study 1993

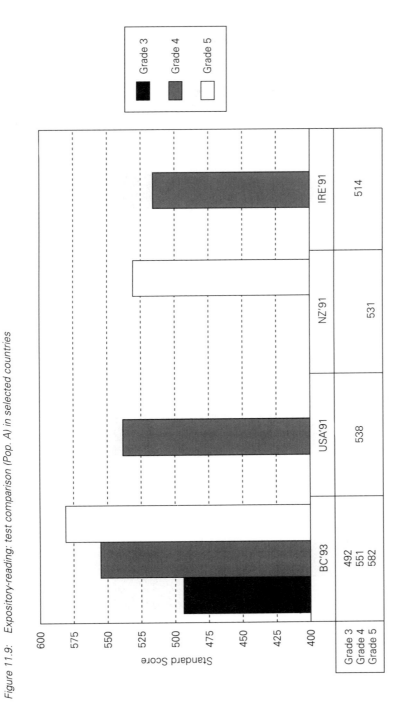

Figure 11.9: Expository-reading: test comparison (Pop. A) in selected countries

Source: BC Growth Study 1993

V. Froese

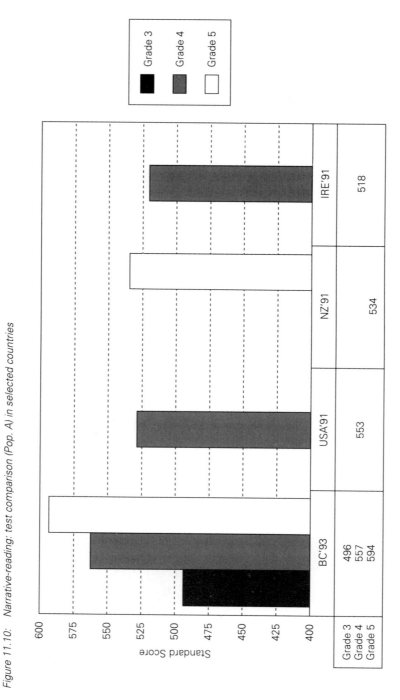

Figure 11.10: Narrative-reading: test comparison (Pop. A) in selected countries

Source: BC Growth Study 1993

182

Figure 11.11: BC students' growth of achievement in response to same passages (Pop. A and B)

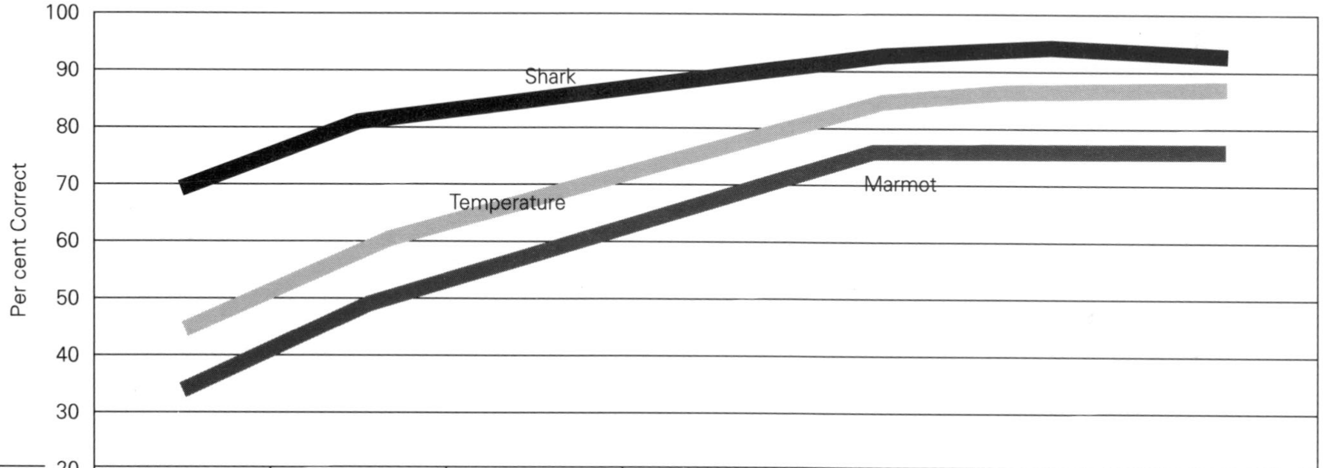

Grade Level	3	4	5		8	9	10
Shark	70.3	81.4	85.5		92.9	94.0	92.7
Marmot	34.4	48.5	58.1		76.5	76.2	76.3
Temperature	45.1	58.7	68.1		85.0	87.0	86.9

Per cent Correct

Shark   Marmot   Temperature

Note: Shark = narrative items; Marmot = expository items; Temperature = document items

Note by Editors

Because literacy enriches the individual and the State, both culturally and economically, it is not surprising that the IEA reading-literacy study has aroused considerable international interest and controversy. Explicit and public accountability for the considerable investment made by countries in their state educational systems is a political high priority.

Increasingly, the nations of the world acknowledge their membership of a global community in which children are entitled to an education. The mass-media have made it possible for more people than ever before to gain an appreciation of life in other cultures, including the variety of their educational systems. The relative standards of literacy of pupils being educated in different social and economic contexts and under a variety of pedagogic philosophies and their related curricular activities, are of both theoretical and practical importance. This has been demonstrated in the present chapter.

Quite clearly, the assessment of reading attainments and the comparison of standards across thirty-two school systems poses important and challenging conceptual and empirical problems to the test developer. The twenty-one different languages involved in the IEA study further compounded these difficulties. Interpreting the results requires expertise.

To assess the standards and progress in literacy of their pupils and also to identify and alleviate individual difficulties, teachers in many countries use a wide range of tests and assessment techniques. Frequently, these instruments are devised and constructed by specialists in measurement theory and practice. To the majority of teachers, 'test theory' probably has the appeal of fillet steak to a vegetarian. Whereas there are dietary substitutes for meat, an understanding of test theory is essential to professional accountability in education.

In the interests of the pupils and parents that the teaching profession exists to serve, it is important that its members become familiar with the concepts underpinning the Rasch model on which the IEA reading-literacy study reading scales in each domain were constructed. If the results obtained are to be understood by the teacher, the assumptions and rationale underpinning the Rasch model have to be appreciated. So too has its strengths and weaknesses.

Acquiring such understandings requires a willingness of the reader to venture into relatively unfamiliar conceptual areas. The exposition presented in the following chapter, by the head of the Danish National Institute for Educational Research, provides a fitting continuation and technical exposition of ideas central to the present chapter.

References

BRITISH COLUMBIA MINISTRY OF EDUCATION (1989) *Year 2000: A Curriculum and Assessment Framework for the Future* (Draft), Victoria, BC, BC Ministry of Education.

EDUCATION PRODUCT INFORMATION EXCHANGE (1977) *Report on a National Survey of the Nature and the Quality of Instructional Materials Most Used by Teachers and Learners* (Technical Rep. 1, 76), New York, EPIE Institute.

ELLEY, W.B. (1992) *How in the World do Students Read?*, The Hague, Netherlands, IEA.

FROESE, V. and CONRY, R. (1993) The IEA Literacy Growth Study in British Columbia: Report to the BC Ministry of Education, Unpublished.

GOODMAN, K., SHANNON, P., FREEMAN, Y. and MURPHY, S. (1988) *Report Card on Basal Readers*, New York, Richard C. Owen Publishers.

LUNDBERG, I. and LINNAKYLÄ, P. (1993) *Teaching Reading Around the World*, The Hague, Netherlands, International Association for the Evaluation of Educational Achievement.

POSTLETHWAITE, T.N. and ROSS, K.N. (1992) *Effective Schools in Reading: Implications for Educational Planners*, The Hague, Netherlands, IEA.

STAHL, N.A., HIGGINSON, B.C. and KING, J.R. (1993) 'Appropriate use of comparative literacy research in the 1990s', *Journal of Reading*, **37**, 2, pp. 104–13.

THORNDIKE, R.L. (1973) *Reading Comprehension Education in Fifteen Countries*, New York, Halsted Press.

Chapter 12

The IEA Study of Reading Literacy

P. Allerup

Summary

This chapter provides a brief overview of the initial statistical analyses of student data employed in the IEA reading-literacy study conducted in the years 1990–1. Attention is drawn to how reading theories may relate to the design of the study and the construction of test materials. The test booklets and questionnaires relating to reading related factual information such as 'number of books in home', used in the study are described. The investigation found that no single variable or set of variables can 'explain' variation in children's reading performance but certain trends are identifiable.

Introduction

It is the aim of this chapter to present a brief overview of the initial statistical analyses of student data employed in the IEA reading-literacy study conducted in the years 1990–1. From the point of view of a statistician the intention is, accordingly to emphasize merely technical aspects raised during the analysis of student data rather than addressing theoretical aspects of the process of reading and, eventually, how reading theories might be related to the design of the study, the construction of test materials, questionnaires etc. The following will summarize the design of the study; the construction of three international reading scales used for comparing student abilities all over the world; and finally how student reading performances were related to background factors sampled jointly with the test results.

Design and Method

The Study

The idea of setting up an international study, like the IEA reading-literacy study, originated from the ambition to study 'reasons' for being a high or low achieving student in terms of 'explaining' background factors. In fact, many national studies aiming at revealing proper 'explanations' fail to succeed, because the variation of background factors *within* a country is limited due to homogeneous educational systems — and, hence, a study on an international basis can bring about adequate variation in these factors in order to reinforce the relation between reading performance and background.

The study was conducted as a pilot in 1990 and a main study in the years 1990–1 on two populations of students: 9-year-olds from grades 3/4 (called Pop. A) and 14-year-olds from grades 8/9 (called Pop. B) in thirty-two countries around the world:

Belgium	Finland	Hong Kong
Italy	The Philippines	Sweden
Venezuela	Botswana	France
Hungary	The Netherlands	Portugal
Switzerland	Zimbabwe	Canada
Germany(W)	Iceland	Norway
Singapore	Thailand	Cyprus
Germany(E)	Indonesia	Nigeria
Slovenia	Trinidad	Denmark
Greece	Ireland	New Zealand
Spain	The USA	

The major aims of the study adopted by the National Research Coordinators (NRCs) included the following:

- to describe the voluntary reading activities of 9 and 14-year-olds;
- to identify differences in policies and instructional practices in reading, and to study the ways in which they relate to students' achievement and voluntary reading;
- to produce valid international tests and questionnaires which could be used to investigate reading-literacy development in other countries; and
- to provide national baseline data suitable for monitoring changes in reading-literacy levels and patterns over time.

The study should also be seen as a continuation of earlier IEA reading studies (Thorndike, 1973); it was not initiated from a set of strictly formulated reading hypotheses which, like in other smaller studies are tested directly, one by one, by adopting relevant statistical tests. The data were collected in all participating countries according to sampling procedures accepted by all NRCs and were, later on, sent to the International Coordinating Centre (ICC) situated in Hamburg, where all subsequent data analyses were undertaken. The sampling of data was carried out in such a way that conclusions drawn from data could be considered as representative for students and teachers in the countries at the specified grades. Throughout the study period several meetings between the NRCs and the Hamburg ICC were held and decisions as to the analysis strategy, forming of conclusions, publication plans etc. were discussed during such conferences.

The complete test materials comprised test booklets to the students, questionnaires to students; questionnaires to teachers and school principals and, on local initiative, a series of so-called 'national options' to be added to test booklets and questionnaires. The information provided by national options was, however, not subject to the international cross-country analyses but is now available for further within-country analyses.

Immediately after completion of the first international statistical analyses on all data, three books have been published: *How in the world do students read?* (Elley, 1992), which is the main reference for this chapter, *Teaching reading around the world* (Lundberg and Linnakylä, 1992) and *Effective Schools in reading* (Postlethwaite and Ross, 1992). A book containing detailed descriptions of all technical aspects during the study will appear soon (Beaton, 1994).

The international books will be succeeded by a number of national reports in the future, after the data were available to all countries as a consequence of publication of the first international books.

The student test booklets consisted of text passages to be read by the students and, after having read the passage, a number of questions — which are the items of the test — were then presented in either closed multiple response-category form (mc) or as open-ended questions. The mc-questions were constructed usually with four answer categories, only one of which could be considered to represent the correct answer. An example is given in Figure 12.1.

The passages were, for both populations A and B, grouped in advance into three so-called domains:

Figure 12.1: Text passage from population A, expository domain

The Walrus

The walrus is easy to recognize because it has two large teeth sticking out of its mouth. These teeth are called eye teeth.

The walrus lives in cold seas. If the water freezes over, the walrus keeps a hole free of ice either by swimming round and round in the water, or by hacking off the edge of the ice with its eye teeth. The walrus can also use its skull to knock a hole in the ice.

The walrus depends on its eye teeth for many things. For example, when looking for food a walrus dives to the bottom of the sea and uses its eye teeth to scrape off clams. The walrus also uses its eye teeth to pull itself onto the ice. It needs its eye teeth to attack or kill a seal and eat it, or to defend itself if attacked by a polar bear.

The walrus may grow very big and very old. A full-grown male is almost 4 m long and weighs more than 1000 kg. It may reach an age of 30 years.

The walrus sleeps on the ice or on a piece of rock sticking out of the water, but it is also able to sleep in the water.

1. Where does the walrus live?

A☐ In very cold water
B☐ In tropical countries
C☐ On the bottom of lakes
D☐ In cold forest country

2. How long can a walrus live?

A☐ 2 years
B☐ 4 years
C☐ 30 years
D☐ 100 years

- *Narrative* text types: Texts that tell a story or give the order in which things happen (Pop. A: twenty-two items, Pop. B: twenty-nine items).
- *Expository* text types: Texts that describe things or people or explain how things work or why things happened (Pop. A: twenty-one items, Pop. B: twenty-six items).
- *Documents* text types: Tables, charts, diagrams, maps (Pop. A: twenty-three items, Pop. B: thirty-four items).

The intention behind the grouping of items into domains was to be able to assess and compare student abilities using index values or score values as outcomes for each specific domain.

The questionnaires filled out by students, teachers and school principals encompassed a variety of aspects ranging from questions to students like 'Number of books in home', 'Hours TV-watching' over instructional strategies for the teachers like 'Use of materials you have prepared yourself', 'Ask questions to deepen understanding' to factual school information like 'Size of school library' and 'classroom size'.

Altogether 656 variables containing test results and responses to questions were transferred back to the national centres after the completion of the international analyses. Counting about 200,000 participating students all over the world located in the two populations, the total number of observations quickly adds up to approximately 100 million bits of information. No doubt, one might say, that it should be possible to find at least a few significant relations since, using conventional levels of significance for statistical tests, around 5 per cent type-I erroneous conclusions should anyway occur. One of the major technical issues was, in fact, to assess true levels of significance, when carrying out so many statistical tests as intended in the study.

A Statistical Model for Analysis of Item Responses

Although responses to the test items were originally sampled as multiple choices and, certainly, important studies can be undertaken to see why and how 'distractors' (i.e., the wrong answer categories) are used, it was an early decision to conduct the international analyses on the levels: correct/non correct/missing for each item. Furthermore, in complete accordance with the very idea behind the concept of a domain, it was decided to construct index values, or domain scores, for each domain, when measures of student 'performance' were ready to be analysed in relation to background variables, rather than analysing single-item information in relation to background variables. By this, it was tacitly assumed that all items within a fixed domain actually belong to one common, latent continuum of 'difficulties' defined by the domain. The basic set of observations within a domain can be visualized by the following frame of reference displayed in Table 12.1.

Let the number of correctly solved items $r_1, \ldots, r_n$ across all k items in a domain be the manifest measure of student ability and, likewise, let the total item-scores (across all n students) $s_1, \ldots, s_k$ be manifest measures of the item difficulty in the sense, that these scores exhaust *all information* about the student abilities and the item difficulties, respectively. This is equivalent, in statistical terms, to acknowledging these two sets of scores as sufficient statistics for student abilities σ_v v

Table 12.1:   Item-responses model within a domain

		Item No.	Scores
		1 . . . . i . . . . k	(r_v)
Student No.	1		
	2	1 0 1 1	a_1.
	.	1 1 0 . 0	a_2.
	v	. . . . a_{vi}	a_v.
	.	.	
	.	.	
	.	.	
	n	.	
Item totals (s_1)		a_i . . . . a_1 . . . . a_k	$a_{..}$

Note: Responses a_{vi} = 0,1 from n individuals to k domain items with individual ability parameters σ_v v = 1, . . . , n and item difficulty parameters θ_i i = 1, . . . , k

= 1, . . . , n and item difficulties θ_i i = 1, . . . , k. At the same time a user–defined statistical model for analysing such schemes of n by k correct–non correct observations has been requested. In fact, Rasch (Rasch, 1971) proved, that the statements of joint sufficiency of the item scores and student scores are unambiguously associated with the following probabilistic model (1) for the single-item response a_{vi} = 0 (non correct) or a_{vi} = 1 (correct) provided by student No. v to item No. i, with θ_i denoting item difficulty (or easiness) and σ_v denoting student ability:

$$(1) \quad p(a_{vi} = 1) = \frac{e^{\theta_i + \sigma_v}}{1 + e^{\theta_i + \sigma_v}}$$

If the Rasch model (1) — also called the one parameter logistic model — fits the data in Table 12.1, the items are said to be *homogeneous*. One of the major problems for the initial item analyses in the IEA study was two-sided: to test for item homogeneity *within* each country and *across* the countries. In fact, oniy if consistent item difficulties θ_i i = 1, . . . , k across *all* countries could be identified, would one, indeed, have a common reading scale acting as a fixed 'ruler' for measuring student ability in every country. It is, however one of the essential attributes of the Rasch model, that if the model fits data the responses to *any* subset of homogeneous items can be used for assessing student abilities σ_v v = 1, . . . , n; therefore, if a few items fail to be homogeneous across all countries — typically in a way that an item 'works' (i.e., is homogeneous) *within* some countries but has to be omitted internationally e.g., because of strongly varying difficulty — a reading scale still exists. This is formed, then, by a set of core items applicable to all countries and, depending on the country, extended by

Figure 12.2:   Item characteristic curves for the Rasch model (1), the two-parameter model (3) and the three-parameter model (4)

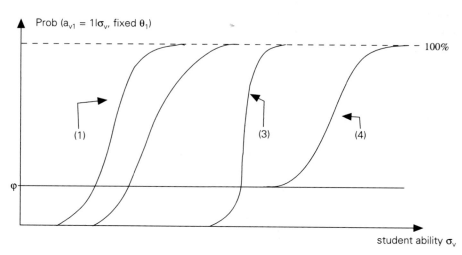

extra homogeneous items. The International Reading Scale for each domain is, consequently, a total reference set of items which, in part is used from one country to another. Underlying these technical efforts is, of course, a wish to utilize as much of the item information as possible in each country.

The struggle for homogeneous items is far from being just an academic exercise, since it is easy to demonstrate (e.g., through computer simulations) that a standard t-test for equal means of two populations judged by student scores, can be significant exclusively from the fact, that the two sets of student scores are outcomes from group-specific inhomogeneous items and, hence cannot be properly ascribed to differences in levels of ability.

The Rasch model (1) is a member of the class of Item Response Theory (IRT) models, where differences between the models can be characterized by differences in the Item Characteristic Curve (ICC), i.e., the probability of a correct response to item No. i with difficulty θ_i examined as a function of the student ability σ_v:

(2)   ICC (σ_v) = Prob $(a_{vi} = 1 \mid \sigma_v$, fixed $\theta_i)$

The Rasch model — or the one parameter model — has parallel ICCs for all items, the position on the X-axis being determined by the value of the item parameter θ_i, see Figure 12.2. The two parameter model (3) (Lord and Novick, 1968) is characterized by intersecting ICCs — i.e., slopes of the ICCs differ from item to item. Many psychometricians consider items with high slope values — viz., high discrimination power — being an advantage, because such items 'discriminate' well between abilities on the X-axis, but only under the one-parameter model is the concept of student ability related in a simple way to the number of correct responses across items.

Finally, the three-parameter model (4) includes yet another feature of the ICCs; when the ICC is not approaching the X-axis completely but smooths out on a horizontal line, φ above the X-axis, it is interpreted as 'the probability cannot be lower than φ due to guessing'.

$$(3) \quad p(a_{vi} = 1) = \frac{e^{\delta_i(\theta_i + \sigma_v)}}{1 + e^{\delta_i(\theta_i + \sigma_v)}}$$

In model (3) the item *discrimination parameters* $\delta_1, \ldots, \delta_k$ must be estimated from data together with the θ — and σ parameters.

In the three parameter model (4) the parameter φ, which measures the probability for obtaining a correct response *by chance* is introduced:

$$(4) \quad p(a_{vi} = 1) = \frac{e^{\delta_i(\theta_i + \sigma_v)}}{1 + e^{\delta_i(\theta_i + \sigma_v)}}(1 - \varphi) + \varphi$$

For a number of technical reasons the three-parameter model was abandoned as a basis for analysing the IEA data (the model is outside the family of exponential distributions and the interpretation of the parameters is ambiguous). A measure of the degree of guessing was, however constructed under the one-parameter Rasch model.

When analysing the IEA data it became clear, that if the Rasch model (1) were to be the one and only theoretical frame of reference for evaluating item homogeneity, quite a number of items would have been dropped from the test booklets. One quite often met cause for misfit was the observation that the empirical ICCs across (independent) samples of data showed consistently biased values of the item discriminations, δ_i being significantly different from unity, which is the value required by the Rasch model (1). For this reason the reference model for the IEA item analyses became the two-parameter model (3), provided that the item discriminations were *not* very *far from unity.*

Test of Fit — Creating Three International Reading Scales

Statistical tests of fit were conducted by means of conditional inference, where the set of ability parameters are eliminated by conditioning (student scores are sufficient statistics for the abilities). Some test statistics are referring to all items *simultaneously* but most of the statistics are referring to one item at a time using the Item Characteristic Curves (ICCs) or, more precisely using CICCs which are the conditional ICCs, the probability of a correct response *given* the value of the student score, which is dependent on complex functions of the item difficulties but independent of the ability parameters σ_v $v = 1, \ldots, n$.

The test statistics used in the study for testing the Rasch model (1) or the two-parameter model (3) were the following:

1. DIST — distance measure
   For each item and for each score level the observed number of students with correct responses to the item are compared with the model expected number.

2. DIFINT
   This is the internal difference between item difficulties estimated from the 50 per cent lowest scoring students and the 50 per cent highest scoring students. DIFINT should be (stochastically) equal to zero if the model fits the data.

3. TESHAPE
   This is the test of shape of the item characteristic curve 'ICC.' It is tested if the ICC is compatible with the one-parameter Rasch model or, alternatively, the two-parameter model with item discrimination different from unity. If this test is rejected the ICC is beyond any 'reasonable' shape for the analyses (e.g., decreasing probability of correct response with increasing ability).

4. TEEXT
   This is the test of external variable, viz., test of sex bias. A Fisher exact test (conditional on score group) compares the frequency of correct responses across sex in a 2 by 2 contingency table. A chi-square statistic aggregated across all score groups is calculated.

5. THETOT
   This is the theta parameter for the total data set, i.e., the estimated item difficulty for each item; items must have consistent item difficulties across all countries. Although one item could be homogeneous *within* a country, it may happen that the item shows varying difficulties *across* different countries, and students in one country could, then, profit from such nonhomogeneity when comparing student abilities. In such cases the item should be omitted from the International Reading Scale.

6. ITDISCR — item discrimination

   If the item discrimination (slope of ICC) is unity it conforms with the one-parameter Rasch model (1). If not, one might accept the item for inclusion in the international scale — provided the TESHAPE test is not significant, the item discrimination is not very far from unity and consistent values across all countries is observed. The estimation of student abilities can then take place in accordance with the two-parameter model.

The results of applying the test statistics Nos. 1–6 to the item responses *within* each of the three domains were that some items had to be dropped from all further analysis because they revealed misfit using most of the test statistics. Such items were not considered for inclusion in The International Reading Scale. Besides, some items had to be dropped from specific countries, mainly due to varying item difficulties across countries. Such items could be included in the reference set of items for The International Reading Scale and be used in the specific countries. According to simple Rasch model (1) the use of different sets of items for estimation of student abilities across different countries is not a statistical problem, since, as said, *any* subset of a homogeneous set of items can be used for the estimation of student abilities. Of course, the accuracy by which student abilities are estimated is dependent on the number of items (but very little on the level of difficulties).

By these procedures, three subsets of the original sets of items were identified as the three reference sets of items called the International Reading Scales.

Estimation of Student Abilities

The estimation of student abilities takes place *after* having estimated the domain-specific item parameters approved by the six test statistics. The maximum likelihood equations for estimating the student-ability parameters $\sigma_v, v = 1, \ldots, n$ are then the following (5) and (6) — showed for the one and the two-parameter model, respectively:

$$(5) \quad r = \sum_{i=1}^{K} \frac{e^{\theta_i + \sigma_v}}{1 + e^{\theta_i + \sigma_v}} \qquad r = 1, \ldots, K-1$$

$$(6) \quad r = \sum_{i=1}^{K} \frac{e^{\delta_i(\theta_i + \sigma_v)}}{1 + e^{\delta_i(\theta_i + \sigma_v)}} \qquad r = \delta_1, \ldots, \sum \delta_j - \text{Min}(\delta_j)$$

If a student fails to respond to an item *in between* two other items, obviously considered (correct or non correct), one may agree to 'non correct' as a fair coding of such a 'missing' response. If, on the other hand a series of 'missings' are observed *in the end* of a test session, with no intermediate correct or non-correct responses, one would certainly have as a valid hypothesis, that the student has never considered these items — maybe because of lack of time. The 'not reached' items can, accordingly, be identified by simply counting backwards from the end of the test, until an item is observed, which is either correct or non-correct.

Several views on whether 'not reached' items would be properly scored as non-correct or 'missing' were forwarded during the discussion of the statistical analyses; a purely statistical judgment of the 'not reached' items is, however available, by asking, whether the test of fit of the model (being at the same time a test of item homogeneity) 'accepts' a scoring of the 'not reached' items as non-correct (zero) responses. The structure of item homogeneity (= accepted model) 'predicts' the expected values of the 'not-reached' items and ordinary comparisons between observed and expected responses can then be undertaken.

The data files containing all data originally collected by each country and the estimated student abilities based on both 'principles' of evaluating the 'not reached' items were later on sent back to each country. All international analyses, and the first international report in particular were, however, based on the coding of 'not reached' as non-correct responses (Elley, 1992). One reason for the low rank of e.g., Denmark and Germany (E) in the leading league tables (see Figure 12.3) in the report can be ascribed to this mixing up of speed and comprehension.

Simple Comparisons of Students in Thirty-two Countries

Using the estimation technique described above, estimated student abilities for approximately 100,000 students in Pop. A and 100,000 students in Pop. B were obtained — yielding three domain-specific estimates. For technical reasons the measures of abilities σ_v $v = 1, \ldots, n$ were re-scaled to mean = 500 and standard deviation = 100 on an international basis. Six tables arising from three domains by two populations emerge directly for each country, and Figure 12.3 shows, as an example, how the student abilities for the Narrative domain Pop. A were presented as ranked performances for twenty seven of the thirty-two participating countries (Elley, ibid.). Using Bonferroni adjusted-confidence limits for the evaluation of differences, the picture

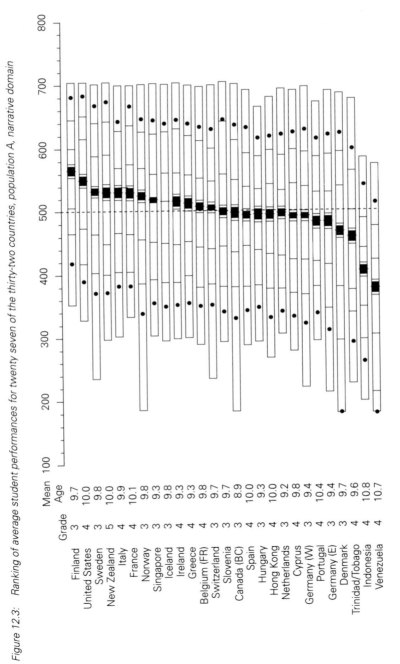

Figure 12.3: Ranking of average student performances for twenty seven of the thirty-two countries, population A, narrative domain

Source: Elley, 1992

leaves no doubt of significant differences between the levels of performance across the countries.

Conclusive comparisons between the thirty-two countries by means of the directly estimated student abilities σ_v v = 1, . . . , n were, however inappropriate considering, among others, the highly distinctive socio-economic conditions in which the various national educational systems are embedded. As a consequence, the crude comparisons of the abilities between countries were initially modified by accepting six different indicators of national development:

- GNP per capita;
- public expenditure of per student on education;
- life expectancy;
- per cent low birth rate;
- newspapers per 1,000; and
- per cent adult literacy as a framework for comparing the σ_v's.

In practice, the six indicators were combined (equal weight) into *one* CDI-index value (Composite Development Index) which was, then, through a simple linear regression of ability on CDI used to calculate CDI-*expected* reading performances. This is done in order to see if, on average, a country is performing 'less' or 'better' than expected by the value of the CDI index. Some countries, by this exercise, could then 'move' from a relatively low position to a position where a global judgment of the results would be 'good' or, even 'better than expected'.

Reading Performance in Relation to Background Factors

The background factors include a number of variables, collected through ordinary questionnaires, devised to reveal systematic background information at the level of analysis given by a student, at the level of a class and, even, at the level of a school. A first issue was, therefore, how one could relate *individual* student performance σ_v v = 1, . . . , n to background information defined on other levels of analysis. A rigorous solution would, e.g., require an appropriate definition of the performance of a *full* class — when analyses on the level of classes are in question. The practical solution was, however to relate to *average* student reading performances, whenever performance was related to background — the average calculated across the relevant 'unity', it being within a class or across all students in a school.

The statistical analyses of relationship between student performance and background factors used a mixture of several strategies but

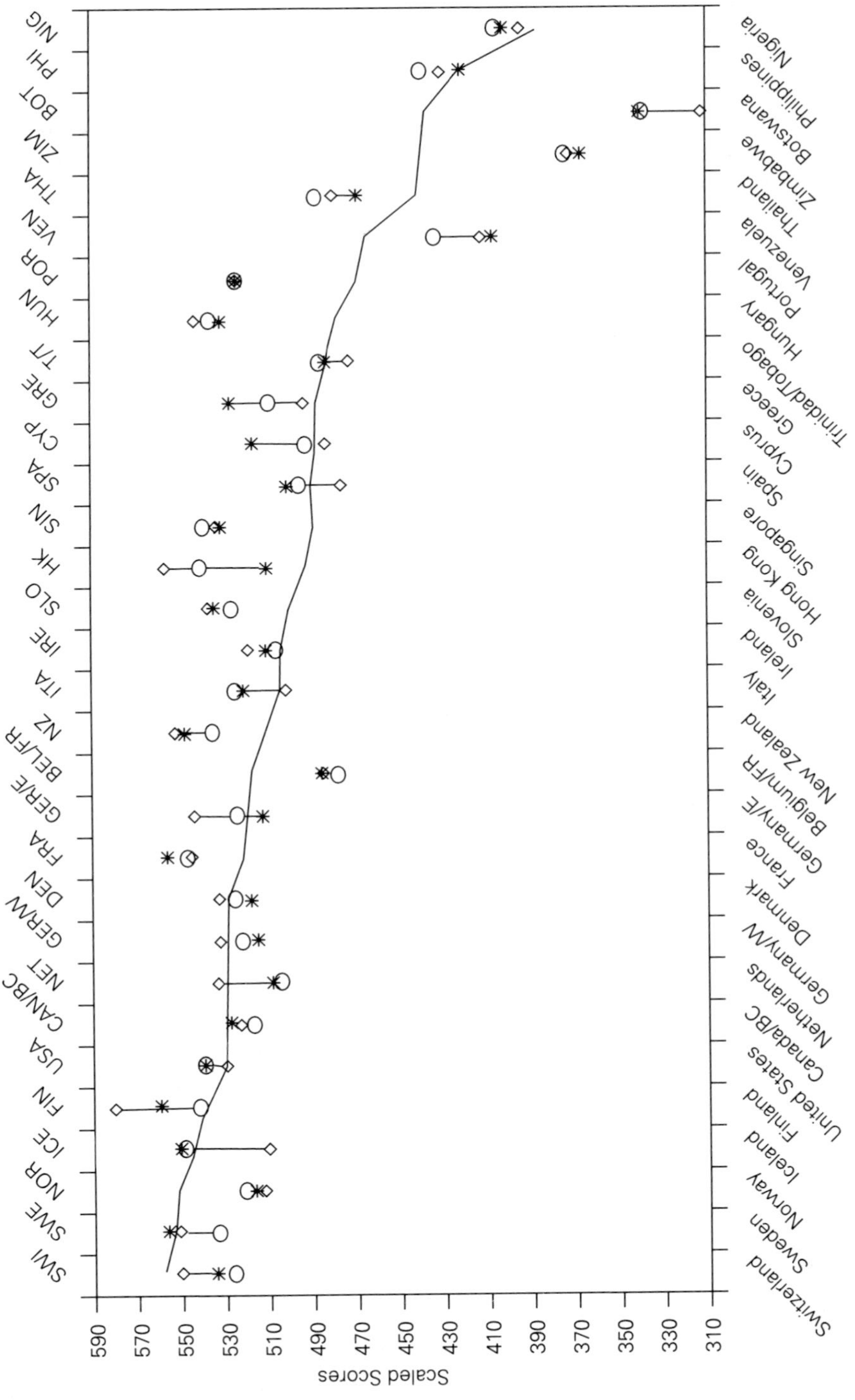

Figure 12.4: Scaled scores by domain compared with Composite Development Index (CDI), population B (31 Countries)

Source: Elley, 1992

underlying all attempts was the fact that performance measured by Rasch scores σ_v $v = 1, \ldots, n$ was related to background factors *one by one*. By this, one could, unfortunately, be overlooking the likelihood that several background factors themselves are intercorrelated. In fact, in order to illustrate this point, imagine that the correlation between a variable A and a background variable B is studied, and data on a third background variable C are available:

B =	1	2	3	4	
A = 1	396	840	1273	1153	
A = 2	102	198	424	381	for C = 1 and C = 2 together

$p = 0.001$ significant correlation between A and B (Chi-square test)
— same table sub divided according to C:

	C = 1						C = 2			
B =	1	2	3	4		B =	1	2	3	4
A = 1	304	666	894	720			92	174	379	433
A = 2	38	85	93	84			64	113	321	297

$p = 0.60$ $p = 0.14$

The (marginal) correlation between A and B is seen to be significant ($p = 0.001$) while analysed for each of the two levels of the third variable $C = 1$ or $C = 2$, the correlation between A and B becomes nonsignificant ($p = 0.60$ and $p = 0.14$). This situation is described as 'conditional independence between A and B', i.e., the simple correlation between A and B ($p = 0.001$) can be 'explained' by the third variable C. It will be part of future statistical analyses to conduct such multivariate analyses; the initial statistical analyses in the first international report are all built upon marginal analyses (Elley, 1992).

One attempt to investigate the influence of educational factors on the national-achievement levels was to select a series of background variables which were *a priori* known to vary across the thirty-two countries. The idea was simply to isolate the values from the ten highest scoring countries and the ten lowest scoring countries from these variables in order to look for differences. The differences between high and low-scoring countries were expressed in standardized terms (relative to a standard deviation), since the scales behind each background variable differ in nature. The top of the table summarizing these analyses for Pop. A is shown in Table 12.2.

Table 12.2: *Differences between ten highest and ten lowest-scoring countries*

Policy indicator	Highest 10 countries	Lowest 10 countries	Diff/SD	Proportion of SD	Advantage for...
1 Starting age of instruction	6.3 yrs	5.9 yrs	0.40/0.65	0.62	Later start
2 % Students in pre-school	68.7	53.8	14.9/31.36	0.48	Preschool enrollment
3 Class size in sample	25.1	24.9	0.2/5.72	0.03	No difference
4 % Female teachers in sample	79.7	76.3	3.4/16.53	0.20	No difference
5 School days per year	178.9	191.6	12.7/19.08	0.67	Shorter year
6 Hours instruction per week	21.7	20.6	1.1/3.49	0.32	More hours instruction
7 Phonic regularity of language	2.6	3.2	0.6/1.21	0.50	Less regular language
8 % Multigrade classes	20.3	24.4	3.1/23.2	0.18	No difference
9 Years teaching this class	1.57 yrs	1.56 yrs	0.01/0.60	0.02	No difference
10 Years teacher education	13.80	12.6	1.2/1.75	0.69	More education for teachers
11 % Other language speaking teachers	10.7	9.8	0.9/21.32	0.04	No difference
12 Easy access to books in community	74.2	62.0	12.2/15.2	0.80	Easy access to books
13 Size of school library	3.50	2.56	0.94/1.97	0.48	Large school library
14 Large classroom libraries	45.6	22.8	22.8/22.7	1.00	Large classroom library
15 Textbooks per student	1.74	1.59	0.15/0.47	0.32	More textbooks
16 Frequency borrow books from library	3.25	2.95	0.30/0.51	0.59	More books borrowed
17 Time on teaching the language	8.12 hrs	7.07 hrs	1.05/2.41	0.44	More time on language teaching
18 Frequency silent reading in class	3.43	3.36	0.09/0.93	0.08	No difference
19 Frequency teachers read to class	2.76	2.25	0.51/1.18	0.43	More teacher reading to class
20 % teachers give frequent reading tests	38.0	51.4	13.4/29.0	0.46	Fewer tests
21 Speed of word recognition	86.9	77.4	9.53/6.32	1.51	Faster word recognition

Note: No adjustments for CDI
Source: Elley, 1992

Interestingly, a similar table based on the CDI-adjusted performances can be constructed and, as expected by parallel arguments forwarded for the A,B,C table, a different picture emerged. A summary of the conclusions for Pop. A with and without CDI-adjustments is shown in Table 12.3.

Whenever a difference between the top-ten and the lowest ten countries was evaluated for a specific background factor, a tentative

Table 12.3: Evaluation of differences between ten highest and ten lowest-scoring countries

Advantage shown for:	Population A		Population B	
	Unadjusted	Adjusted for CDI	Unadjusted	adjusted for CDI
1. Smaller classes	—	no	yes	—
2. More female teachers	—	yes	no	—
3. Shorter school year	yes	yes	yes	yes
4. More hours per week	yes	yes	no	—
5. More years teacher education	yes	yes	yes	yes
6. More textbooks per student	yes	—	yes	no
7. Larger school library	yes	yes	yes	yes
8. More formal tests	no	yes	no	—
9. Earlier starting age	no	yes		
10. High preschool enrollment	yes	—		
11. More multigrade classes	—	—		
12. More years with same class	—	no		
13. More books in community	yes	—		
14. Larger classroom library	yes	yes		
15. More library books borrowed	yes	yes		
16. More time teaching language	yes	yes		
17. More silent reading in class	—	yes		
18. More teacher reading to class	—	yes		
19. Students faster word recognition	yes	yes		
20. Better pupil-teacher ratio			yes	—
21. Principal evaluates teachers more often			no	—
22. More general homework given			yes	yes
23. More reading homework given			no	—
24. More resources for reading			yes	yes
25. More individual tuition			yes	yes

Note: With and without adjustments for CDI
Source: Elley, 1992

t-test, using 0.30 as cut point, was applied for classifying the particular difference as 'important' or 'not important'.

More conventional statistical approaches were used when factors like gender and home versus school language were analysed; in fact, such analyses were conducted as ordinary two sample t-tests. The results of analysing gender differences in Pop. A are presented in Table 12.4.

Another set of important background factors for understanding differences in achievement levels is defined by 'size of school library', 'number of books in home', 'hours of daily TV watching,' 'degree of voluntary reading' and a variable measuring how urbanized the environment of the school is (on a scale with 'village' at the one end and 'city' at the other end).

Typically, such analyses give rise to statistical judgments where whole 'curves' are analysed, see Figure 12.5 for an example.

Table 12.4: *Statistical evaluation of gender differences in score levels, population A*

Country	Average score (s.e.)		Difference	Standard score difference
	Boys	Girls		
Belgium/Fr	503 (4.5)	512 (4.5)	9	.12
Canada/BC	495 (5.4)	506 (5.4)	11*	.14
Cyprus	479 (3.2)	484 (3.2)	5	.07
Denmark	463 (5.5)	489 (4.9)	26*	.34
Finland	564 (4.5)	575 (4.5)	11*	.14
France	530 (5.7)	533 (5.6)	3	.04
Germany/E	490 (6.3)	509 (6.1)	19*	.24
Germany/W	501 (3.9)	508 (3.8)	7	.09
Greece	499 (4.4)	510 (4.2)	11*	.14
Hong Kong	512 (3.7)	524 (3.6)	12*	.15
Hungary	495 (3.8)	504 (3.6)	9	.11
Iceland	508 (0.0)	528 (0.0)	20*	.24
Indonesia	394 (3.6)	397 (3.7)	3	.04
Ireland	502 (5.2)	517 (5.0)	15*	.19
Italy	525 (5.2)	537 (5.1)	12*	.15
Netherlands	483 (5.4)	488 (5.2)	5	.06
New Zealand	519 (4.1)	539 (4.0)	20*	.25
Norway	517 (4.6)	533 (4.0)	16*	.18
Portugal	474 (4.5)	483 (4.5)	9	.11
Singapore	510 (1.3)	521 (1.3)	11*	.14
Slovenia	491 (3.3)	506 (3.4)	15*	.19
Spain	500 (3.4)	508 (3.3)	8*	.10
Sweden	533 (4.4)	546 (4.3)	13*	.16
Switzerland	507 (4.2)	517 (4.2)	10*	.13
Trinidad/Tobago	443 (4.3)	460 (4.1)	17*	.21
United States	543 (3.6)	552 (3.4)	9*	.11
Venezuela	379 (4.2)	392 (3.9)	13*	.16

Note: * = significant difference (.05 level)
Source: Elley, 1992

In Figure 12.5 a couple of countries are displayed having similar curve patterns; other patterns (e.g., constant curves) could also be identified, and a discussion was undertaken of the distinctive shape of the curve, valid for a group of countries with the specific curve pattern, in relation to the levels of student performance.

Messages for Teachers

In the introduction to *How in the world do students read?* (Elley, 1992) a brief summary of the findings in the first international screening of the data is presented. If one would have hoped for the finding of a few, important key factors which could account for most of the variance found in the student achievement levels around the world, one would have been disappointed. It turned out different. No single variable or

Figure 12.5:   Pattern of decreasing reading achievement with increasing daily TV viewing, population A

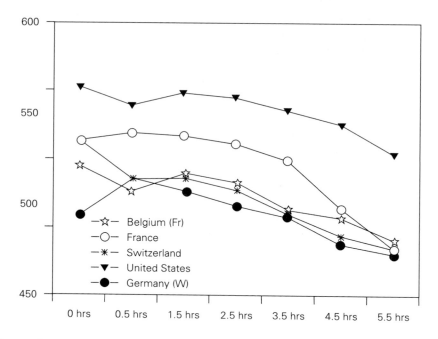

Source: Elley, 1992

small group of variables can 'explain' why the students performed well or not so well; future analyses will, however proceed to investigate more details in the national-data sets and may reveal structures which provide useful information to national educational planners.

The principal content of the executive summary was the following:

1. National achievement levels
    The students of Finland showed the highest reading literacy levels at both 9 and 14 years of age in almost all domains.
2. Domain profiles
    The levels of reading literacy achieved in each country are highly correlated across all three domains, and across both age groups.
3. Economic and social context
    For most countries, the levels of reading literacy are closely related to their national indices of economic development, health, and adult literacy.

4. Home language
   The students of Singapore achieved high levels of literacy in spite of the fact that they were instructed in a non-native language from the beginning of their schooling. This finding is unexpected and potentially important.

5. Age of beginning instruction
   Formal instruction did not begin until age 7 in four of the ten highest scoring countries at each level. Apparently a late start is not a serious handicap in reading instruction, when judged at age 9. However, when achievement scores were adjusted for economic and social circumstances across all countries, an earlier start was generally found to be an advantage.

6. Differences between high and low-scoring countries.
   Factors which consistently differentiated high-scoring and low-scoring countries were large school libraries, large classroom libraries, regular book borrowing, frequent silent reading in class, frequent story reading aloud by teachers, and more scheduled hours spent teaching the language. Several countries with low scores reported very little experience with formal tests, but above a threshold level, this factor was not found to differentiate high and low-achieving countries.

7. Less important differentiating factors
   At the 9-year-old level, no perceptible advantage was found in reading literacy levels of countries which had high enrolment ratios in preschool, or generally smaller classes, or large numbers of multigrade classes, or longer school years, or policies of keeping the teachers with the same class through successive grades. While many of these policies were found regularly in high-scoring countries, the data suggest that their importance may well be only a function of relative affluence and community factors outside the school.

8. Gender differences
   Girls achieved at higher levels than boys in all countries in population A, and in most countries in population B.

9. Language differences
   Children whose home language is different from that of the school show lower literacy levels in all countries at both age levels.

10. Urban–rural differences
    Urban children achieve at higher levels than rural children in most education systems. However, in a few highly developed

countries, rural students show literacy levels which are as good as, or even better than their city age mates.

11. Importance of books

The availability of books is a key factor in reading literacy. The highest scoring countries typically provide their students with greater access to books in the home, in nearby community libraries and book stores, and in the school.

12. Links with television

Television viewing occupies much of students out-of-school discretionary time. In a few countries large numbers of children watch TV for more than five hours per day. Those who watch TV often tend to score at lower levels than who watch less, as a general rule.

15. Voluntary reading

The amount of voluntary out-of-school book reading that students report is positively related to their achievement levels. The relationship is clearer at the 9-year-old level, and in the developing countries at age 14.

Conclusion

The technical underpinnings of the IEA study of reading literacy have been briefly outlined. Within the text are included references that will enable the reader to follow up the ideas presented. As in so much of education, for both teachers and pupils, one of the best ways of checking whether or not a particular line of argument has been understood is to see whether one can explain and justify it to others.

References

ALLERUP, P. (1994a) 'Development of the reading scales', in BEATON, A.E. (Ed) *IEA Reading Literacy Study; Technical Report*, International Association for the Evaluation of Educational Research, The Hague.

ALLERUP, P. (1994b) *Rasch Measurement Theory of The International Encyclopedia of Education*, 2nd ed., Pergamon Press.

ELLEY, W.B. (1992) *'How in the World do Students Read?'*, The International Association for the Evaluation of Educational Achievement, The Hague.

LORD, F.M. and NOVICK, M.R. (1968) *Statistical Theories of Mental Test Scores*, MA, Addison Wesley.

LUNDBERG, I. and LINNAKYLÄ, P. (1992) *Teaching Reading Around the World*, The International Association for the Evaluation of Educational Achievement, The Hague.

Postlethwaite, T.N. and Ross, K. (1992) *Effective Schools in Reading — implications for Educational Planners*, The International Association for the Evaluation of Educational Achievement, The Hague.

Rasch, G. (1960) *Probabilistic Models for Some Intelligence and Attainment Tests*, Danish Institute for Educational Research.

Rasch, G. (1971) 'Proof that the necessary condition for the validity of the multiplicative dichotomic model is also sufficient', Dupl. note, Statistical Institute, Copenhagen.

Thorndike, R.L. (1973) *Reading Comprehension Education in Fifteen Countries*, Uppsala, Almqvist and Wiksell.

Notes on Contributors

Pamela Owen has worked as a primary teacher and as a secondary School English teacher before moving into literacy research at the Centre for Formative Assessment Studies, School of Education, University of Manchester. Here she worked on the development of a literacy assessment scheme and then moved into the development of SAT English material for the STAIR consortium. From 1991 she has been senior lecturer at S Martin's College with responsibility for the design and delivery of reading and language courses in ITT. She has run several courses on reading for serving teachers and was conference coordinator of the 1993 International Reading Conference held in Lancaster.
Contact address: English Department, University College of St. Martin, Lancaster LAI 3JD. FAX: 0254 68943

Peter D. Pumfrey is professor of education and head of the Centre for Educational Guidance and Special Needs at the University of Manchester. He is a qualified and experienced teacher having been employed in mainstream schools and Remedial Education Services for fourteen years prior to training and working as an LEA educational psychologist.

His research and training interests are in the identification and alleviation of literacy difficulties in general and of reading difficulties in particular. In addition, he is concerned with the assessment and improvement of reading standards.

Professor Pumfrey is a fellow of the British Psychological Society and a Chartered Psychologist. He has served on the Committee of the Division of Educational and Child Psychology, and also on the Society's Committee on Test Standards.

He has published over 250 papers and written and edited fourteen books.
Contact address: Centre for Educational Guidance and Special Needs, School of Education, University of Manchester, Manchester M13 9PL. FAX: 061 275 3548

Christy L. Foley is an associate professor who teaches graduate and undergraduate courses in reading. Her recent research in the area of international education focuses on classrooms in the USA territory of Guam.
Contact address: 119 Tate Page Hall, Western Kentucky University, Bowling Green, Kentucky, 42101, USA. FAX: 010 502 8424722

Bridie Raban-Bisby has taught children and adults to read and write during thirteen years before entering university-sector work. She has worked at the Universities of Bristol, Reading and Oxford conducting research and working with teachers. More recently she has worked at the University of Warwick where she has been the director of the Centre for the Study of Early Childhood. Currently she holds the Foundation Chair of Early Childhood Studies at the University of Melbourne in Australia.
Contact address: Department of Early Childhood Studies, Faculty of Education, University of Melbourne, Private Bag 10, Madden Grove, Kew Victoria, 3101, Australia. FAX: 010 613–854–3358

Tom Gorman has taught applied linguistics in universities in East Africa, the U.K. and the U.S.A. He joined The National Foundation for Educational Research (NFER) in 1975 and has directed over thirty projects in the fields of language and literacy. He has written or co-authored over fifty books and articles in this field and now works as an independent consultant.
Contact address: Childswickham House, Childswickham, Nr. Broadway, Worcestershire, W12 7HH. TEL. 0386 853214

Meta Bogle is a lecturer in language education and literacy studies. Her research interests include knowledge acquisition, conditions and processes of literacy acquisition, and processes of change in teacher performance with respect to instruction.
Contact address: Faculty of Education, University of the West Indies, Mona, Kingston 7, Jamaica, West Indies. FAX: 010 809 9277581

Christopher Upward is senior lecturer in the modern languages department, Aston University, Birmingham, England, where he teaches 'Writing Systems and Written English'. He is also the Simplified Spelling Society's editor-in-chief and author of *Cut Spelling: a handbook to the simplification of written English by omission of redundant letters.*
Contact address: Department of Modern Languages, Aston University, Aston Triangle, Birmingham B4 7ET. FAX: 021 359 6153

Nick Atkinson has many years experience as a specialist reading teacher. He has worked as an educational researcher in the Centre for Fomative Assessment Studies in the University of Manchester School of Education and has also taught statistics and psychology to students. Latterly he worked as a teacher for Islington Learning Support Service, Lough Road, London.
Contact address: 31, Bonnington Avenue, Liverpool L23 7YJ. TEL: 051 924 7417

Tom Christie is professor of educational assessment and evaluation and director of the Centre for Formative Assessment Studies in the School of Education, University of Manchester. He is deeply involved in the development of the assessment system for the National Curricula of England, Wales and Northern Ireland. He was consultant to the Task Group on Assessment and Testing (TGAT) and has subsequently directed national development projects at both the primary and the secondary stages.
Contact address: CFAS, School of Education, University of Manchester, Oxford Road, Manchester M13 9PL. FAX: 061 2753552

Patricia Smith is an associate researcher in the Assessment Research Centre at the Royal Melbourne Institute of Technology. She is particularly interested in the assessment and reporting processes in support of teacher judgement. She is a Life Member of the Australian Reading Association.
Contact address: Pat Smith, RMIT, P.O. Box 179, Coburg, 3058, Victoria, Australia. FAX: 0015 44 282 779099

Eli Meiselles is a graduate of the University of Manchester, England. Since 1979 he has been Chief Examiner in the North Division of the Ministry of Education and Culture in Israel. His research interests include teaching methods, students' reading difficulties, enrichment programs and teacher training.
Contact address: Eli Meiselles, Ministry of Education and Culture Northern Division, Nagareth, Israel. FAX: 972–4–983 1788

Victor Froese is a professor and head of the Department of Language Education at the University of British Columbia in Canada. He has published over thirty articles and authored or edited four books, the latest of which is *Whole Language: Practice & Theory* (Allyn and Bacon, 1994). He was the research coordinator for the IEA reading-literacy

study for the Province of British Columbia (referred to as Canada [BC] in IEA publications).
Contact address: Department of Language Education, UBC, Vancouver, BC, Canada, V6T 1Z4. FAX: 010 604 8223154

Peter Allerup is a mathematical statistician, specializing in Rasch models. He is employed at the Statistical Institute under Georg Rasch. From 1972 he has been employed at the Danish Institute for Educational Research, and is a lecturer at the University of Copenhagen. He has been working for many years as a statistical consultant.
Contact address: Danish Institute for Educational Research, 28 Hermods-gade, 2200 Copenhagen, Denmark. FAX: 010 45 31814551

Index